PELICAN BOOKS

WHOSE LAND?

Rev. James W. Parkes, M.A., D.Phil., Hon. D.H.L., D.Litt., was brought up in Guernsey and received a full Victorian education in the classics. He joined the Army in 1916 and was gassed. On recovering he became a Brigade Gas Officer engaged in the protection against gas. After the war he took a degree in Theology at Oxford, with architecture as his special subject. While an undergraduate he organized the League of Nations Union in the University. He joined the Student Christian Movement in 1923, after which he worked for the International Student Service until 1935. However, his unconventional approach to politics and religion put him at odds with theologians and eventually the S.C.M. He is a leading authority on Judaism, and Jewish –non-Jewish relations in Europe and the Middle East. In 1933 he helped emigrés from Nazi Germany. His research into antisemitism led to his involvement with the fate of German Jewry, and in 1935 his seven-year residence in Geneva ended with the discovery that the Nazis had ordered his liquidation. He has been a notable best-seller both under his own name and under 'John Hadham'. *Good God*, a controversial best-seller, was published as a Penguin Special in 1940, and *God in a World at War* was published during the Battle of Britain. The war years brought marriage, work at Chatham House, and more publications. Post-war travels followed, notably to Palestine in its most critical years. In 1964 he presented his books and archives to Southampton University. He was President of the Jewish Historical Society (1949–51).

James Parkes

WHOSE LAND?

A History of the Peoples
of Palestine

Penguin Books

Penguin Books Ltd, Harmondsworth, Middlesex, England
Penguin Books Inc., 7110 Ambassador Road, Baltimore, Maryland 21207, U.S.A.
Penguin Books Australia Ltd, Ringwood, Victoria, Australia

—

First edition published by Gollancz in Great Britain,
and by Oxford University Press Inc. in the U.S.A., in 1949
This completely revised edition first published 1970
Reprinted 1971

—

Copyright © James Parkes, 1949, 1970

—

Made and printed in Great Britain
by Hazell Watson & Viney Ltd
Aylesbury, Bucks
Set in Linotype Juliana

Contents

Contents

PART FOUR

The Restoration of the Balance

List of Maps

Preface

AT the very beginning of this book I am confronted with a problem. What am I to call the territory with which it deals? If I call it 'the Land of Israel', 'the Promised Land', 'the Holy Land', even 'Palestine', each name has a slant in favour of one hypothesis or another. So I have called it 'The Land', with a capital T and a capital L, except for two periods when Palestine was its correct political title. The first is that from the second Jewish war with Rome to the Arab conquest, when it formed the province of *Palestina*, and the second is that of the British Mandate for *Palestine*.

The story of The Land presents several peculiar qualities. Some of these it shares with certain other countries; some are unique. Some are due to its geographic position; some, and the more important, to the activities of the peoples who have inhabited it.

Its geographical position on the Mediterranean sea-coast between Asia and Africa, between the river valleys of the Nile and the Euphrates, has meant that when these valleys were in the possession of different empires it was the bridge between them, along which passed the influences of culture, the wealth of caravans, or the armies of war and occupation. Such was its situation in the ancient world, until Rome came and reduced it to an unimportant minor province; for Rome controlled both the Nile valley and the western approaches to Mesopotamia. Such was its situation again when the unity of Islam was broken and rival caliphs and princes ruled from Baghdad, Cairo or Damascus, until the Osmanli Turks conquered both the Euphrates and the Nile, and it again lost its cultural and strategic importance. But for substantial periods in its long story, it has not belonged to the East, but has been part of the European-Mediterranean world, whether as an insignificant, if turbulent, province of Rome, an uncertain Latin kingdom under the crusaders, a neglected area of several Turkish provinces, or a modern Mandate of Great Britain.

One peculiarity it would be difficult, if not impossible, to equate with the situation of any other area. The Land is the mother of two religions, Judaism and Christianity, which in turn possess a unique relationship to a third, Islam. Though the immense majority of Jews and Christians have long ceased to dwell within its narrow frontiers, and though it was never a primary Islamic homeland, yet to none of the three has it become a matter of indifference. But the interests of the three religions differ in both emphasis and intensity.

Christianity has become indigenous in many parts of the world; it is represented by powerful Christian states. There is nowhere a desire of homeless Christians to return to the original land of their religion. Yet its Holy Places have been a constant attraction for Christian pilgrims, and their protection and maintenance has been a religio-political interest of Christian powers at many periods of history. For two centuries there were efforts of Christendom, again half religious and half economic or political, to regain The Land by force, and the crusades have left a permanent mark on the country.

The Jewish interest has been both more intense, and more productive of complications. For Jewry has nowhere established another independent national centre; and, as is natural, the Land of Israel is intertwined far more intimately into the religious and historic memories of the people; for their connexion with the country has been of much longer duration – in fact it has been continuous from the second millenium B.C.E. up to modern times – and their religious literature is more intimately connected with its history, its climate and its soil. The Land therefore has provided an emotional centre which has endured through the whole of their period of 'exile', and has led to constant returns or attempted returns, culminating in our own day in the Zionist Movement.

The Land is not in the same sense the homeland of the third religion with whose history its own is intertwined. The homeland of Islam is Arabia. But for many centuries Islam has been the religion of the majority of its inhabitants and in Jerusalem stands the third holiest shrine for Muslims throughout the world. Moreover in a general sense The Land forms a portion of those territories which the Arab feels to be part of the patrimony allotted to his people by Allah.

However, from the Arab conquest until the British Mandate it was never even a name on the political map of the world. It was a portion of some larger unit, whether Arab, Mamluk, or Turkish; and its people were never conscious of themselves as a national unit, nor did they ever attempt, as they had done in early and later Israelite days, to form an independent kingdom. During the long period of Islamic rule, with its kaleidoscopic changes of dynasty, no claimant to the throne of the caliphs, or even to a separate sovereignty, ever emerged from its population. It was the alternate prey of dynasties ruling from Damascus, Baghdad, Cairo or Istanbul. Only in the twentieth century has it resumed a separate identity, and that by the will of outsiders rather than of the majority of its own population. The result has been conflict, uncertainty and one of the most delicate and difficult problems of modern international politics.

*

It remains only to add three points.

The present volume is to a very large extent based on A *History of Palestine from 135 A.D. to Modern Times*, which was published in 1949 in the United States by the Oxford University Press Inc. and in Great Britain by Victor Gollancz. That book was actually written before the end of the British Mandate, when the future was still uncertain; and the mandatory period was therefore described in much more detail than present historical perspective warrants. The present volume concentrates on the actual peoples who live, or have lived, in the country, and has reduced its confused political history to the minimum necessary framework.

As to the spelling of Arabic and Hebrew names, I have adopted a compromise; trying (where a name is not so well known as to make the conventional spelling inevitable) to approximate to the present use of scholars. But I have refused all dots, accents and breathings, believing that those who are familiar with Arabic and Hebrew do not need them, and that those who (like myself) are not, pronounce names according to the written letters and have not the slightest idea what to do with the impedimental aids with which it is the present fashion to encumber them. I must, however, add that no system will guarantee that references in the index will be found under the letter where individual readers expect them; there is too much variety in contemporary use. I can only recommend further search between C, K and Q, between P and F, and between O and U, A and E, when first efforts are unsuccessful.

As this is a book to be read by both Jews and Christians, I have dated events as 'B.C.E.' and 'C.E.', standing for 'Before the Common Era' and 'Common Era'. It proved too complicated also to use the dates of the Islamic calendar.

Finally, it is a pleasure to record my gratitude to the many scholars who have most generously answered questions and made comments. They are too numerous to mention individually, but I would like them to realize that their help was very sincerely appreciated.

JAMES PARKES

Iwerne Minster,
Blandford, Dorset.
1969.

PART ONE

The Makers of its History

CHAPTER ONE

Jewish: The Children of Israel

THE Land consists of a maritime plain, varying in width from twenty miles to a few hundred yards, backed by high, rounded, limestone hills, whose western slopes catch the rainfall, and whose eastern boundaries sink imperceptibly, with ever increasing dryness, into the desert wastes. Today these hills are largely barren, their rocky skeleton showing everywhere through the thin coating of soil. In ancient times, before destruction and neglect had led to the continuous erosion of the soil, large areas were fertile or covered with forest.

The Land has been inhabited since paleolithic times. Traces have been found of the presence of paleolithic man two hundred thousand years ago; but it is only with his neolithic successors, dwelling in caves and mud-built houses and practising primitive agriculture as well as pastoral occupations, that its present history begins. For there is not only no known link between paleolithic man and his successors, but the remains of animals which have been discovered show that in paleolithic days the country enjoyed a very different climate from that which it has known for the past ten thousand years.

It is probable that remnants of the neolithic population form part of the ancestry of the present Arabic-speaking population, as well as of the Jewish people of today. For they were still there when the ancestors of the Jews first appeared in the land, although they inspired a certain fear and superstitious horror among these later settlers, as the names which they gave them suggest. They called them 'the ghosts', 'the horrors', 'the howlers', or 'the long-necked ones'. In exactly the same way the ancestors of present-day Europeans embodied the older inhabitants in their folklore as giants and goblins, ghosts and evil spirits, whose power and hostility filled the night and the solitary place with danger.

It is only with the migrations into the country which took place around the second millenium B.C.E. that its recorded history begins. But from then on there is a continual dual thread running through its story which forms an essential part of its peculiarity. On the one side is the life of its actual inhabitants; on the other is their relation to nomadic or semi-nomadic peoples, or to the powerful empires of the river valleys of the Euphrates and the Nile between whom their land formed a barrier or bridge. The story of The Land is never exclusively the story of the men and women who actually dwelt within its borders. In the earliest period of which we have records, the contact with external empires was naturally light and transient. For they were not yet organized to exercise regular supervision over areas through which their armies passed, and from which their kings claimed tribute. The external interest during this time is provided by migrations into and through the country.

The first of these migrants are described in the biblical story of Abraham, and came from the north-east. They may have included the ancestors of both the Jewish and the Arab peoples, the former wandering no farther than The Land, the latter penetrating farther south and joining the nomads moving around the great trade routes of Arabia. But the origin of both Jews and Arabs is regarded by contemporary scholars as more obscure than was thought in the days of nineteenth-century pioneering. In any case the 'cousinship' of the two peoples rests on language and culture rather than on identity of physical ancestry in what is now southern Arabia.

The second millenium witnessed also movements into The Land of a number of peoples coming from the north and north-west. The first of these were the Hyksos, a people of uncertain origin, who actually succeeded in penetrating into the Nile Valley, and in maintaining for some centuries a kingdom in the Lower Nile. They were expelled from Egypt between 1600 and 1500 B.C.E., and disappear from history. Their place was taken by Hittites who moved into the country from the north at about the same time as 'Abrahamites' were appearing on its eastern frontiers. Their earlier home was in Asia Minor, whence, presumably under pressure from the movements of more northerly peoples, they began to spread southward about 1500 B.C.E. As they were not by nature a nomadic people, they settled down all along the eastern shores of the Mediterranean, where their physical type can still be seen today. For it is from a Hittite ancestry that many Turks, Jews and Syrians get the fleshy noses, full lips and heavy build which contrast with the more aquiline features and lighter build of the Semite.

Their domination of the country lasted for but a short time; for there followed in their wake other migrants from the north-west, the Philistines. Though the latest arrivals, and though they only exercised control over the whole country for a few uncertain decades, they have been the cause of its name of Palestine. These Philistines were an Aegean people, driven out of Greece and the Aegean islands round about 1300 B.C.E. They moved southwards along the Asiatic coast, and in about 1200 attempted to invade Egypt. Turned back, they settled in the maritime plain of southern 'Palestine', where they founded a series of city states. At the end of the period of Hebrew 'judges', their combined power extended over the greater part of the country.

The Hyksos had managed to get control of the lower Nile valley through the weakness of the native Egyptian dynasties. But round about 1600 B.C.E. they were expelled, and Egypt began to assert herself once more along her frontiers. For a hundred years she contented herself with the possession of a few strategic garrisons, and with periodic military operations which prevented any local power from becoming too strong. Then in 1479 B.C.E. Tutmose III, or Thotmes, a strong and powerful ruler of the Eighteenth Dynasty, undertook more serious operations against a kingdom which was centred in Kadesh on the Orontes in northern Syria. Their complete defeat ensured an unchallenged Egyptian occupation of the country for several centuries. Later a weakening of Egyptian power coincided with the movements southwards of the Hittites and westward of the Abrahamites; and from 1150 to 850 B.C.E. The Land was in the unusual position of being almost free from foreign control. That period coincides with the settlement of the country by the Israelites, as well as with the short period of their imperial expansion as a united kingdom.

While nomadic peoples from a distance may provide much of the interest in the second millennium B.C.E., the ancestors, or predecessors, of the indigenous nomads of today are already to be found in the area. In fact, the story of Cain and Abel, the sons of Adam and Eve in the Book of Genesis (chapter iv), reflects a permanent element in the local situation. It is a confused story, reflecting probably many different legends. But one thing is clear. It reflects the enmity between the pastoral and the agricultural life. Abel, so to speak, the bedouin shepherd, is killed by Cain, the fellah. In fact in one version Cain was even more representative of the settled life. He is the creator of the city (iv, 17). Not only the indigenous nomad, but also his camel appears in the stories of the patriarchs of Israel. Abraham possessed camels. It was her watering of his camels that showed the servant of Abraham that Rebekah was the divinely chosen wife of Isaac, his son (Genesis xxiv). The nomad tribes appear sometimes as the friends, sometimes as the enemies, of the Israelites. Those who rescued Joseph are called indifferently Ishmaelites or Midianites (Genesis xxxvii). The wife of Moses was a Kenite nomad, and the Kenites appear as friends. But the camel-owning Midianites or Amalekites are reckoned as ingrained enemies (1 Samuel xv, 3).

At what stage the nomads came to call themselves *Arabs*, it is impossible to say, but a whole social judgement exists in the fact that the word meant *noble*, and until the present century it was confined to the nomads and those of nomad descent. Moreover the word *bedouin* was likewise confined to those who bred camels among the 'Arabs', and camel breeding was considered a nobler occupation than the herding of sheep or goats. Again it is only in modern times that the word has been used loosely for all the indigenous nomads. In its strict use it is familiar to Biblical writers. The wealth of Solomon is shown by his receiving gifts from the kings of Arabia (1 Kings x, 15); and the destruction of Babylon in an anonymous prophecy (Isaiah xiii) is to be so complete that not even an Arab will pitch his tent there. In New Testament times, the most prominent Arab group is composed of the Nabatean traders, the relatives of King Herod.

It is impossible to fix the actual date of the removal of Terah and his son Abraham from Harran or from Ur of the Chaldees, nor does it matter that we cannot. For this uncertainty does not throw doubt on the belief that in the saga of Abraham are contained actual memories of a real person who, for real reasons, was regarded as the founder of the Israelite people. The stories of the patriarchs, Abraham, Isaac and Jacob, are in their main elements consistent with what we know of the lives of the nomadic peoples moving from east to west around the fertile crescent during this period. They may already have been distinguished from others by the tribal appellation of 'Hebrews' from a reputed ancestor, Eber. What distinguished them from other nomads were their religious beliefs and practices. The origin of this distinction might lie in the fact that the group was not of nomadic origin. It had taken to the nomadic life after experiencing that of settled city-dwellers. Whether it was some internal compulsion, or the downfall of their city, or both, which persuaded them to return to the more primitive ways of their remote ancestors does not matter. For one reason or the other they did so; but they brought with them relics of their urban experience, which showed itself in the religion, the folklore and the legal system which they bequeathed to their descendants.

What may have been the origin of Abraham's peculiar religion has been suggested by Sir Leonard Woolley, the discoverer of Ur, the city whence Abraham probably came. He points out that, in leaving the city, Abraham inevitably left behind the civic deities, whose jurisdiction did not extend beyond the area controlled by their worshippers. But just at this period the worship of a family, or private, tutelary deity had become common among the inhabitants of Ur, and this family god would accompany its worshippers, even though they left the city. In the absence of the other territorially limited, though more important, deities this one faithful guardian came to be regarded by Abraham and his people as the only god for them to worship. The idea fell far short of conscious monotheism, of the belief that there is only one God of the whole universe, and it was many centuries before the descendants of Abraham reached so lofty a conception. But it contained the germ of the idea, and preserved the Hebrews from following the normal habit of nomads and adopting in each locality the gods whom that locality worshipped. Around their one God clustered other memories Abraham had brought with him from Ur, the folklore of the creation and the flood, and the earliest code of laws.

The patriarchal and nomadic period lasted for several centuries. By this time the migrants of the previous wave had largely settled down, occupying an area east of the river Jordan and stretching northward to Damascus. Others had possibly settled west of Jordan, being known to us in the Bible as Canaanites. At a later stage both intermingled considerably with the Hebrews, and memories of this Canaanite ancestry persisted for many centuries. The Hittites were likewise settled in The Land, and it was from a Hittite that Abraham is recorded to have purchased the cave at Hebron where the graves of the patriarchs are still believed to exist (Genesis xxiii). After some centuries the descendants of Abraham had grown into a group of tribes related not only by their common ancestry, but by their common worship.

At some time in the middle of the second millennium B.C.E. a series of droughts and crop failures led them to follow the example of other nomads of the district and seek permission to pasture their flocks in the eastern fringes of the Nile estuary. Whether all the tribes together went down to Egypt it is difficult to establish, for there are suggestions in the Biblical narrative that the group of whom Judah later became the leader remained in the southern part of The Land, or at least returned to it separately and before the group of 'Joseph' tribes, led by Ephraim. Some, at any rate, made a prolonged sojourn in Egypt, and were reduced to a state of semi-servitude from which they were rescued by a national leader, Moses, who led them out of Egypt. This period made a profound impression, which was never forgotten in their subsequent history.

Scholars differ considerably as to the date of this emigration ('Exodus'). Some throw the whole of the period already described further back, and believe that it took place between 1600 and 1480 B.C.E. Others place it between 1380 and 1300 B.C.E. But there can be no doubt as to the fact that it was a historical event, and that during the generation which separated the slave life of Egypt from the conquest of the central hill country of The Land, some experience took place in the mountainous region of Sinai – and scholars differ even as to where it is to be found – of vital importance to the religious and national future of that group of Abrahamite tribes, and through them gave to the subsequent history of The Land a significance in the story of mankind far greater than that of its more powerful contemporaries in the valleys of the Euphrates and the Nile.

The events associated with Sinai were a creative focusing point of all the previous experiences of those who received them, not an unrelated and inexplicable irruption into the normal tenor of their development. In the words of Browning: 'Out of three sounds was made, not a fourth sound, but a star.' But the three 'sounds' were 'real' sounds, even though the roles of historian and theologian differ as to the interpretation of the making of the 'star' therefrom. The 'sounds' were their loyalty to the God worshipped by their group of tribes, the ethical traditions of the codes of Babylon, the wisdom of Egypt, the customs of their ancestors which formed the background of their corporate experience, and the spiritual purging which the desert freedom and stringency brought to them after the slavery and 'fleshpots' of Egypt. And the historical significance of the 'star' was the establishment of belief in a link between the ethical conduct of a community and divine guidance and approval, which marks the religious development of Israel during all her subsequent history. And it is this relationship which forms the bond of union with the daughter religions of Christianity and Islam. All three are distinguished among the world's religions as 'ethical monotheisms'.

No 'miraculous' or sudden change in conduct followed from the events of Sinai. To outward appearances the conduct of this group of tribes differed in nothing from that of others of their kind. The seed implanted in them grew slowly and naturally. Their invasion of The Land was often accompanied by the same savagery and ruthlessness that characterized the activities of their neighbours. History records that Moses, the desert leader, died before the tribes reached the Jordan, and it was under the leadership of Joshua, of the 'Joseph' tribe of Ephraim, that the invasion of the central hill country was successfully undertaken.

The conquest was a slow affair, and involved a much greater intermingling with the existing population – known by the general term of Canaanites – than the Biblical narrative would often suggest. There was nothing which corresponded to a central government, and it was only the menace of external pressure which normally drew the separate tribes into temporary, and often unwilling, cooperation. So long as the main issue was resistance to what amounted to but temporary raids, such a method of action might suffice. What compelled closer unity and organization was the need to meet the menace of the growing power of the Philistines who, from their position on the southern maritime plain, had gradually acquired a predominant position in the central hill country, and even established a stronghold at Bethshan overlooking the Jordan valley.

After initial successes the first attempt at united action ended disastrously. Somewhere about the year 1000 B.C.E. the Israelites, under the leadership of Saul of the little tribe of Benjamin, met the Philistines in battle on Mount Gilboa above Bethshan, and were totally defeated. Saul was killed, and the Philistines remained masters of the country for a number of years.

After the death of Saul the mantle of kingship fell on his far greater successor, David, who remained for all subsequent history the ideal of a Hebrew king. More legends may have clustered round his son Solomon; but it was David who remained the ideal of a king and the prototype of the expected Messiah. Moreover, it is in the time of David that we first find two most important developments firmly established: the writing of history, as expressed, for example, in the record of the revolt of Absalom, and the literature of personal religion expressed in the early psalms.

Unlike Saul, David was a southerner, and he enjoyed good relations with some at least of the Philistine cities. When exiled by Saul, it was to the land of the Philistines that he fled, and when he became king it was of Philistines that he formed his personal bodyguard. Nevertheless, he brought the war against this people to a successful conclusion, expelling them from their conquests and leaving them only the strip of coastland in the south where their original cities had been founded. Having dealt with the menace of the Philistines, David proceeded to secure himself against the other neighbours of Israel. His capture of Jerusalem gave him a strong fortress capital, traditionally belonging neither to the northern nor to the southern group of tribes, and so an excellent centre for their new unity.

It is extraordinary how quickly Jerusalem became in the

national thought not just a symbol of unity but an embodiment of the whole conception of the covenant relationship between God, land and people. Allowing the Philistines to remain in the south, David added to his kingdom all the coast north of Ashdod as far as the frontiers of Tyre. Inland he conquered the southern parts of the Lebanon, extended his authority as far as the Euphrates, and reduced Damascus to a dependent position under a governor of his own appointment. He did the same with Edom in the extreme south, and made Moab and Ammon into vassal principalities. These were the widest boundaries Israel ever possessed, and were only made possible by the fact that both Assyria and Egypt were so occupied with home affairs that they had no strength to spare for the extension or even maintenance of their frontiers.

The kingdom of David fell apart after his death, and the subsequent political story is of little interest until the northern half fell victim to Assyria in 721 B.C.E. and the southern to Babylon in 586. The independent kingdoms were finished, the religious and social upbuilding of Israel had only just begun.

In the period from Saul to the fall of Jerusalem, there had been a remarkable development in every aspect of the religious life of the Hebrew community. Even the conception of kingship which had grown with Saul and David was different from that of their neighbours. David was no absolute oriental monarch. The absolutist conception of Solomon had no place in Hebrew ideas. The king was king by a contract with his people which left them free men and his brethren. He was not above the common law – his function was to see to its just administration – and the community had a kind of representative, not under royal control, whose business it was to denounce, openly and in the royal presence, any infringement of this royal duty. This is one of the basic points in which Jewish and Arab thinking are identical, even when differently expressed.

These representatives were not, like the tribunes of republican Rome, officers elected by the community to supervise the executive, but the order of prophets, whose beginnings appear to lie towards the end of the previous period. Eastern religions have constantly brought into existence bodies of ecstatic fanatics, similar to the dervishes of medieval and modern Islam. It seems that such were known in pre-Israelite Canaan; and it is not surprising if the worshippers of Yahweh developed a group of such men in opposition to the devotees of the local Baal. All that could be said of them in early days was, perhaps, that they were devotees of Yahweh and kept his religion alive. They seem to have had little political or ethical interest. They lived in communities, supported by popular gifts and, presumably, by tilling the soil. Saul, the first king of Israel, was at least closely connected with such a group.

With the establishment of the monarchy and an ordered administration the king took the place of these ecstatics as the guardian of the national worship. But in the meantime a change was taking place within the body of prophets. They began to produce men who were concerned with the fulfilment of Yahweh's will by the king and people, and with the ethical laws of which Yahweh was believed to be at once the author and the sanction. The functions of 'prophet' and 'priest' separated, and the concern of the prophets turned from the worship of the altar to the life of sovereign and people. It was in this way that they became a unique series of censors of royal and national conduct, representing unafraid the religious and popular opinion at their highest. At times they interfered in the political life of the kingdom, making and unmaking kings, and giving advice on the highest policies of the state.

All this is well illustrated in two of the earlier members of the group. The first is Nathan, a prophet of the time of David. When David took to himself Bathsheba, Uriah's wife, and arranged for the death of Uriah in battle, he was doing what would have been regarded as perfectly normal and unexceptionable by any of his royal contemporaries. But not only did Nathan dare to rebuke him to his face; but David recognized the justice of his rebuke. Even more striking was the career of Elijah in the northern kingdom. He not only denounced the sovereigns for their personal immoralities, but intervened on behalf of Yahweh in their public policy and action. In his challenge to the priests of Baal, he was challenging, and subsequently massacring, royal protégés. Elisha, his successor, followed in his path and openly advocated policies which involved the overthrow of the royal house. Here again we have a parallel when the Turkish political sovereignty was compelled to listen to the voice of religion on two occasions in the seventeenth and nineteenth centuries (pp. 120 and 183).

The new prophets were individuals of the highest spiritual development of their time. They belonged to no order or succession, but appeared in every rank of society, from the royal family to the peasantry, and in both the northern and southern kingdom. The religious development for which they were responsible in the eighth and seventh centuries B.C.E. has been a permanent enrichment of the spiritual understanding of mankind. Their teaching as to the holiness and love of God, and as to moral responsibility in public as well as private life, form the background of both Jewish and Christian theology and social teaching.

Parallel with the development of prophecy was an equally important development of law. As with prophecy, it is possible to trace the beginnings of written codes of law to the predecessors of Israel, both in Mesopotamia and in the land of Canaan. But also, as with prophecy, Israelite law took on a development which had no parallel in the codes of the neighbouring peoples, but which has many parallels in the development of Islamic law based on the Koran. In some ways the codes which are embodied in the first five books of the Bible represent a more primitive stage of development than those of which we have knowledge from Mesopotamia or elsewhere. They reflect the life of a more primitive and agricultural society, still possessing some nomadic features; they make very little reference to monarchy, to trade or industry. On the other hand, they reflect a much greater concern with persons than with property, and a sensitivity to the unfortunate which has no parallel. The fatherless, the widow and the stranger are the objects of constant solicitude to the lawgivers. The laws are also unique in their constant association of human and divine sanction in their enactments. The whole basis of their ethics is ascribed to the will of God; need for obedience to them is ascribed to religious motives, and in some cases the only sanction of an order or prohibition is divine disapproval.

All this formed a natural complement to the work of the prophets. But it is necessary to recognize in relation to both that they formulated ideals which were very far from being realized in the actions and customs of the people to whom they were proclaimed. There was still idolatry in Jerusalem when it fell into the hands of Babylon, and the denunciations of social corruption in such prophets as Amos show how far his people fell short of the ideal society which his prophecies and the codes of law proclaimed.

The end of the two kingdoms of Judah and Israel was more than merely the temporary or permanent loss of independence. A large proportion of the population of the two kingdoms was transported to various spots in Mesopotamia and in the mountains east of it, and never returned. Those who remained in the northern kingdom, mixed with immigrants settled by the conqueror, became known as Samaritans. The population which remained in the southern kingdom, much enfeebled in numbers and deprived both of political and social leaders and of skilled craftsmen, might well have been expected to lose themselves gradually in the surrounding population. It is the fact that neither of these things happened that gives to Jewish history characteristics which begin by being unusual and end by being unique. For the religion which was developing into a universalistic ethical monotheism never lost its roots in The Land; and the people, increasingly dispersed, considered residence in any other part of the globe, however prosperous it might be, to be 'an exile', or at least 'a dispersion'.

The first return followed the fall of Babylon. Its conqueror, Cyrus, king of the Persians and Medes, followed a very different policy towards the subject peoples of his empire. He allowed all those deported from various provinces by the Babylonians to return to their homes, did they so wish. Taking advantage of this opportunity, a small company of Jews, under the leadership of a scion of the royal house, Sheshbazzar, returned to Jerusalem in 538. In 520 a further company arrived, led by Zerubbabel, and set about the restoration of the Temple. The Temple was completed in 516, and thereafter there is silence about the Jerusalem community for some seventy years. A further company of Babylonian Jews came under the leadership of Nehemiah, who had received a high appointment at the court of the Persian king, and who came armed with royal letters appointing him governor of Judea. Nehemiah rebuilt the walls of Jerusalem, in spite of a good deal of opposition, and set himself to secure a stricter enforcement of the Law, as understood by the Babylonian Jews. This involved an attack on the friendship existing between the local community and its Samaritan neighbours, and for some time the question of mixed marriages was violently disputed between Nehemiah and local elements. After twelve years Nehemiah returned to Babylon for a period, but at some unspecified date he returned to Jerusalem to continue the fight for strict conformity.

In 397 yet another group came from Babylon to help to build up Jewish life. This was led by a religious, not a political, officer, Ezra, and he brought with him the text of the Law (Torah*) as codified by the scholars of Babylon. The whole, or sections, of this he solemnly read to an assembly of the people, who thus had their first opportunity of getting a general picture of the scope of their religious law. The result was a good deal of eager work of reformation; how far it went we cannot say, for again the sources fail, and the community passed into obscurity. But it is in that obscurity that the foundations of essential forms and lines of development for subsequent Judaism were laid.

Religion was for the first time made the subject of the education of the whole people. The Law was read regularly wherever Jews lived, and a body of scribes was formed whose business was both to make copies of its text and to explain that text to the people. This involved the choice of what books should be so treated and a 'canon of Scripture' was thus built up. The books chosen emphasized the perpetual paradox of Judaism, a particularism which fenced in a particular discipline of life for a single people, and an ethical monotheism of universal significance with a technique, also of universal significance, by which it could be developed.

The technique was twofold: the religious education already described, and the establishment of the synagogue, providing a centre for regular worship wherever a Jewish community existed. Its combination of prayer, praise, and teaching has formed the basis of the worship of both church and mosque.

In the period which followed Judaism began to take different forms as one aspect or another of its increasingly rich tradition

---

*Hebrew for 'The Law', and expressing much more than legal enactments. It means 'revealed teaching'.

was emphasized. The radical Pharisees and the conservative Sadducees are familiar from the New Testament. The ascetics have become famous from their scrolls discovered near the Dead Sea. Those concerned with the coming of a Messiah found the answer either in nationalist fanaticism, or in acceptance of Jesus of Nazareth.

So far as Jewish life was concerned the Persian Empire passed away almost unnoticed, overthrown in 331 B.C.E. by the Macedonian conqueror Alexander the Great. But he died eight years later, before he had had time to organize his vast conquests stretching from Greece to India. The new shape of Asia only emerged gradually out of the subsequent contests and rivalries of his generals. The Land fell to Ptolemy, who had been wise enough to concentrate his energies on the possession of Egypt, even before Alexander's death, and to remain satisfied with a compact and manageable acquisition. It remained under the rule of the Ptolemies for 130 years, and during this period the returned community maintained, though with some difficulty, its organization as a theocratic nation ruled by a high priest. Though inevitably the country suffered from the passage of armies, yet these years were relatively tranquil.

After long conflict, hegemony passed in 199 B.C.E. from Ptolemaic Egypt to Seleucid Syria. In 175 there came to the throne of Syria Antiochus IV, Epiphanes, a man who had a passionate admiration for all things Greek. In the first year of his reign he was solicited by a member of one of the wealthy and hellenizing priestly families to grant him the high-priesthood. Antiochus, considering the high priest to be nothing more than the governor of one of the dependencies of his crown, made the appointment, and subsequently unmade his candidate and substituted another – all this in violation of the Law, by which the selection was made for life, and could only be made from a single family.

The result of his action was a rebellion of the more orthodox section of the population, which was suppressed with violence, and punished by the plundering of the Temple. When that had no effect, Antiochus proceeded to the deliberate suppression of Judaism. All Jewish observances, including the rite of circumcision, were forbidden, and the Temple was desecrated by a heathen altar. But the carrying of this policy from Jerusalem into the rural districts in 166 provoked an act of rebellion which had momentous consequences. When the emissaries of Antiochus came to the town of Modin, in the foothills between the mountains of Judea and the maritime plain, a member of a priestly family living in the town, Mattathias of the house of Hashmon, killed the official, as well as a Jew who had begun to offer heathen sacrifice. This act was the beginning of a flare-up of religious enthusiasm throughout the country which produced the first example in history of ordinary people accepting death rather than the denial of their deepest religious convictions. Humanity's noble army of martyrs begins with Judean peasants in the time of Antiochus Epiphanes. Mattathias had five sons, three of whom in turn came to the leadership of the national and religious revival. Though only one of them, Judas, actually had the title of 'Maccabee', this name, as well as 'Hasmonean', is usually attached to the whole family which succeeded in establishing an independent monarchy lasting a century until it was thrust aside by the expansion of Roman colonization.

All that Rome destroyed when she wiped out the independence of the Maccabees was an oriental kingdom already corrupt and impotent. The House of Herod, which succeeded the House of the Hasmoneans, ruled only by the most complete subservience to Rome. The Herodians were appointed and dismissed at the whim of the Roman emperor, and not even that Herod whom we call 'the Great' made any significant contribution to either the cultural or religious life of the people. Had the writers of the historical books of the Bible survived to chronicle his reign and the reigns of his successors, they would have had nothing to record save that 'he did evil in the sight of the Lord', and it is doubtful whether they would even have waxed enthusiastic over the pompous hellenistic shrine which he erected on the site of the Temple of Solomon and Zerubbabel.

During the centuries which followed the conquests of Alexander a new factor was introduced into the population of the country. A number of Greek cities were established. Some had been settled by soldiers of the armies of Alexander; some grew up in subsequent centuries. Along the coast was a chain of such cities, and east of the River Jordan a further group was built at convenient points on the great trade routes which passed west and south from Damascus. These latter cities, once freed from the yoke of the Maccabees by the Romans, formed the League of the Ten Cities, the Decapolis. City States were familiar to the Romans, and many of these cities retained their autonomy under Roman rule; and their population, varied in origin, provided yet another element in the permanent amalgam of The Land.

The stages by which Rome had come to a direct government of The Land faithfully reflect the traditional methods of her imperial expansion. Her hand was far heavier, as well as far more efficient, than had been that of any of the previous imperial rulers of the country. With Judaism and its exclusive monotheism the wisdom of Julius Caesar found it possible to make an intelligent accommodation. It was made easy for the Jewish communities scattered throughout the Greek and Italian cities to practise their religion and at the same time to be loyal to the empire. But in The Land itself the temper of both sides made such an accommodation difficult. Jews there had too recently known independence, and this independence had been accompanied by too many bitter internal feuds, always likely to disturb the peace. Local governors did not possess the wisdom or tolerance of a Caesar, and the result was a constant series of explosions between Rome and some section of the Jewish populace. At one time it was the Pharisees intent on rejecting some insult to their religious scruples; at another the nationalists, fired with messianic enthusiasms and foolishly convinced of divine assistance in a war with Rome. The situation deteriorated steadily, and in 66 C.E. Rome found herself engaged in full scale war with the nationalists. Too late the Pharisaic leaders realized the rashness of some elements of their teaching and withdrew from the doomed Jerusalem. They saved Judaism but were unable to save the Jewish commonwealth. For three years the Romans were kept at bay. But the end was inevitable. In 70 C.E. Jerusalem was laid waste after months of siege, and the Temple was destroyed, never again to be rebuilt. The ruins of the unwalled city provided little more than accommodation for the camp of the Roman garrison, though as the years went on some of the population, Jews and Judeo-Christians, crept back and settled in the south-west corner round the hill of Zion. Hundreds of thousands of Jews either perished or were taken away to be scattered as slaves through the empire, even to the Rhineland.

Even after this bitter lesson The Land had but an uneasy peace. Sixty-two years later, under a pseudo-Messiah Bar-Cochba, revolt flared up again, only to end in 135 with the destruction of the city and the prohibition to any Jew to set foot within its boundaries. It was then that The Land was named *Palestina* by the Romans to eradicate all trace of its Jewish history, so that it is legitimately used until the end of the Roman-Byzantine supremacy. But the interval between the two destructions had allowed both religions of the country, Judaism and Christianity, to become independent of geography, while at the same time a new and unique relationship with the country itself was slowly built up by the former, and to a lesser extent by the latter also.

To some readers it may seem inappropriate to have devoted so much time to 'a situation which passed away two thousand years ago'. But it is only *politically* that the defeat by Rome, and the scattering of the Jewish population, made a decisive change in the history of The Land. That which had been created by more than a thousand years of Jewish history remained, as did that which was beginning to be created in the thoughts of the young Christian Church. Both grew in significance as the centuries passed, because both led to continuous action, in the one case to settlement and in the other to pilgrimage, and for both, *whatever* were the difficulties, the action was regarded as a necessary part of their religion. That is what makes The Land unique. Yet it remains true that, even though The Land be unique, the human beings who inhabit it are no different from the inhabitants of any other region of the earth. To all alike peace will only come when they accept that justice has been done.

CHAPTER TWO

Jewish: Judea under the Romans

THE most significant fact in the sixty years which mark the end of the Jewish commonwealth is that they mark also the development of Judaism and Christianity into world religions. For Christianity the *organizational* break was complete. In all its subsequent history it never again regarded the Holy Land as either its intellectual or geographical centre. No bishop of Jerusalem ever contested the primacy of the Pope of Rome or the Patriarch of Constantinople; no special authority ever attached to the opinions of the scholars of the Holy Land; and no permanent centres of learning came into existence in the country. But as a centre of pilgrimage for ordinary Christian men and women it enjoyed an unquestioned pre-eminence.

With the Jews and Judaism the development was quite different. The destruction of the Temple only confirmed an already established change in Jewish religious practice which had been built up through several centuries. The synagogue had grown naturally out of the geographical dispersion of Jewish communities. Every synagogue in every city was already equally a centre of Jewish teaching and worship. There was no religious papacy to compare with that of Rome for the Christians, just as there was no hierarchically and geographically organized priesthood to compare with that of the Christian tradition. Judaism had no provinces or dioceses; and spiritual primacy passed freely from centre to centre according to the actual merits of the spiritual leaders existing in any generation. But The Land was much too closely interwoven into the whole fabric of the Jewish religious tradition to require either Temple or hierarchy to maintain its uniqueness.

It was impossible to forget that it was within the Land of Israel that the religious formation of the Jewish people had taken place; certain formal acts, such as the fixing of the calendar, were for a long time the exclusive privilege of its rabbis; a certain sanctity remained inherent in its soil. The conception of a 'return' was never absent from Jewish thought, and there was no alternative but the holy soil of The Land to which a 'return' could be envisaged. Jews did not forget that once before there had been an exile and a restoration. Finally, though the concept of a Messiah did not occupy the central place in Judaism that Jesus Christ had come to occupy in Christianity, yet there was no doubt in Jewish minds but that at some period a Messiah should come and there was no land to which he would lead his people but to their ancient home. What happened to the two religions, therefore, as a result of the events of 70 and 135 C.E. was that Christianity's centre moved away from Jerusalem and never looked back to its first home, while Judaism, deprived of the Temple and the priesthood, evolved a new and more spiritualized relationship to a centre which had not changed.

The agency of this evolution was Pharisaism. A change of emphasis from Temple to Torah had been taking place during the centuries of voluntary migration. When, therefore, just before 70 C.E., Jochanan ben Zakkai and the other Pharisaic leaders came to the conclusion that the nationalist resistance to the Roman armies of Vespasian and Titus carried no divine sanction or religious obligation they retired, with the permission of the Roman authorities, to Jabne (Jamnia). Jabne was originally a Philistine city; then it had acquired a Greek population; it had fallen to Alexander Jannaeus in the Maccabean period, and had later become a private appanage of the Empress Livia, whence it passed to Tiberius. Its population was mixed, but at the time when the Pharisees made it their headquarters it was predominantly Jewish, and Jews possessed equal civic rights with its non-Jewish inhabitants. It would seem that it was because it already possessed a seat of Jewish learning that Jochanan asked to be allowed to go thither, and it remained the centre of Jewish life until after the deaths of Jochanan and his successor, Gamaliel II. At some date after the revolt of Bar-Cochba the centre moved from Jabne and Judea to Usha, a town in western Galilee, and it was there that the new arrangement took definite shape. The president of the rabbinical school received the title of *nasi*, or prince, and came to be recognized by the Roman authorities as the spiritual head of Jewry with the Greek title of Patriarch. This recognition did not take place in a day, and the same is true of the acceptance by the Jewish population of the authority of the religious courts and ordinances of the rabbis. Nevertheless it was in The Land during this period that Judaism assumed the intricate form which enabled Jews to survive the nearly two thousand years of total dispersion.

The two wars seriously diminished the numbers of the Jewish population, and modified its distribution; but they did not alter its character. The Jews remained a people of peasants and landed proprietors, dwelling in the hills rather than in the plains of the country. We have from Josephus a fairly clear idea of the destruction wrought after the victory of Rome; for he gives us lists of the towns, villages and districts ravaged and left deserted by the Roman conqueror. Jerusalem itself was left empty; and in Judea the main losses were in the Hebron area and around Thamna, a town founded in the Hasmonean period some twenty miles north-west of Jerusalem. In Transjordan the land was ravaged around Machaerus east of the Dead Sea and around Bethennabris, a place whose site has not been identified. In Galilee parts of the plain of Esdraelon were destroyed, and villages around Jotapata and Gamala. After 135 most of the destruction was in Judea where the revolt originated. The result was that the centre of Jewish population shifted from the south to the north, and this was further accentuated by voluntary migrations, for example of the priestly families who had lived around Jerusalem, and of the rabbinical scholars who had been in residence in Jabne.

The Christian situation was different. On the whole it would seem that Christianity had grown more in the cities than in the countryside, and that it had thus become hellenized to some extent even before it left The Land. We know of Christian communities in the first century at Joppa and Caesarea, at Lydda and Samaria and other cities of the plain and the sea coast. There were probably similar urban Christian communities in Transjordan. The one area which seems to have been an exception was the southern (Idumean) Shephelah, between Lydda and Beit Jibrin, where there were many Christians in the villages. The inhabitants of this region had been forcibly converted to Judaism two centuries earlier by John Hyrcanus, and were still scarcely treated as equals by the stricter Jews. This may have disposed them to listen to the Christian message, and it is interesting that Idumeans are expressly mentioned among the earliest followers of Jesus (Mark iii, 8). On the whole the Church seems to have grown mostly in the less Jewish districts of the country, and in this there is nothing surprising.

It is the period from 70 to 135 which marks the development of the characteristic Christian institution of episcopacy, although this took place more naturally in the Gentile Churches of Asia and Greece. While local organization was coming to take definite shape, no generally recognized pre-eminence yet belonged to any one church. So long as Christians were compelled to live under cover and exposed to periodic persecution, a localized and decentralized institution linked by travelling 'apostles' was almost inevitable. But as a central authority came into existence its seat was not Jerusalem but Rome. Even when eastern and western theology came into conflict the centres of interpretation in the east were Antioch and Alexandria. The Christians of The Land never provided a third competitor.

The two developments in which it played the predominant role, in one case as actor and in the other as victim, were the break with Judaism and the condemnation of the Judeo-Christian Church as heretical. The break between the two religions was a gradual process taking about a century to complete. Judaism was accustomed to a variety of sects and tolerant of great differences of belief; while Christians, so long as their beliefs were not interfered with, had no reason to refuse the protection which membership of the Synagogue gave them. They needed, as much as did other Jews, exemption from any act which involved idolatry, and they could obtain it only through synagogue membership. But the mixed Jewish-Gentile membership of the new sect inevitably precipitated a crisis.

It would seem, moreover, that the religious leaders of the Jewish community as well as their civic heads had their own reasons for wishing to have done with any direct connexion with the new and rapidly growing sect. It is a fair assumption that one of the objectives of the rabbinical group in Jabne, faced with the task of providing an alternative to the Temple as a centre of Jewish religious life, was to bring some order out of the multiplicity of

beliefs of the Greek and Maccabean periods. The codification of
the Law, which culminated in the production of the Mishnah in
the following century, was begun at this time; and its effect was
to define more precisely what was and what was not tolerable as
Jewish belief and practice.

In the break between the Gentile and Jewish wings within the
Church The Land was the main victim. It was natural that it
should have been in The Land that Christian congregations should
have had the largest proportion of Jewish members; and when
these members were excluded from communion, first with the
Synagogue, then with the Gentile Church, an almost fatal blow
was struck at the development of local Christianity. This is the
natural explanation of why the original home of the religion so
early lost all importance in the affairs of the growing Church.
The Judeo-Christians, excluded from synagogue by the Jews and
looked at with suspicion in church by the Gentile Christians,
were also excluded from Jerusalem by the Romans. In Aelia
Capitolina arose a wholly Gentile Church, and the last home of
the Judeo-Christians seems to have been in Transjordan. By the
third century the group was proscribed as heretical, and its
literature was so completely destroyed that we have but the most
meagre knowledge of its developments. A couple of hundred years
later it had vanished.

Between the two sections of the Jewish population in Judea and
Galilee the land of the Samaritans stretched from the mountains
of Ephraim down to the maritime plain in the neighbourhood of
Caesarea. In the centre of the region was the ancient political
capital of the northern kingdom, Samaria, which had been refounded by Alexander the Great and settled with a colony of
Macedonian veterans in punishment for the murder by the
Samaritans of his governor of southern Syria. It remained a pagan
city when Herod the Great rebuilt and extended it, and made it
one of his favourite residences. A few miles south-east of Samaria
was the more ancient city of Shechem, which was the centre of
the Samaritans as a religious group. Here also a pagan city was
built by Vespasian, and named Flavia Neapolis (Nablus), but it
seems gradually to have returned to Samaritan hands.

The possibility of a reconciliation between the two religious communities scarcely existed. Although modern scholarship has shown that the Samaritans were basically a Hebrew people, practising the Hebrew religion, they had taken no direct part in the post-exilic developments of Judaism. So long as the Sadducaic party remained, some reconciliation might have been dreamed of, for there had been friendly relations between the Samaritans and the Jerusalem priesthood in the days before Nehemiah; Sanballat, the Samaritan high priest, was related by marriage to the Jewish high priest. But with the reforms of Ezra and the subsequent rise of the Pharisees to power, they came to be considered the bitterest enemies of the Jews, and the Jewish hatred was returned with interest by the Samaritans. Nevertheless they were equally restive under Roman rule and equally oppressed by procurators such as Pontius Pilate. In fact his recall was due to the brutality with which he had ordered his troops to massacre the participants in a purely unarmed and religious march to Mount Gerizim, where a religious enthusiast had promised to reveal to them the ancient vessels of the Temple. In 52 the smouldering hatred against the Jews broke into open violence, and a group of Galilean pilgrims were massacred on their way to Jerusalem; the Jews retaliated; and mutual reprisals continued until the Governor, Cumanus, intervened. Yet the Samaritans rose at the same time as the Jews against Vespasian, and 11,000 are said to have been slaughtered. In the second Jewish rising they took the opposite side and supported the Romans who, in return, assisted them to rebuild their temple on Mount Gerizim which had been destroyed by John Hyrcanus and had since lain in ruins.

While there exists a historic link between the Jews, the Christians and the Samaritans, an important element in the life of the country was wholly foreign to all the experiences which linked those three peoples. These were the 'Greek' cities, and the agricultural regions depending on them, which were to be found in various parts of the country. Even more than the cities of the medieval merchants, these cities lived a life extraordinarily independent of the countryside outside their particular territories; but like the medieval cities most of them possessed relatively complete communal autonomy and were related to some higher authority mainly by the payment of a single corporate tribute.

They were thus – as again was the case of the medieval cities – frequently given as presents, or taken as spoils of war, so that they constantly changed ownership. But in most cases the change was confined to a change in the recipient of the corporate tribute; and the life and administration of the city went on unchanged.

The cities of Palestine owed their origin to three main causes. The most important lay in the trade routes which crossed the country; next were the strategic needs of successive rulers who established colonies of veterans either to police the countryside or to defend the frontiers; finally, there were the charm or impregnability of certain sites and the desire of a ruler to build himself a palace in some spot whose beauty or strength appealed to him. Of the first class there are two main groups. There was a line of cities up the sea-coast from Raphia through Strato's Tower (Caesarea) to Dora along the coastal caravan route from Egypt to Tyre and beyond. A second group of cities lay east of the Jordan where another important caravan route ran from Damascus to Petra and the Gulf of Akaba. This group was known as the League of the Ten Cities (Decapolis) and was organized by Pompey out of cities founded in the Greek period. One city of the league, Scythopolis (Beisan), lay west of the Jordan guarding the most important east–west link between the two caravan routes at a point where the river could be forded just below the lake of Tiberias.

Cities of veterans were founded and refounded by all the successive rulers of the country. Alexander the Great settled Macedonian soldiers in the ancient capital of Samaria. Herod rebuilt it as Sebaste, bringing in a fresh population. Herod likewise converted Strato's Tower into a magnificent Roman city which he named Caesarea. After 70 Vespasian gave it a new charter and population as a Roman colony. The Herods were also active in founding similar cities in the heart of the country, such as the Galilean Sepphoris and Tiberias. Others they built for strength or pleasure, such as Antipatris in the maritime plain, Phasaelis in the Jordan valley north of Jericho, Caesarea Philippi at the sources of the Jordan on the slopes of Hermon, as well as Massada in the wilderness west of the Dead Sea, and Machaerus, the desert fortress of Transjordan.

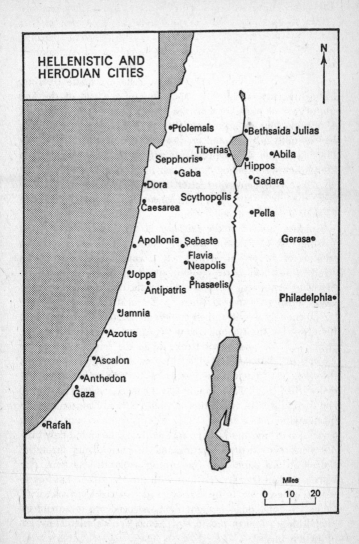

HELLENISTIC AND
HERODIAN CITIES

N

•Ptolemais   •Bethsaida Julias

          Tiberias   •Abila
Sepphoris•   Hippos
      •Gaba   •Gadara
•Dora
      Scythopolis
•Caesarea
                  •Pella

•Apollonia •Sebaste   Gerasa•
          Flavia
          •Neapolis
•Joppa   •Phasaelis
  •
Antipatris   Philadelphia•

•Jamnia

•Azotus

  •Ascalon
•Anthedon
•Gaza

•Rafah

                    Miles
              0   10   20

The population of these cities was, as was to be expected, extraordinarily mixed. A few came to be largely Jewish, such as Jabne, Tiberias or Sepphoris. In some, such as Jabne or Joppa, all the population had equal rights; in some, such as Ascalon or Ptolemais, civic rights were confined to the original settlers and their descendants. Some, such as Joppa, Pella, or Sebaste, certainly had Christians among the population by the end of the first century; some probably remained wholly pagan. As will be seen, it is impossible to make any generalizations about them; each had its individual life and privileges. It is also impossible to say to what extent their descendants survive in the country. In so far as they were trading cities, their inhabitants probably moved elsewhere as trade declined after the Muslim conquest. As to the rest, they probably form an element in the present Jewish, Christian, or Muslim population.

Another product of the existence of the great caravan routes passing east of Palestine was the emergence along the eastern frontier of an organized and settled community of Nabatean Arabs, which had moved up gradually from the south during the preceding centuries. We meet it first in the time of Alexander the Great; during the period when the Seleucids or Ptolemies were strong enough to control their borders and protect their commerce, there is little information about these Arab settlers; but as the power of Syria and Egypt weakened in the century before the whole area fell under Roman domination, the Nabateans were able to carve out a kingdom for themselves covering an extensive area east of the Jordan. Their capital was the inaccessible city of Petra, and their authority at one time extended beyond Damascus in the north and to the sea at Gaza in the west. Pompey accepted them as a vassal state and the Romans apparently did not mind how matters went between the Nabateans and their neighbours; for in the time of St Paul there was a Nabatean governor in Damascus. The Nabateans had friendly relations with the Maccabees, but less so with the Herodians. In the war of 70 they helped Vespasian with troops. In 106 Trajan brought their independence to an end by establishing a Roman province of Arabia Petraea stretching east of the Jordan.

To what extent the kingdom of the Nabateans was an organized commercial state and to what extent it existed by various forms of depredation on the caravan routes from Damascus southwards, scholars disagree. Probably both views are true of different periods. Certainly brigandage is mentioned in almost every complaint about conditions in these regions in the days before the establishment of Roman rule; and the evidence of monuments suggests that the greatest period of prosperity followed and did not precede the establishment of the Roman province. That the Arabs of that day prided themselves on their independence would appear to be indicated by the pleasant title adopted by many of their kings. While in flattery of the West it was common for an eastern princeling to call himself 'friend of the Greeks', 'friend of the Romans', or 'friend of the Emperor', the Nabatean kings called themselves 'friends of the people'. Another Arab people, the Iturians, had created a kingdom in the southern Lebanon and extended their interests into northern Galilee. Finally, there was always a certain bedouin element in the Jordan valley and the south; but there is little record of the bedouins at this time, apart from the references to brigandage at any period at which the central or local government was weak.

Over this heterogeneous population a Roman or Byzantine governor presided from Caesarea until the Arab conquest. Thereafter there were many different governors. But in two points all were alike. They were governors on behalf of a foreign power, and they were themselves foreigners.

CHAPTER THREE

Pagan and Christian: Rome and Byzantium

DURING the five hundred years of Roman rule from the end of
the revolt of Bar-Cochba to the Muslim conquest the peoples of
Palestine enjoyed an unusual measure of security from external
pressure or invasion. None of their frontiers were frontiers of the
empire, and to the east they had no dangerous enemy menacing
them as Parthians and Persians menaced the neighbouring province of Syria. In 211, in common with all other provincials, they
received from Caracalla the privileges of Roman citizenship without discrimination. Both Jews and Christians benefited from the
friendly feelings towards their religions of two of the best emperors of the third century, Septimius Severus (193–211) and
Alexander Severus (222–235). The latter is said to have placed
statues of both Moses and Christ in his palace chapel. Yet, in spite
of these local favours, the third century was a period of general
political and economic decline; and the incompetence of the
emperors came to a climax in 260 when the Persians overran Syria,
captured Antioch, and took the emperor Valerian prisoner. In the
north and west also the frontiers of the empire were breached,
and its end appeared near.

The Persians were only driven back by the skill of Odenathus,
prince of Palmyra and nominally 'Dux Orientis' for the young
Emperor Gallienus, son of Valerian. But it was in his own interest
that he extended his authority as far as Egypt; and when he was
murdered in 266, his famous widow Zenobia succeeded him,
nominally on behalf of his son, and ruled an independent state
comprising parts of Asia, Syria, Palestine and Egypt. But in 270
the Roman army, which made and unmade emperors at will,
conferred the purple on one who was also a skilful general,
Aurelian (270–275); and in the brief space of five years he restored
the frontiers and gave to the whole a specious appearance of
restored prosperity and unity. But military victories could not
arrest the economic decline which a long period of oppression and

misrule had rendered inevitable. Nor was the political restoration solid; the old belief in the 'pax romana' was shaken, and Aurelian showed himself no stranger to the prevailing feeling that the old order was passing, when he fortified Rome itself against possible invaders.

Ten years later the army raised to the throne an even greater leader, Diocletian (284–305), and the empire really took a new lease of life. Diocletian undertook a thorough reorganization of the whole imperial administration and provincial system; and, though the result was a somewhat top-heavy bureaucracy, it at least gave the Western Empire another hundred and fifty years of life, and the Eastern more than a thousand.

The division of the empire into four equal sovereignties broke down on the abdication of Diocletian in 305. Almost twenty years of civil war followed until Constantine reunited the whole under a single prince, and retained sole power until his death in 337, when it broke up again. The reputation of Constantine, however, does not rest on his being the last successful emperor of the whole empire, but on the fact that at long last an emperor accepted Christianity as his own personal faith. During the reign of Constantine recognition still meant equality with all other religions; the exemptions which were given to Christian clergy were given, for example, also to Jewish rabbis. But Christianity could ill brook a rival. Recognition was quickly followed by the demand for a position of privilege, and before the end of the century Theodosius the Great (378–395) had made the orthodox Christian creed promulgated at the Council of Nicaea the sole belief which his subjects were entitled to hold.

In 364 the two brothers Valens and Valentinian divided the empire into east and west; and for the next 250 years Palestine's destiny was bound up with that of the Eastern Empire from Constantinople. It was a period of much-diminished prosperity and tranquillity. Burdened with the huge bureaucracy of Diocletian, society could not, even with long periods of peace, recover from the century of economic distress which had preceded his re-organization; the population dwindled, a ferocious caste system tied men to the place and occupation of their parents, and the oppression of the masses steadily increased.

The population of the country was undoubtedly much larger in the days of the Roman Empire than it has ever been since, except in completely modern times; but many of the cities must have been little more than market towns for the neighbouring agriculture; they had no special reason for existence, commercial, industrial or strategic. Most of them had the privilege of minting, and it is from their coins that we are able to trace much of their history, or even their existence. Of the occupations of the inhabitants during these five hundred years there is little to add to the picture we receive from the New Testament, or, indeed, from the prophets. As has already been said, the province shared the general distress of the empire in the third century, and laboured under the burden of Byzantine taxation from the fourth century onwards; but in the last period before the Arab invasion it enjoyed a certain prosperity from the mass of Christian pilgrims attracted to Jerusalem, and the number of Christian communities in the country. Jerusalem itself became one of the richest cities of the East. But, on the whole, it remained a land of peasants and landlords, owners of vineyards, corn lands or flocks of sheep and goats. There was a certain amount of local industry in or near the caravan cities. We hear of glass factories, of linen weaving, of purple dyeing, and of pottery manufacture; and the wines and olive oil of the land were famous. All alike, merchant and peasant, benefited from the suppression of brigandage, and from the excellent roads which the Romans built and policed.

While the political history of the period is relatively unimportant, these centuries gain their significance from the developments which they witnessed in Judaism and Christianity. During the first period it is the Jews who present the more interesting picture; during the second it is the Christians. The years from 135 to 400 witnessed the creation of the patriarchate and the completion of the Mishnah and the greater part of the Talmud of Jerusalem; while the period between 300 and 640 witnesses the Arian and monophysite controversies, the emergence of separate eastern Churches which still survive, the growth of eastern monasticism, and the new attraction of Palestine as a centre for Christian pilgrimage.

Undoubtedly the Jewish community took some time to recover

the confidence of the Roman authorities after the violence of the revolt of 135. For a generation or more the two cities, Sepphoris and Tiberias, which were to be centres of Jewish life in the succeeding centuries, and which certainly retained a substantial Jewish population all through the second century, showed openly pagan emblems on their coinage, indicating that the Jews were at that time disfranchised. By the end of the century Tiberias has reverted to the neutral emblems used on Jewish coinage; and literary evidence tells of Jewish town-councillors in Sepphoris. The main centre of the Jewish population shifted during this period to Galilee. Some Jews remained in the villages of Judea, especially in the southern hills; but there were none resident in Jerusalem until the Empress Eudocia (394–460), widow of Theodosius II, secured permission for them to return. Jewish travellers passed through the city; a few lived in villages overlooking it, and in the fourth century they were allowed to enter it on the ninth of the month of Ab, the day of the destruction of the Temple, to mourn over its ruins. There were Jewish communities in many of the maritime cities, and in the caravan cities and villages of Peraea. But the bulk lived in Galilee. Thither the rabbinical schools had moved from Jabne, and many of the priestly families which had formerly lived for convenience in the neighbourhood of Jerusalem had also moved northwards. The first centre of the community was at Usha, a short distance inland from the bay of Haifa; then it moved to Shefar Am, a village a few miles north-east of Usha, thence to Sepphoris and finally to Tiberias. The population remained as it had been before the loss of independence, primarily peasants and landowners; and the rabbinical descriptions of the wealth and selfishness of the landowners of this period exactly parallel the prophetic denunciations of their predecessors a thousand years earlier. Jewish villages were thickly scattered in the hills and valleys of the region; there is one, Peki-in (Buqeia), in the wildest hill country, which claims a continuous Jewish settlement from Biblical to modern times.

The Roman recognition of a hereditary patriarchate in the House of Hillel was of the utmost importance for the Jewish community. It not only gave them a large measure of political autonomy in Palestine; but secured two other results. The Romans accepted the patriarch as the supreme authority for the whole Jewish community within the empire, and so provided it with a centre in place of the Temple and Jerusalem; and the patriarchate itself was a religious as much as a political office, so that it retained in existence the theocratic conception of the Jewish people, and the intimate association between their political survival and their religious loyalty.

It was this combination which was to provide them with the foundation on which they have survived. The Patriarch, Judah the Prince (c. 135–c. 220), was responsible for the collection and codification of the interpretations of the Law and the judgments handed down by his predecessors in the Pharisaic tradition. This collection is known as the Mishnah, or Instruction, and became the standard basis of Jewish orthodoxy for the future. It was also the text on which the vast commentaries of the Jerusalem and Babylonian Talmuds were built. Although a number of the rabbis of the period were men of wealth, drawn from commerce or land-owning, one problem which had to be solved during this period was the support of the poor student who wished to give his life to religious study. The monastic solution, with its celibacy and exaggerated asceticism, was alien to Jewish thought, and the tradition had to be gradually created that it was an honour to a man of wealth to support such a student. The men of wealth at first certainly did not take kindly to the suggestion, and we may assume that it was only as the rabbinical courts and the rabbinical method of judgement gradually came to supersede the Roman or local tradition that the rabbinical schools came to receive the honour which was theirs in later times.

Although the patriarch was recognized by the Romans as the legal head of the Jewish community, and was able to receive an income from all the synagogues of the diaspora, actually the effective leadership in Jewry passed in the fourth century from Palestine to Babylon, where the Jewish communities were far more numerous than in Palestine and enjoyed from their Persian rulers even greater local autonomy. This process was accelerated by the anti-Jewish legislation which began to appear once the Christian Church had the power to express its theological views in the laws of the state; and there were even migrations of scholars and others from Palestine to the more congenial freedom of Sura, Pumbeditha and the great Mesopotamian academies. Here was observed for the first time the feature of all subsequent Jewish life, that the religious centre moved spontaneously to the place in which the outstanding Jewish scholars and interpreters were to be found, and quitted it and moved elsewhere when it declined. During the first two hundred years after the loss of Jerusalem, that centre was undoubtedly Palestine; it returned to the country again nearly six hundred years later.

The last three centuries of Roman rule were centuries of increasing tragedy for the Jews. Legislative action was followed by popular violence, conversions to Christianity doubtless took place in small numbers, and the community dwindled in both numbers and wealth. In the fourth century it is probable that Jews still formed a majority of the population of Galilee, but only a minority in the south where they had not recovered from the losses of 135. We cannot establish the fact statistically, but several Christian writers of the period, especially Jerome who lived in Bethlehem, reported that there were few Christians and that most of the people in the country were Jews. This evidence might have appeared conclusive, did we not know how easily men magnify numbers when stating that a district is full of people they dislike! By the seventh century the Jewish population of the whole country had probably dwindled to under a quarter of a million and possibly less. It depends on the accuracy of the statement that 20,000 Jews joined the Persians in 614. If the figure is correct it would imply a population of 200,000 or more, but ancient figures are notoriously difficult to check.

The legislation which was the basic reason for this decline came gradually to impose on the Jews a second-class citizenship; it went far beyond religious intolerance. Not only were synagogues forbidden to be built; not only was a synagogue, seized by a Christian mob and consecrated in haste, irrecoverable, but public offices and professions were forbidden to them; and the language in which these prohibitions were expressed was an invitation to popular violence; in the heyday of eastern monasticism that invitation met a quick response.

The centuries which witnessed the decline of Jewry witnessed

the increasing prominence of the country as the Holy Land of
Christianity. Unhappily this was not accompanied by a creative
Christian activity parallel to that of the Jewish rabbinical semi-
naries of Galilee. Though there were a few eminent scholars of
Palestinian origin, and doubtless many tens of thousands of sincere Christians living out their lives in its towns and villages, that
which history has to record is mainly continual religious controversy leading even to bloodshed; physical violence against Jews
and pagans; and a profitable traffic in Holy Places, often wholly
imaginary.

For two hundred years after the apostolic age the story of
Christianity in Palestine is relatively obscure. It is easy to understand that the pagan city of Aelia Capitolina had none of the
spontaneous associations of Jerusalem, and there seems to have
been no objection to the transference of the organizational centre
of the Church to Caesarea. The bishop of Jerusalem was, until the
fifth century, merely a suffragan of the metropolitan of Caesarea,
in the patriarchate of Antioch, though from at least the third
century he began to enjoy a courtesy eminence outside the metropolitan diocese. Thus we find him at the council of Antioch (about
270), sitting among the patriarchs; at Nicaea (325) he signed
before his metropolitan, and was granted precedence within the
diocese next to the metropolitan, to the great indignation of the
latter. Only in 451 did he become himself a patriarch, with
authority over all the Holy Land, and later over Arabia.

It is in the persecution initiated by Decius (249–251) and carried on by Valerian (253–260) that we first get evidence of the
vitality of the Palestinian Christians. By this time the Church
had made such strides that the empire could no longer ignore the
mass of citizens of all ranks who would not participate in the
ordinary demonstrations of loyalty and solidarity which (rather
than any religious emotion) characterized the official sacrifices and
religious ceremonies of the court, the army, and the municipali-
ties. In spite of their genuine protestations of loyalty the Christians were suspect, largely because they were incomprehensible.
Much of their activity must still have seemed to the authorities
to identify them as a secret society, and autocrats and bureaucrats
alike fear what they cannot keep wholly under their eyes. More-

THE PATRIARCHATE
OF JERUSALEM

Archbishopric: CAESAREA
Bishopric: Dora
Monastery: *S. Saba*

N

Zabulon Jotapata
Sycaminion Hippos
Diocaesarea Abila
Nazareth Exaloth Gadara
Dora Maximianopolis
SCYTHOPOLIS
CAESAREA Pella
Sebaste
Neapolis

Antipatris

Joppa
Lydda Archelais
Jamnia Emmaus *Quarantania*
Gadara Jericho
Azotus JERUSALEM
Bethlehem *S. Theodosius*
S. Saba
Ascalon Eleutheropolis
Bethelia
Anthedon
Maiuma
Gaza
Raphi Gerar

Minois Arad
Elusa Zoar
Sodom PETRA

Miles
0 10 20

Eboda Phana Augustopolis Arindela

over the empire was going through a severe political and economic crisis, and in such times men are exceptionally apt to resent a minority which will not conform. The edicts of Decius and Valerian were directed against those who would not take part in a national supplication to the gods of Rome to avert the dangers which surrounded the state. They were designed to secure apostates, not martyrs. They did not ask the Christian to abjure his own faith, but to recognize also the faith of the empire. If he would do that, his private beliefs were not inquired into. But most Christians would not accept the compromise and there were many martyrs.

In this persecution Alexander, the aged bishop of Jerusalem, who had already spent nine years in prison for his faith in an earlier persecution in Cappadocia, was so ill-treated that he died in prison in Caesarea. Many others were tortured and imprisoned, but none seems to have been executed until three youths from the countryside near Caesarea, seeing the sufferings of their fellows in the city, boldly came before the governor and proclaimed themselves Christians. They were given to the beasts in the amphitheatre. When Gallienus succeeded to the empire in 261 he called a halt, but Palestine had yet one more martyr, a predecessor to St George of Lydda and perhaps more historical than that more famous saint. An officer, Marinus, had been appointed centurion; a rival denounced him as ineligible because he was a Christian. Marinus admitted the charge, and after being given three hours to change his mind, was executed.

In the profound peace which followed these ten years the Church evidently thought that such times had passed for ever. Church buildings of considerable architectural dignity began to rise openly in the cities of the bishops; high officials and members of the imperial family had no hesitation in avowing their Christian faith. In everything the Church acted as though the danger was over for good and all.

It would be interesting if we were able to say what proportion of the empire was Christian at this time; but the estimates of different scholars vary enormously. Somewhere between five and ten per cent may be as near as we can get, but the distribution was uneven. In Palestine the proportion was probably smaller, possibly much smaller. In the regions where Jews were numerous it is unlikely that there were many opportunities for the development of Christian communities. The Jewish authorities were both hostile and powerful and frowned on any contact with Christians. There must have been such contacts in the economic field, for the country is too small for the inhabitants to remain rigidly segregated, but it is doubtful if they went beyond the social-economic sphere. In any case there is little record of prominent Christian buildings in Palestine when the persecution of Diocletian fell on the unsuspecting Church.

Of the events which followed in Palestine, Eusebius, the most prominent church historian of his time and resident at Caesarea through much of this period, has left an invaluable record. He himself escaped martyrdom, but his great friend and teacher, Pamphilus, a presbyter of the church in Caesarea, died in prison. The struggle lasted for six years; when the attack on the bishops and clergy failed, new edicts were directed either by Diocletian or his imperial colleague against the laity, as well as against all Christian buildings, property and sacred writings. Many yielded, but still more stood firm, and endured horrible tortures at Caesarea, at Gaza and at Scythopolis. The number who gave their lives was relatively small; but the number who were imprisoned, mutilated and sent for long periods to work in the mines was very large. The last executions took place in the spring of 310; but by that time it was evident to all that the persecution had failed; there remained nothing for the empire to do but to make peace with this new force which had grown up within the citizenry; and in 311 the inevitable step was taken of proclaiming religious toleration throughout the empire.

The end of external persecution was but the signal for the outbreak of internal violence and disorder. For nearly half a century the Church was rent over the Arian controversy, which was itself but a phase in the long drawn out effort to reconcile the divinity and humanity of Christ. The controversy became so violent and widespread that in 325 Constantine summoned a council of the whole Church to deal with the issue, and 318 bishops met in the imperial city of Nicaea to settle the matter. One of the leading figures at the council was Eusebius of Caesarea, who had become the trusted friend of the emperor; and the creed of Caesarea, as brought forward by Eusebius, formed the basis of the famous creed of Nicaea.

The Arian controversy was the first struggle in which the Church engaged after the empire had made its peace with her. The use which she made of this friendship was, therefore, a precedent for the future. Unhappily, she succumbed entirely to the idea that theological questions can be settled by the short cut of imperial legislation and civil punishment – aided by violence which the side supported by the imperial court could be sure would be overlooked. Within a couple of centuries the Emperor Zeno could write of the effects of another controversy on the same issue that 'thousands have perished in the massacres and not only the earth but the air is red with blood', while Christians attacked each other with a ferocity 'such as a savage would not dare to use to a pagan or a Jew'.

In the fifth century Palestine was to realize to the full the significance of the moral disaster which had befallen the Church; for the protagonists of intolerance and violence were the eastern monks and Palestine had become their main centre. The two attractions which the land provided were Holy Places and deserts; at Sinai and in the region of the wilderness of Judea both were combined in unique measure. The cult of Holy Places spread side by side with that of relics. The Church of the first three centuries grew up in the Jewish belief that a dead body was unclean; and there is little trace of any veneration being paid to bodies, even the bodies of saints and martyrs, until the fourth century. The remains of martyrs were collected and reverently buried where they had died; to do so was indeed a pious duty linked to the belief in a bodily resurrection; but that their bodies should be divided into bits in order to give special sanctity to other places, this was the distortion of a later age, but a distortion that, once admitted, spread like fire. By the eighth century it was impossible to consecrate an altar which did not contain the relics of a saint, and the collection of heads, arms, legs and other single bones became the natural ambition of a pious prince or churchman. Naturally relics connected with Biblical events, and with the life and person of Jesus and of Mary, were worthy of the highest veneration; and there was no place where they could be so convincingly produced as in Palestine.

The real beginning was made by the determination of Constantine himself to recover the 'true cross', and to build a suitable shrine on the sites of the Crucifixion and the Resurrection. The present Church of the Holy Sepulchre covers but a small part of the ground occupied by the magnificent buildings of Constantine; though what was the evidence on which Macarius, Bishop of Jerusalem, decided that this was the actual site of those events has never been known. The only church built by Constantine which retains, partially at least, the form in which he built it, is the Church of the Nativity at Bethlehem. By the end of the Byzantine period magnificent churches had been built in many parts of Palestine; and relics of every instrument mentioned in the gospel narrative of the Passion had been provided, together with many other similar marvels from the Old and New Testaments. As early as the end of the fourth century an important lady on pilgrimage from Gaul, visiting Jerusalem and Sinai, saw the site of every incident of the Exodus, including such details as the stone on which Moses broke the tables of the Law. And around all such relics clustered the monks, whether in monasteries when the relics were in towns or in hermitages when they were in the deserts.

The origins of monasticism (or rather monachism, from the Latin *monachus*, a monk) can be found in the pre-Christian asceticism which was a recurrent expression of the eastern belief that matter is inherently evil. It appeared in the Judaism of the Greek period as Essenism; it reappeared in the Judeo-Christian sect of Ebionites; and it has a rational basis in reaction against the corruption and sexual indulgence of many oriental cults. In an organized form monachism first appeared in the Christian Church in Egypt towards the end of the third century, when Anthony, who had retired to the desert at the age of twenty and had attracted many followers, consented to organize them under a loose rule of life. He was followed by Pachomius, who produced a much more careful rule, based on a common life, and on the performance of useful work, both for the community and for society in general. The ideas of Anthony were early transferred to Palestine by a young man named Hilarion, who, at the age of

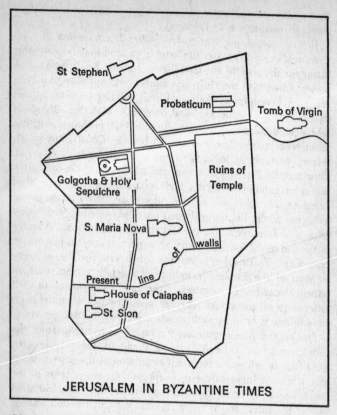

JERUSALEM IN BYZANTINE TIMES

Map labels: St Stephen, Probaticum, Tomb of Virgin, Ruins of Temple, Golgotha & Holy Sepulchre, S. Maria Nova, Present line of walls, House of Caiaphas, St Sion

fifteen, established himself near Gaza and likewise drew many followers.

A better element was introduced in the middle of the century by Basil (330–379), son of a wealthy Cappadocian family who, after visiting the monks of Syria, Egypt and Palestine, introduced a new tradition – it was not a formal rule – in Asia Minor. Basil's monks followed a strictly ascetic discipline; but they were forbidden to allow asceticism to weaken them to the extent of being unable to do useful work for their own community, or charitable and educational work for those around them. These works made the monks beloved of the local population, and many of them were rightly admired for their useful lives and genuine piety.

Among the Palestinian monks of the fifth century were to be found examples of all the types so far described, and two of the writers who tell us most of these early monks, Cyril of Scythopolis and John Moscus, were both Palestinians. Both lived at the end of the sixth century, one stayed at Mar Saba and the other began his career in Jerusalem and died at Rome. There were hermits, and followers of extravagant asceticisms; there were 'lauras' or houses following roughly the discipline of Pachomius which was regulated in Palestine by St Sabas (439–531), founder of the still existing monastery of Mar Saba by the Dead Sea; and there were many regular monasteries, especially in and around Jerusalem, following the tradition of St Basil. The presence in Bethlehem from 386 till his death in 420 of St Jerome brought added lustre to the monasticism of the country. But it also provides an early example of the other side of monasticism – the consequences to be expected from theological disagreement. Jerome took a vigorous part in the controversy raging at that time over the views of the first recorded British puritan, Pelagius (*c*.360 – *c*.420), on the basis of salvation, and so enraged the supporters of the latter that they fell on his monastery at Bethlehem, murdered one of the deacons, burned down the buildings, and would unquestionably have killed Jerome himself had he not managed to escape to a neighbouring military post.

A few years later there appeared in the country a Syrian monk, Barsauma, with forty companions, who terrorized whole districts, especially Jewish districts, burning down synagogues, and laying waste towns and villages. When in 449 one of the periodical attempts was made at a council at Ephesus to settle the question of the nature of Christ, Barsauma and his gangster-monks terrorized his opponents to the extent of so misusing Flavian, the patriarch of Constantinople, that he succumbed to his injuries. To the rage of the monks the decisions of Ephesus were reversed two years later by the Council of Chalcedon (451); and when they learnt that its decisions had been supported by Juvenal, Bishop of Jerusalem, whom the council had elevated to the dignity of

Patriarch, they raised a riot, prevented Juvenal from entering Jerusalem, consecrated one of their number to take his place, and others to replace all the suffragans who supported him, and were only reduced to obedience by the action of both the emperor and the pope, aided, if the chronicler Zechariah of Mitylene be correct, by Juvenal himself, who, with a mixed force of Roman soldiers and Samaritans, massacred all the monks he could find.

While such was the spirit in which religious disagreement might be conducted, it is not surprising that permanent schisms followed the different interpretations of the nature of Christ which were put forward in the fifth and sixth centuries and which go under the name of the monophysite controversy (from those who held that the divine and human elements made one nature – *mono-phusis*). It is necessary to say something of the controversy, because it explains the diversity of Christian Churches present in contemporary Jerusalem. With one exception, those eastern churches which still reject the authority of both Rome and Constantinople grew out of the bloody persecutions and vile abuse which marked the conduct of the disputants.

The exception is the Church of Persia, which asserted its entire institutional independence of Constantinople as a political necessity of its acceptance by the Persians. The Christians in that country had undergone persecutions as long drawn out and as painful as those endured by their brethren in the Roman Empire. As they began to win toleration it was in the highest measure desirable that they should be able to assure the Persian sovereign that they owed no political or other allegiance to the Byzantine emperor, and in view of the intimate association of Church and State, this involved owing no allegiance to the patriarch of Constantinople. It was thus on political and not doctrinal grounds that the Church of the East became separate, acknowledging only its catholicus, the bishop of Seleucia. But the Byzantine system of securing religious uniformity inevitably created refugees; and such refugees naturally fled to Christians outside the reach of Byzantine governor or bishop. The defeated party of the fifth century were the followers of Nestorius, ex-Patriarch of Constantinople, who had so distinguished the divine and human natures of Christ that he considered Mary should be called 'mother of

Christ' but not 'mother of God'. The Nestorians fled to Persia and were there accepted; and so, almost inadvertently, the Persian Church came to be considered, and ultimately to be, Nestorian in its doctrine, and is so to this day.

Those who went to the other extreme proclaimed a complete assumption of the human nature into the divine nature, so that in the union Christ had only one nature (*mono-phusis*). This view was held by almost all the Christians of the eastern provinces, except in the patriarchate of Jerusalem, whose bishops, apart from brief periods, were firm 'Chalcedonians' – i.e. accepted the formula of the Council of Chalcedon which avoided the two extremes, and declared Christ to be one person in two natures. In the issue undoubtedly a certain Syrian and Egyptian nationalism and dislike of the heavy hand of Greek bureaucracy came into play; and the result was that the Church of Egypt (the Coptic Church), with its Abyssinian daughter, became and remain monophysite, while they coined the word 'Melkite' (semitic, *malk*: king) for those who adhered to the 'royal' view of Chalcedon–Constantinople. Such was the strength of monophysitism in the East that at the beginning of the sixth century it caused a complete, if temporary, breach between the Churches of Rome and Constantinople.

The conflict reached another peak of bitterness and violence when Justinian (527–565) became emperor. A brilliant ruler and no mean thinker, Justinian possessed to the full the narrowness and intolerance which was a feature of the Christianity of his age. He was determined that every subject of his should be absolutely faithful to the Chalcedonian formula, and the ferocity with which he persecuted heretics (as well as Samaritans and Jews) surpassed that of his predecessors. As his particular enemies were the monophysites, one result of his action was to create a monophysite Church in Armenia for exactly the same reasons that had produced a hundred years earlier a Nestorian Church in Persia. The kingdom of Armenia, uneasily wedged between the two great empires, with its loyalty suspect by each, had to make the difficult decision as to which represented the greater danger. Having decided for Persia, they took the easiest step to reassure the Persians that they were not secret allies of Constantinople;

they adopted the monophysitism detested by the Byzantine emperors. But the situation had a comic side.

While Justinian ruthlessly enforced his Chalcedonian orthodoxy, his empress, the beloved and brilliant Theodora, secretly sympathized with monophysitism. She took advantage of the fact that her husband had locked up a large number of monophysite bishops in Constantinople to get them, in their prison, to consecrate a certain Jacob Baradai bishop, with secret authority over all the eastern provinces, where the population much preferred monophysitism to Chalcedonianism (or, as the emperor called it, orthodoxy). This intrepid man travelled in disguise as a beggar for thirty-five years (543–578) through the eastern provinces, secretly consecrating bishops, maintaining the courage of the faithful, and leaving behind him a fully organized monophysite Church. An interesting fact is that this Church included not only the Romanized Nabatean Arabs, but also the Arabs on the fringe of the empire, especially the great clan of the Abu Ghassan whose territories stretched round the desert fringe of the fertile crescent between the Byzantine and Persian territories. From Jacob Baradai, this Church appropriately took the title of 'Jacobite'.

The intolerance which the Christian Churches showed to each other they all showed equally to those who were outside the Christian fold. The lot of a provincial in the Byzantine Empire was rarely an easy one, for the burden of taxation was usually exceedingly heavy and the exactions of personal avarice, whether in governor, subordinate or soldier, had to be added to the load. When to this economic extortion were added the special burdens of religious nonconformity time was ripe for revolt. Justinian's exclusion of pagans from citizenship – which could only be obtained by baptism – must have been the last straw.

The legislation against Jews had been explicitly extended to include Samaritans by Theodosius II. In 438 he excluded them from all honorary office; prohibited the building of new synagogues and all but essential repairs to existing buildings, and forbade conversions among slaves and freedmen. But a good deal of oppression probably went on in addition to these formal laws, and in 484 the Samaritans rose, raided Caesarea, and both massacred a considerable number of Christians and destroyed a number of churches before they were overpowered by the garrison. In consequence they were expelled from their sanctuary on Gerizim, and it was turned into a church of the Blessed Virgin. Some years later the Samaritans rose again, expelled the small garrison in Neapolis (Nablus) and seized the church; but they were quickly expelled by the governor. They rose once more in 529, following still more oppressive legislation from Justinian which, addressing them (together with Jews and various brands of heretics) in the most insulting language, promised them all the sweat of office and none of the sweets, dismissed them from any honourable offices they had already received, excluded them from the bar, and confirmed all previous laws against them.

The previous laws may have fallen into desuetude or been ignored; Justinian's were meant to be enforced. The Samaritans rose in desperation, but the forces of Justinian were too strong; they were completely crushed; many thousands were forced into the Church; they were deprived of all administrative autonomy; their synagogues were destroyed, and their property confiscated by their being only allowed to will it to an heir who was a member of the Orthodox Christian Church. Two years later they were excluded from pleading in a lawsuit, or even from giving evidence, except in favour of an Orthodox suitor. This was the end of the Samaritans as a national, or political, unit. What their numbers were at that time we have, as usual, no means of knowing; but the belt of country which they inhabited was extensive and more fertile than it is today, and it may well have supported a population equal to that of the Jews. There survived for many centuries Samaritan communities in various parts of Palestine, Syria and Egypt; but as a national community they never recovered from the catastrophe of 529. There was another rising in 556, but it was easily suppressed.

The hopes of the Samaritans had to some extent been based on the possibility of indirect help from the Persians; the eyes of the Jewish community were often fixed on the same region. There was little doubt in the minds of Jewish leaders that in the long duel between Rome and Persia Jewish interests lay with the latter. But it is doubtful if there was any serious Jewish rising during the sixth century. Some chroniclers imply that the Jews rose with the

Samaritans, but this is doubtful. In any case their power was substantially diminished; their political autonomy, their civil rights, and even their religious freedom had all been reduced by the bullying orthodoxy of the Byzantine emperors, and in particular by Justinian, who added insult to injury by constantly empowering their chief enemies, the orthodox bishops, to assist the civil government in the enforcement of the humiliating burdens imposed upon them. In the fourth century Cyril of Jerusalem had complained that 'Jewish serpents and Samaritan imbeciles' had attended his addresses to Christian converts 'like wolves surrounding the flock of Christ'. Neither Jew nor Samaritan would have dared to exercise such freedom in the time of Justinian and his successors.

The day of a brief relief and revenge was, however, approaching. Justinian's grandiose dreams of imperial magnificence, and his passion for building – including several churches in Palestine – had heavily overstrained the empire's weak economic resources. His successors could not possibly maintain what he had so rashly conquered; and the empire fell a prey to disorder. Then occurred a repetition of the superstitious fears which had led Valerian and Diocletian to persecute the Christians, only this time the infidels who were said to be angering the Almighty were the Jews. Phocas (602–610) and his successor Heraclius (610–641) were said to have been warned that the empire was menaced by 'the circumcised', and both in consequence ordered the Jews of the empire to accept baptism. What numbers submitted we have no means of knowing. In any case their submission was probably of short duration, for in 611 the Persians swept through the eastern provinces, and in 614 they took Jerusalem after a siege lasting only twenty days.

There is no doubt that the Persians received substantial help from the Jews of Galilee. One chronicler mentions a figure of 20,000 Jewish soldiers, another 26,000. While the actual figures are as unreliable as all ancient figures, there is no reason to question the fact that the Jews aided the Persians with all the men they could muster, and that the help they gave was considerable. Once Jerusalem was in Persian hands a terrible massacre of Christians took place, and the Jews are accused of having taken the lead in this massacre. It would not be surprising if the accusation were true, even though the fantastic stories told of Jewish revenge by Christian chroniclers are certainly exaggerated. The Jews seem to have hoped that the Persians would allow them the full possession of the city, and even the re-establishment of an autonomous state. But the Persian occupation was too short for such plans to develop. It lasted only fifteen years.

In these fifteen years, however, changes occurred which centuries were not to repair. The country had been desolated by the Persian armies; agriculture had come to a standstill; cities were empty, while their inhabitants had fled to the mountains; churches and monasteries were in ruins, and much of Jerusalem itself was burnt. All the treasures collected in its shrines, including the 'true cross' itself, had been taken away, and the Patriarch Zacharias sent with thousands of others as prisoners to Persia. It was a half-empty country filled with ruins which, by a supreme effort, Heraclius managed to reoccupy in 629. Though he himself seems to have been inclined to spare the Jews for the part they had played as allies of the Persians, the clergy of Jerusalem thought only of revenge; and as bloody a massacre took place of Jews as had previously taken place of Christians. But that – and the recovery of the 'true cross' – was all the satisfaction that the Christians got. A far more powerful enemy was approaching. In the year in which Heraclius regained Palestine, Muhammad was completing his conquest of Mecca. In 636 his followers entered the country; in 640 Caesarea surrendered and Byzantine rule was at an end.

CHAPTER FOUR

Muslim: The Arab Conquest

THE Persians in 614 were the first foreign invaders to cross the frontiers of The Land for more than six hundred years. Twenty years later the victory of the Arabs over the Byzantines at the battle of Yarmuk in August 636 finally brought that long period of political peace to an end, and for nearly a thousand years The Land was to know once again the continual passage of armies in foreign and civil wars with many of which the inhabitants had no direct concern; and, for much longer than that, to realize the insecurity of her eastern and southern frontiers whence raiding bedouins descended to devastate her fields, destroy her trees, and often massacre her people.

The primary motive which inspired the Arab conquest was economic. It was made possible by the weakness of the Mediterranean–Middle Eastern world in which the great empires of Rome and Persia had wasted too often their strength in internecine strife. Everywhere on their fringes new peoples were on the move, from the scanty pastures of the north and east as well as from the sandy deserts of the south; and everywhere the motive was the same, the desire for booty, for the control of the rich lands which centuries of peasant industry under stable, if exacting, governments had raised to a level of productivity which The Land itself, and many other lands as well, have never known since. Those who find it a subject of congratulation that among the Arab peasants of today are to be found unchanged the economy and customs of the Bible ignore the fact that this is only possible because of the regression which has resulted from centuries of Muslim rule. It is only the most backward and impoverished parts of the Holy Land of Jesus and the apostles which are recalled by the modern fellaheen. The busy cities, the caravans of merchants, the thriving forests, the prosperous estates, and the rural industries with which Jesus or the apostles would have been familiar, have perished beneath the combined assaults of the bedouin, the goat and the tax-collector.

So little was the first wave of the Arab conquest an exclusive product of religious fanaticism, offering the conquered Islam or the sword, that many of the bedouin bands who formed the armies of Islam were in all probability still pagans when they took part in the first great surge out of the peninsula. Moreover their whole economy was so completely based on the payment of tribute by their non-Muslim subjects that when later the subject populations tended to accept Islam in large numbers, there was a severe crisis in the finances of the state, and the whole system of taxation had to be revised. There is no doubt that within a very short time a religious *élan* was developed; but it was akin to that of the Puritans of Cromwell. It made magnificent warriors, but not missionaries.

The ease with which the Arabs advanced was due to the exhaustion of the Byzantine and Persian empires. But another factor was the religious intolerance of Orthodox Christianity* and Persian Zoroastrianism, both of which had created in their respective empires large and dissatisfied minorities only too willing to accept a change of masters. Here again a correction of traditional views is necessary. If the motive of Arab expansion was not religious neither was its conduct characterized by fanaticism. The conquerors were looking for tribute rather than converts, and their attitude to those who did not resist them was characterized by generosity rather than arrogance. Among the instructions which the first caliph, Abu Bakr (632–634) is said to have given the army when it first marched out of the peninsula are the following:

Be just, for the unjust never prosper. Be valiant: die rather than retreat. Keep your word, even to your enemies. Be merciful: slay

---

*In this and succeeding chapters the word 'Orthodox' is used to denote those Christians in communion with, or sharing the doctrines of, the ecumenical patriarch of Constantinople. From the doctrinal standpoint every Church naturally claims orthodoxy for its views – otherwise it would scarcely hold them.

neither the old, nor the young nor the women. Destroy no fruit trees, no crops, no beasts. Kill neither sheep, nor oxen nor camels, except it be for food.

So also most of the stories which later ages told of his successor, Umar (634–644), deal with his simplicity, his generosity, and his lack of pomp; and if the stories about both these caliphs be partly apocryphal, they reflect what later ages knew of them, and they are borne out by the ready obedience which the conquerors found among the conquered. Jews and non-Orthodox Christians in Byzantine territory, or Orthodox Christians in Persia, all alike found the change of ruler a benefit, once the sufferings endured in the years of the conquest had been overcome. For once they had paid their tribute – and it was no more onerous than the previous taxes – they were free to manage their own affairs, and their new masters were indifferent to their religious beliefs.

Muhammad died in 632. His successor, Abu Bakr, was fully occupied in extending his authority over the Arabian peninsula, for not more than a third had accepted the political or religious leadership of the Prophet in his lifetime. Only raiding parties went further. It was under the second caliph, Umar, that the conquest of both Byzantium and Persia was undertaken. The occupation of Palestine was a minor incident of that conquest. The Arabs advanced along both borders of the desert, up the western banks of the Euphrates and along the Mediterranean coast. When it became evident that the forces of Heraclius would be in the field before the Persians, those advancing along the Euphrates, by a brilliant forced march, crossed the desert, joined up with the western Arabs north-east of Palestine, and completely routed the Byzantine army in 636 on the river Yarmuk.

The fall of Damascus took place in the following year, and the rest of the cities of Syria and Palestine fell like ripe plums into the conqueror's mouth. Jerusalem, after a short siege, surrendered in 640. The year 641 saw both the final defeat of Persia and the conquest of Egypt. Scarcely any attempt was made to organize this vast empire. The main, almost the only, interest was to assure the regular payment of the tribute, and governors were appointed not as administrators but as soldiers or as tax-collectors. So long as the centre remained in distant Arabia there could, indeed, be no question of a full administration: the caliph lived too far away; and it was only after the murder of the aged Uthman (644–656) that his successor Ali (656–661) moved the capital to al-Kufah on the Euphrates.

Ali was the last of the 'orthodox' caliphs who had been companions of the Prophet and succeeded by some sort of election. But his tenure of power, short though it was, was a tragic presage for the future. He came to the caliphate through the murder of his predecessor, not by the enemies of Islam, but by those in his own household; and he only secured his position by civil war. By civil war he lost it, and he was himself murdered by one of the dissenters in his own army. He was the unintentional cause of a schism which has endured to this day; for his followers refused to accept the religious supremacy of his successor, Muawiyah, governor of Syria, and founded the Shiite sect (the sectaries) in opposition to the Sunnis (the followers of tradition, or orthodox) who accepted Muawiyah.

Announcing that Ali had forfeited his rights through complicity in the murder of Uthman, Muawiyah (661–680), who was descended from Umayyah, nephew of the great-grandfather of Muhammad, announced himself caliph at Jerusalem, and made his capital Damascus. He introduced the principle of hereditary succession, but his Umayyad descendants ruled the empire for less than a century. Yet in this period, under the caliph Walid (705–715), it reached its greatest extent, and stretched from Spain to India. The Umayyads were the only dynasty which could be called purely Arab. For when they fell and power passed to the Abbasids, it was Islam and not Arab blood which formed the basis of unity; and a little more than another century saw the passage of effective power to successive usurpers who were wholly or largely of Turkish origin.

There is, however, a factor which remained constant until modern times and in all the territories once ruled by the caliphs. Government was personal government; elaborate written laws and constitutions played but little effective part, and nothing like an ordered development of political institutions is to be looked for. Action and attitude varied according either to the social traditions or religious ideas of the tribe, group or sect in power, or, more simply, to the whim of a ruler, which might differ from evening to morning according to his mood. It is only on the widest canvas and over long periods of time that generalizations can be made which have anything like universal validity. The many records of nineteenth-century writers on the Middle East describe situations and behaviour identical with those of the earliest caliphs and their governors, in the sudden changes from kindness to oppression, from indifference to intolerance. Though there were many just and God-fearing rulers, bribery and personal predilection were too often the basic determinants of action and inaction, not laws, written privileges or to some extent even custom. This general consideration is of special importance in treating of The Land in which there were throughout important non-Muslim elements to whom custom itself gave no equality with Muslims or rights against Muslims; but it is in fact equally true of the treatment of the general Muslim population by governors and tax-collectors throughout the Islamic East.

During the first century after the Arab conquest the caliph and governors of Syria and The Land ruled almost entirely over Christian and Jewish subjects. Apart from the bedouin, in the earliest days the only Arabs west of the Jordan (not all of whom were themselves Muslims) were the garrisons of the capitals of the two provinces into which it was divided. Al-Urdunn, with capital at Tiberias (Tabariyah) occupied roughly the area of Galilee; and Filastin, with capital at Lydda (later Ramleh) occupied all the area south of that down to the frontiers of Egypt. These garrisons were small, and two years after the capture of Jerusalem they were decimated by epidemics and only gradually replaced. At first they were not even allowed to own land, but this was rescinded by Uthman. Thereafter a good deal of the country passed into the ownership of rich Arabs. Doubtless there were cases where the Christian owners had fled and others where they were dispossessed. But this change of owners did not involve any extensive change in the nature of the population. The land was still worked by the same peasants, for the Arabs were not only entirely inexperienced in agriculture, but heartily despised the tiller of the soil.

We can, then, assume for at least a hundred years that the

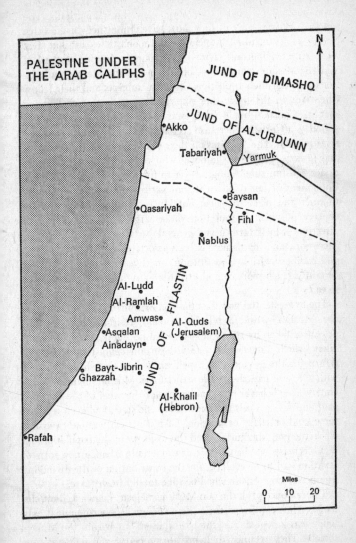

PALESTINE UNDER
THE ARAB CALIPHS

JUND OF DIMASHQ

N

JUND OF AL-URDUNN

Akko

Tabariyah
Yarmuk

Baysan

Qasariyah
Fihl

Nablus

Al-Ludd
Al-Ramlah
Amwas
Al-Quds
(Jerusalem)
Asqalan
Ainadayn

JUND OF FILASTIN

Bayt-Jibrin
Ghazzah

Al-Khalil
(Hebron)

Rafah

Miles
0   10   20

majority of the population continued to be Christians – Orthodox or monophysite – and the minority Jews and Samaritans. The number of both of these latter must have diminished during three centuries of Byzantine intolerance and monastic excess, but they were still an important factor in the country. In view of the fact that the Muslims would have been in no position to prevent relations between their numerous Christian subjects and their fellow Christians in the Byzantine empire, it is interesting to discover that at Constantinople Islam was regarded for a considerable period as a Christian heretical sect akin to Arianism, and not as a rival religion. The Muslims on their side regarded both Christians and Jews as 'People of the Book' who were entitled to protection under Muslim rule, though never to full equality with Muslims. The extent of fair or ill treatment varied enormously from ruler to ruler and place to place; but Umar, the first caliph directly concerned with the question on a large scale, issued certain directives which formed the general basis for the policy of his successors, and his name has been associated by Muslim lawyers and codifiers with a 'constitution' or 'covenant' which is almost certainly much more complicated than anything which existed at so early a period.

The first essential was that the non-Muslim should surrender to the Muslim without offering violent resistance. Cities and provinces taken by the sword possessed no rights. Cities like Jerusalem which surrendered received certain defined privileges, in return for the payment of a poll tax (*jizya*) on which, together with the land tax, the whole structure of Muslim finances rested. For the true believer only paid a tax for the relief of the poor. He paid nothing towards the expenses of the state, and even received some kind of salary or pension. Such a system was only possible while the non-Muslims formed the majority of the population. As they decreased at the expense of converts to Islam, a new form of taxation had to be evolved, for the contribution of the dwindling number of non-Muslims had become totally inadequate.

The tax once paid, the non-Muslim subjects, known as *dhimmis*, more or less continued their life as before. Their communal existence was accepted, and they became *millets* within the Muslim society. They retained their private property; and religious communities, Jewish or Christian, retained their churches and ecclesiastical laws and the administration of them, though they were not allowed to put up new buildings. Their religious activities, however, had to remain unobtrusive, so as not to attract the attention of Muslims, and dhimmis had to avoid, either in dress or conduct, appearing to be Muslims, or to be on an equality with Muslims. Dhimmis were gradually excluded from service in the army. As the first capital outside the peninsula was at al-Kufah in Iraq, it is possible that this general system owes something to the position already established in Persia for the Nestorian Christians. They were organized in a similar way as an autonomous religious community, dealing with the government corporately through their catholicus or patriarch. The 'millet' system, which continued up to the end of the period in which Turkey ruled the Arab world, thus antedated the Arab conquest.

The earliest converts to Islam in The Land were probably Christian Arab tribes along the eastern frontiers. Among the many Christian monuments in the territory of the Hauran east of the Sea of Galilee, there are only two which can be dated after 640, which suggests that Christian leaders made a poor struggle for survival in this region. The twin facts that the new conquerors were themselves Arabs, and that the Christianity of the Nabateans and their successors had been monophysite and exposed to continuous persecution by the Byzantine government and the Orthodox patriarchs of Jerusalem, seems to have made them very ready to change their religion. That this attitude was not universal was discovered by Baldwin I, King of Jerusalem, when in 1100 he was able to repopulate Jerusalem with Syrian Christians from this region. In the rest of the country a change of religion was a much slower business; but even while they made no attempt to force conversions the Arabs, from the very first, laid claim to the Temple area in Jerusalem.

A wooden mosque was built near where the Aksa Mosque now stands. In the time of Abd al-Malik (685–705) was built the present glorious shrine, which stands upon the spot whence Muhammad made his legendary flight to heaven. It is the work of Byzantine architects and Greek, local and Egyptian craftsmen. Though the cupola itself had to be rebuilt some centuries later after an earthquake, and the outer wall had to be added for additional strength, the building still stands substantially as al-Malik left it in 691. He probably also built the Aksa Mosque at the southern end of the great enclosure or Noble Sanctuary (Haram* ash-Sharif) but of the original building nothing remains today. It is quite possible that the reason for building so splendid a shrine was at least as much political as religious. The authority of Abd al-Malik had for some time been challenged by a rival caliph, Abdullah ibn al-Zubayr, who was in possession of Mecca and so able to draw a substantial revenue from the pilgrims who came from Abd al-Malik's dominions; and pilgrimage to the Dome of the Rock may have been intended to provide an effective substitute for the pilgrimage to Mecca ordered by Muhammad himself.

The Umayyads built themselves palaces and hunting lodges in the Jordan valley and east of the river. Remains of them still exist at Qeseir Amra, at Amman and at Khirbet Mefjer near Jericho; but the only caliph who made his permanent residence in The Land was the second son of Abd al-Malik, Sulayman (715–717). He built himself a palace and a large mosque at Ramleh.

The period of Abd al-Malik and his successors saw a considerable increase in conversions to Islam. At the turn of the century the official registers were for the first time ordered to be kept in Arabic instead of Greek, and Umar II (717–720), nephew of al-Malik, reintroduced and amplified the legislation concerning the dhimmis. Though the majority of officials were still Christians, the time was coming when it was at last possible to challenge their monopoly – and the temptation to change religion was thereby increased. For an educated class of Arabic-speaking Muslims was coming into existence, and naturally expected priority in employment. Moreover the general temper was changing. At the highest level, at the court of the Abbasids as well as that of the Umayyads, a Christian or a Jew of intelligence and capacity could still live in a very tolerant atmosphere; but at the level of the street and the market place, it would seem that Muslim

---

*The word should be spelt with a dot under the H, to distinguish it from Haram which means pyramid. But here the reader is unlikely to be misled.

intolerance and even fanaticism were beginning to show, and were accentuated by the arrogance and display of those dhimmis, Christian or Jewish, who had obtained wealth and power by official protection. Nevertheless both continued to enjoy the protection of the caliphs and the full control of their communal affairs.

Though the Christians still probably formed the majority of the population up to the beginning of the ninth century, and continued to be an important element right down to the period of the crusades, yet the Christian community was by no means the most interesting of the period. Doubtless they needed time to recover from the devastation caused by the Persian invasion of 614, and also found it difficult to adjust themselves to the second-class citizenship which had become their lot; a difficulty to which the Jewish community may well have adjusted itself, after centuries of a similar treatment by Christianity. But it remains true that little or nothing of the glory of Christianity during those centuries falls to the Church of Jerusalem. Islam cannot be blamed for this; for these centuries witnessed a missionary expansion led by the Nestorian Church from Persia as remarkable as the expansion (partly under the direction of popes who themselves came from Syria) of Christianity among the barbarians of Europe. In the whole eastern field, which stretched from China to South India, there are no prominent figures from The Land. And yet they were less isolated than their brethren in eastern Islam. For pilgrims still came from all parts of the Christian world to the Holy Land, and the Muslims did not interfere with them except for two brief periods in the eleventh century. Furthermore, though they naturally favoured sects which had no connexion with Byzantium, there was no persecution of the Orthodox as such. It seems that at first the Nestorian catholicus in Iraq was recognized as the head of all the Christian Churches; and that when a local head was accepted it was at first the Jacobite patriarch of Antioch. Sophronius died soon after the surrender of Jerusalem, and we know of no further Orthodox patriarch until the end of the century. But in the eighth century two councils were called in Jerusalem (in 726 and 763) by Orthodox patriarchs to deal with the iconoclastic controversy, and a third in 836 dealt with the same subject. As all pronounced in favour of images, it is evident that the councils had freedom of action from their Muslim masters.

Apart from these councils the Christian story continued to be one of monks and pilgrims. Neither class was officially interfered with by the new rulers, who, in fact, professed the greatest respect for both. The instructions given by Abu Bakr definitely forbade any interference with them; and the monasteries and lauras in Jerusalem and the western area of the country were relatively secure. But the same does not apply to those in the eastern deserts and mountains, which began to be subject to bedouin raids from the side of the erstwhile Christian Nabateans and Ghassanids. Actually Mar Saba was first sacked by bedouins during the Persian war; but it was attacked again, and many monks murdered and buildings burnt, at the end of the eighth and the beginning of the ninth centuries; and the same fate befell other desert monasteries, such as the convent of St Theodosius (Deir Dousi) overlooking the Dead Sea. Pilgrims continued to come from the west, and the conversion of Hungary in the tenth century made it possible for them to come by the easier overland route. But this was balanced by the fact that the roads were often less secure than in Byzantine times, for the caliphs were rarely able to keep order in the provinces as effectively as the emperors. As time went on, conditions certainly worsened for all the non-Muslim peoples, but it must be said of the Umayyad and Abbasid periods that life for a Christian was tolerable, and that many Christians were able to rise to important positions without having to conceal their faith.

For the Jewish community the new regime was entirely welcome. That they assisted the Arabs on various occasions during their conquests is only to be expected; but their numbers must have been relatively small. They had suffered three centuries of Christian intolerance, and monkish violence had been spasmodic during at least half of that period. During the Persian invasion they may have been spared the losses which fell on the country as a whole, but many thousands fell victims to the vengeance of the Christians during the brief return of Heraclius. Nevertheless we have evidence that Jews lived in all parts of the country and on both sides of the Jordan, and that they dwelt in both the towns and the villages, practising both agriculture and various handicrafts. During the seventh and eighth centuries Tiberias continued to be their centre; but some Jews began to return to Jerusalem shortly after the Muslim conquest in spite of the fact that in the original negotiations for the surrender of the city, the Christians had wished to insist that no Jews should be admitted to it.

At first Jews lived in the southern quarter near the Wailing Wall; as their numbers increased they began a new settlement in the north east between the Damascus and St Stephen's Gates, where many names still recall them. At some period they purchased the slopes of the Mount of Olives facing the Temple, and there used to be a considerable pilgrimage to this spot at the chief festivals, especially at the Feast of Tabernacles. At these pilgrimages important events were proclaimed; contacts with the Dispersion maintained, and pilgrims from all parts of the world received. When the capital of Filastin moved from Lydda to Ramleh a considerable number of Jews, some of them from Lydda, settled in the new town. There were also large and important communities in such places as Ascalon, Caesarea and above all Gaza, which the Jews of southern Palestine had made a kind of capital during the period in which they were excluded from Jerusalem.

The vigorous spiritual life of the Umayyad and Abbasid periods provoked a similar renaissance among the Jews of The Land which showed itself in various directions. The Jerusalem Talmud was by this time completed, but work was done on collecting and editing the mass of commentaries known as the Midrash. Moreover there remained much work to be done on the actual language of the Bible itself. This led not only to a revival of Hebrew, but also to a close study of the Biblical text, and to the development of a new and more efficient system of pointing and punctuation (Masorah). The eighth and the ninth centuries covered the main work of the Masoretes, and Tiberias was their centre. The Masoretic text of today is largely their work. There was likewise a considerable outpouring of Hebrew poetry, though this may be traced to Byzantine rather than Arab inspiration. For Byzantine hymns bear resemblance to Hebrew hymns, but most of the themes of the Muslim poets were secular. A number of hymns, still used in the synagogue, were the work of Galilean poets of this period. The greatest of them was Eliezer ben Kalir, who flourished at the end of the seventh century. The influence of eastern Christians may, perhaps, also be traced in a revival of messianic and apocalyptic mysticism. The eighth century saw two pseudo-messiahs appear, Serene of Syria and Abu-Isa of Ispahan; and various cabbalistic works probably belong to the same time.

Of the organization of the community in the first period it is difficult to speak with certainty. From the ninth century onwards we have access to the mass of documents discovered in recent decades in the Cairo Genizah, but we have nothing comparable for the earlier period. At first the exilarch of Babylonia seems to have had the same authority with regard to all Jews in the caliphate that the catholicus exercised over all Christians. But a local Jewish successor to the patriarch may have existed even in Byzantine times at Tiberias, and have obtained some recognition of his status from the Muslims. The *gaon*, or president, of the rabbinic academy in Tiberias was certainly recognized and given an official position later. His religious authority was, in certain matters, widely accepted by Jews; for it was the task of the Tiberias academy annually to fix the Jewish calendar for Jews throughout the world. Whether the Samaritans were regarded by the authorities as part of the Jewish community at this time we cannot say; later, when the country was ruled from Egypt, the Egyptian *nagid* or president certainly had authority over them.

The period during which the empire was ruled from Damascus, and can be called an 'Arab' empire, lasted less than a century, and even in that short time it had begun to decline. In the seventh century the frontiers were only violated once, in 678, by a raid of a Christian tribe known as the Mardaites who lived in the mountains of Lebanon. How much damage they did we do not know, though they seem to have penetrated as far as the walls of Jerusalem. But in the eighth century the old divisions between the Arab tribes began to reassert themselves, and civil war in Syria and Filastin left the last Umayyad caliphs no troops to spare to repress a revolt in the east which was headed by Abu b. Abbas al-Saffah (750–754). Playing on the opposition of Iraqi to Syrian, Shiite to Sunni, and Persian to Arab, he overthrew the Umayyads and founded a new dynasty of the Abbasids. In these events The Land had the melancholy distinction that it was at Antipatris that the last of the Syrian dynasty were treacherously murdered by the general of al-Saffah. The new capital was at first at al-Kufah, until al-Mansur (754–775), the successor of al-Saffah, built the new imperial city of Baghdad. Vast as were the territories of the Abbasid caliphs, they were no longer coterminous with Islam. In the extreme west the Umayyads reappeared as caliphs in Spain; and in the extreme east local dynasties arose.

Its distance from the new centre had an evil effect on the state of The Land. It was now but a remote and unimportant province; and though strong rulers might suppress insurrection, yet tribal disorders and bedouin raids might at any time make life insecure for Muslims as well as Jews and Christians. Even in the days of Harun al-Rashid (786–809) such a war between the tribes of the Southern and Northern Arab federations devastated wide areas. Towns and villages were sacked; the roads became unsafe and even Jerusalem was threatened. It was in this conflict that Mar Saba and other monasteries were plundered and their inmates murdered. Further there was often civil war between one reign and the next; on the death of al-Rashid, for example, such a war swept over the country, leading to the burning of churches and the flight or massacre of Christians. Finally, even in times of peace, both Christians and Jews were discovering that the toleration of early days was beginning to wear thin, and unfortunately it was the stronger rulers who tended to be the sternest repressors of the dhimmis. At one moment al-Rashid, deceived by the malicious denunciation of the patriarch of Antioch as a Greek spy by some monks of Aleppo, broke his habitual tolerance to order the destruction of all new Jacobite churches; and al-Mutawakkil (847–861) reintroduced all the humiliating restrictions of Umar II together with new additions.

There is little to show that The Land had much share in the magnificence of the court of Baghdad during the early days of the Abbasids. Christian and Jewish scholars were among its luminaries, but none came from The Land. Their inspiration was Persian rather than western, and in general it may be said that among the Muslims also the Arab and western influences were giving way to increasing orientalism and to new strains from central Asia. Yet the high humane level of civilization to which the early

Abbasids raised the whole of western Asia naturally had local repercussions. In The Land trade and industry flourished as well as agriculture, and the dyeing, weaving and glass-work of the country found a ready market; Arab geographers describe it as one of the most fertile and prosperous regions of the empire.

There still survived from Byzantine times the annual fair at Jerusalem on 15 September, to which merchants from the commercial cities of Europe – Pisa, Genoa, Venice, Marseilles and elsewhere – came half on pilgrimage and half for trade, and readily exchanged the spices and silks of the east for the wares of Europe. When the fair ceased to exist we do not know, but it could scarcely have been held regularly in the long period of intermittent disorder which marked the two centuries before the first crusade. That disorder had its origin at the beginning of the ninth century, when the caliphs began to rely on Turkish mercenaries; for it was not long before these mercenaries and their leaders were in effective control of the state. By the middle of the century the caliphs were little more than prisoners, with a nominally religious primacy, and the governors of provinces were making themselves hereditary and independent princes.

The whole population suffered from this long period of misrule, though naturally Jews and Christians were the primary victims. On a number of occasions Christian churches were destroyed by fanatical mobs of local Muslims. In 923 the Orthodox churches of Ascalon, Ramleh and Caesarea were sacked, and in 937 and 975 the Church of the Holy Sepulchre was damaged; on the latter occasion the Orthodox patriarch himself was burned alive as a Byzantine spy.

At the end of the tenth century a new conqueror arrived, this time from the west, Jawhar, the leading soldier of the Fatimid princes of North Africa. The Fatimids claimed descent from Fatima, daughter of Muhammad, and the claim may have been genuine; though it was, not unnaturally, denied by the Abbasids. They had set themselves up as caliphs in north-western Africa in 909 and established a caliphate of the Shiite sect; for it was through the plots of a vast Shiite secret society, the Ismailites, that they had obtained power. It was the Fatimids who built Cairo, and under al-Aziz (975–996) their rule was extended to the whole of Syria and Filastin. Al-Aziz was a beneficent and very tolerant ruler; and both Jews and Christians were readily employed by him in the highest offices of the state. His greatest vizir, Ibn Killis, was of Jewish origin, and his wife, the mother of the infamous al-Hakim, was the sister of the Orthodox patriarch of Jerusalem. On his death there was civil war between rival generals of his successor, al-Hakim (996–1021). Early in life this caliph began to develop signs of eccentricity, which finally developed into such complete insanity that he declared himself an incarnation of the godhead, and compelled his Muslim subjects to accept him as such. The sect of the Druzes survives from this strange period; they still accept him as a divine incarnation, and expect his messianic return.

In 1009 al-Hakim forbade pilgrimages and ordered the destruction of all churches and synagogues throughout the empire, except the Church of the Nativity at Bethlehem but including the Church of the Holy Sepulchre. According to one account, he ordered this last to be destroyed because of his disgust at the imposture of the Holy Fire at the Easter ceremonies; according to another because of the intrigues of an ambitious monk, John, who, on being refused a bishopric by the patriarch, denounced him to the caliph as a traitor. On the death of the madman the Christians, with the aid of the Byzantine emperor, were allowed to rebuild their churches. But it was some years before the Church of the Holy Sepulchre rose from its ashes. The destruction of a shrine venerated throughout Christendom had serious repercussions in Europe, and prepared the way for the first crusade. Unfortunately it had other repercussions also. The story circulated in the West that it was at the instigation of the Jews that al-Hakim had given the order, and widespread massacres and forced baptisms were the result.

For a brief period after the death of al-Hakim The Land seems to have enjoyed peace, and there was a great development of pilgrimages. We read of the arrival of bands numbering several thousands, and though they were sometimes molested by bedouins, they seem to have been otherwise accepted. But the country suffered during the eleventh century from a series of earthquake shocks, which wrought immense destruction. The most serious were in 1016, when the cupola of the Dome of the Rock fell, in 1034 and in 1068. But yet another army of Turkish invaders was approaching, that of the Seljuks, who, like earlier conquerors, had originally been mercenaries and who came from the far-eastern provinces of Islam, in this case from the actual frontiers of China. It was not until 1098 that the Fatimids re-established their authority for the few months which intervened before the arrival of the crusaders.

While there is little new to be said of the Christian communities during the last two centuries before the crusades, other than that their numbers dwindled continuously under the pressure of Islam, there are a number of changes to be recorded in the life of the Jewish community, which also must be assumed to have lost considerable strength during the period. The two messianic movements of the eighth century, to which reference has already been made, were to some extent connected with a not unexpected reaction against the Talmudic system of interpretation and the elaborate daily discipline which it ordained. This reaction took a fuller development, largely in The Land and in Syria, as a result of the teachings of Anan ben David in the second half of the century. Anan had expected to succeed to the Babylonian exilarchate on the death of his uncle but, being rejected, set himself up as an independent teacher, emphasizing always the laws of the Bible as opposed to those of the Talmud. His followers, known as the Karaites, still exist. Unable to make much headway in Babylon, they made Jerusalem their centre. Other events contributed to bring Jerusalem for a brief period into the centre of the picture of world Jewry. The Babylonian exilarchate had come to an end during the ninth century; the two great Talmudical schools of Sura and Pumbeditha were both in decline. Before their extinction they had a brilliant flicker in two great presidents, Saadiah (892–942) and Hai (969–1038); but Babylonian Jewish life had become too insecure and internally corrupt to maintain its integrity amidst the decay of political and intellectual life into which the Abbasid caliphate had sunk. New schools were springing up in Egypt, Kairouan and Muslim Spain. The Jerusalem Talmud, which had been completely eclipsed by the Babylonian, was in temporary favour in the schools of Kairouan; Jewish philosophy and poetry were to be reborn in Egypt and Spain; but while these were still coming to fruition, for a short while Jerusalem inherited a shadowy supremacy, albeit in a period that lacked both religious and intellectual distinction.

Jerusalem possessed thus the interest both of the Talmudists and the Karaites. The former possessed in the city the academy of Gaon Jacob, whose head was for a brief period heir to the heads of the great Babylonian academies; and the latter had founded in that city an ascetic brotherhood of Mourners of Zion, who, in the manner of Christian ascetics, passed their lives in poverty and prayer for the restoration of the Temple. The Jewish community possessed a somewhat complicated organization, half independent and half dependent on that of Egypt. The successor to the exilarch of Babylon, though with much less general recognition in Jewry, was the nagid of Egypt, and his authority was recognized by the Fatimid caliphs as extending over all Jews and Samaritans within their dominions. The nagid was not necessarily a member of the House of David, as had been the Babylonian exilarch; but there were representatives of the royal house who took the title of *nasi* (prince) and enjoyed some kind of authority in both Egypt and The Land, though what the relationship of this authority was to that of the nagid or the presidents of the local communities it is impossible to say in detail. While the public organization was thus centred in Egypt, the religious authority of the president of the Academy of Jerusalem was recognized for such matters as the fixing of the calendar throughout the Fatimid dominions. But this authority was of short duration. The community had been so utterly impoverished by the natural disasters and the constant political unrest that it was in constant need of help from the wealthier community of Cairo; and the school of Jerusalem had itself to vacate the capital and take to a wandering life in various cities until it too passed into Egypt and disappeared during the period of the first crusade.

It is during the two centuries which preceded the crusades that the main emphasis of Palestinian history passes from the Christian and Jewish communities to the Muslims, though it must be said of them also that they passed into ever-increasing obscurity, poverty and decline. This decline showed its full effects only in the period following the crusades, but it was the failure of the caliphate to build up any kind of continuous security or competent public administration that ultimately led to it. In the centuries before the Arab conquest the Roman-Byzantine provinces of Palestina probably possessed the largest population and the most varied economy of any period of its history. This at least is the evidence uncovered by archaeologists from the study of the innumerable deserted sites to be found in every region of the country. This economy only gradually decayed; during the first two centuries after 640 Arab geographers and travellers could still speak of the many products of both agriculture and industry which were produced in its cities and villages; what we know of its tax payments shows a prosperity little inferior to that of northern Syria and the Lebanon.

To what extent the decline of the economy was produced by a change in the population, as well as by harsh taxation, bedouin raids and civil wars, it is difficult to judge; but it is probable that there was, in some parts of the country at least, an influx of Arabs during the latter part of the period, and that they settled down to a more primitive agriculture than that practised by the other inhabitants, Christians and Jews, whom they supplanted. In any case we hear more as time goes on of disturbances caused by the typical inter-tribal rivalries of Arab life, which would have been unlikely without a considerable influx of Arabs accustomed to those quarrels. There was no reason for their outbreak among a population which had been indigenous over a long period and organized in entirely different ways. The fact that the whole population was beginning to speak Arabic, and that the majority were now Muslims, would have given an impetus to the acceptance of Arab ways and standards in a country so near both to Arabia and the desert, although elsewhere in Islam totally different influences, stemming from Persian or Turkish sources, were becoming dominant. This change did not add to the strength, political or spiritual, of the resistance which the inhabitants were able to offer to the crusaders. The Latin conquest was effected without excessive difficulty, and the reversion of the country to Islam, when it came, was not to come from Arab sources, but from a fresh wave of Turkish invaders represented by Saladin the Kurd.

CHAPTER FIVE

Christian Interlude: The Crusades

THE Arab conquests of the seventh and eighth centuries had destroyed the unity of the Mediterranean world. The sea divided two new civilizations, one in western Europe and one in the east whose centre fluctuated from Baghdad to Cairo. But there was no clear frontier between these new powers, and it shifted as opportunity favoured one side or the other. At first the initiative had lain with the Arabs, and western Europe, together with the relics of the old Mediterranean power of Byzantium, had been compelled constantly to retreat; but the Arab Empire was brittle and unstable, and the initiative passed gradually to the other side. In this world of movement The Land might at almost any time have changed masters.

The particular circumstances which dictated the form which that change should take – a movement of conquest and colonization coming from the west of Europe and not from the nearer Byzantium – were many and complicated. One was the change in direction of the flow of peoples out of the central steppes of Asia. While the Mediterranean and middle-eastern regions were held safe in the power of Rome and Persia, the nomads had moved along the northern fringes of the civilized world, repopulating northern and western Europe with vigorous if barbaric stocks. When Rome broke, the hordes poured down into Italy, Spain and the rich lands of the western Mediterranean basin. That was in the fifth century; and since then the barbarians had themselves formed strong new societies, well able to resist subsequent invaders, and to make counter-offensives into the lands of their enemies. Saxon, Avar, Slav and Arab discovered this to their cost in the triumphant campaigns of Charles Martel (717–741) and Charlemagne (768–814); and though the unity of Europe broke up in the following century, the feudal knight and the feudal castle gradually proved equally successful against the last invaders, the Magyars, the Petchenegs and the Normans. As western

Europe became impenetrable, the whole shock of the later nomad migrations had to be taken by the Byzantine Empire, and the wide, thinly held dominions of the Arab caliphate. The bulwark of Byzantium had for some centuries given western Europe the security in which it could consolidate its strength; and the effort had led to a considerable loss of Byzantine power, a loss accentuated by its own past mistakes. During the seventh century Arab armies and fleets stood on several occasions within sight of Constantinople. In 838 a Byzantine emperor, Theophilus, made the first appeal to the West for help; but the West was not yet strong enough to respond. The appeal was not quickly repeated for the Arab danger was passing, and in the following century the Byzantines went over to the counter-attack. But before new frontiers could be consolidated the balance shifted again, and they lost all that they had regained before advancing Turks.

It was in the middle of the eleventh century that the Seljuk Turks obtained complete control of the capital of the Abbasid caliphs. By 1071 they had become sufficiently powerful for one army, led by their sultan, Alp Arslan, to inflict a decisive defeat on Byzantium at Manzikert, while, in the same year, his general Aziz inflicted a similar defeat on the Fatimids. The former event compelled a fresh Byzantine appeal to the West; the latter interrupted the pilgrimage from the West to the Holy Land. These two events, which were the direct cause of the first crusade, do much to explain the subsequent relations of the crusaders with Byzantium. From the standpoint of the former it was a western European enterprise to reopen the road to the Holy Land; from that of the latter, the crusaders were assisting to re-establish the power of Byzantium over provinces which she had been in a fair way to recapture by herself until the sudden emergence of the Seljuk power confronted her with an enemy who threatened her very existence and was too powerful to meet alone.

The appeal which had failed in the ninth century came at a more apposite moment at the end of the eleventh. Western Europe was everywhere expanding and developing a superabundant energy. The attack on Islam had already begun successfully in Spain and Sicily. The commercial cities of Italy, especially Venice, Pisa and Genoa, were developing navies equal to those of Islam, and were anxious to increase their trade with the eastern Mediterranean ports. The new social order was producing a class of knightly warriors only too anxious for fresh opportunities to carve out a kingdom by the sword, as well as a surplus agricultural population unable easily to find new work at home. Above all the Western Church had set her house in order and had gained a powerful hold over men's actions and imaginations. The call to crusade was primarily the work of the papacy, and if many of the effects of the movement on the life of western Europe have been exaggerated, the part which it played in the development of papal power and policy is incontestable. In consequence of all these causes, the call fell in 1095 on ears ready to accept the appeal from every one of the motives by which men are moved to action.

The plans elaborated by Urban II were for a carefully picked and directed invasion, mainly recruited from those parts of France where experience had been gained by men like Raymund de St Gilles, Count of Toulouse, in fighting with the Muslims of Spain. The mob oratory of Peter the Hermit, and the undisciplined march of the 'poor men' across Europe, spreading ruin and massacring Jews on their route, were no part of the original papal plans. But with this part of the crusade we are not concerned; it perished in Asia Minor without ever reaching the Holy Land. The official army, led by the papal legate Adhemar, Bishop of Puy, comprised a contingent from Provence led by Raymund, three from northern Europe, one led by Godfrey of Bouillon, Duke of Lower Lorraine and son of the Count of Boulogne, one by Robert of Flanders, and one by Stephen of Blois. A contingent from Sicily was led by Bohemond of Taranto. On the naval side the most important fleet was that of Genoa. At Constantinople all the leaders, except Raymund, formally accepted the idea that they were acting as vassals of Byzantium and received in return considerable financial help, as well as guides and provisions, from the emperor, Alexis Comnenus.

Once they had crossed into Asia the personal ambitions and the lack of personal piety among the leaders manifested itself in continual quarrels, especially when the death of the papal legate removed any visible leadership. Several carved out principalities for themselves and abandoned their colleagues. But in January

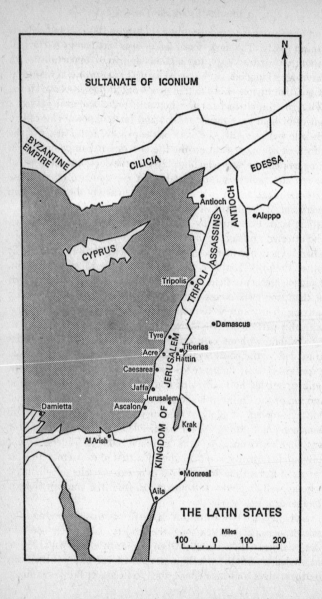

N

SULTANATE OF ICONIUM

BYZANTINE EMPIRE

CILICIA

EDESSA

●Antioch

●Aleppo

CYPRUS

ANTIOCH

ASSASSINS

Tripolis●

TRIPOLI

●Damascus

Tyre●

Acre●

JERUSALEM

Tiberias●
●Hattin

Caesarea●

Jaffa●

Jerusalem●

Damietta●

Ascalon●

●Krak

Al Arish●

KINGDOM OF

●Monreal

Aila●

THE LATIN STATES

Miles
100   0   100   200

1099 the rank and file, equally disgusted by the conflicts and by the rapacity of their leaders, forced them to make a move towards Jerusalem. The advance southwards along the coast met little resistance from the petty and practically independent amirs along the route, and on 7 June the army came in sight of Jerusalem, the first city since leaving Antioch to offer determined resistance. But on 15 July it was captured and there followed a massacre of almost all the Muslims and Jews found within the city. The bloodshed shocked even the crusaders, and had the unfortunate effect of stiffening resistance in all the towns of the coast, whose possession was essential to their security.

With the capture of Jerusalem the objective of the crusade was reached; and those of the crusaders who had no intentions of remaining in the east considered that they had only to arrange for its future government and return home. Godfrey of Bouillon, who had been one of the first to scale the walls of the city, was appointed with the title of Defender of the Holy Sepulchre. The subsequent establishment of the Latin kingdom was the work of no more than a few thousand Franks (as the Muslims called them all, whether they came from France or not). The only prominent leader who remained with Godfrey was Tancred, who had not yet obtained a principality. Together, with an army containing not more than a couple of hundred knights, they set out to secure their position. Tancred operated in the north and was rewarded with the principality of Galilee, while Godfrey secured his position in the south.

Godfrey died very shortly after, and the barons, supported by some of the clerics themselves, resolved on offering the throne to his brother Baldwin, Count of Edessa. Baldwin accepted and the kingdom of Jerusalem was established. The only real protection of the crusaders thereby came into existence. For the House of Boulogne, and the House of Anjou which succeeded it, produced a series of excellent monarchs. It was a kingdom on a perpetual war footing; as soon as it produced a ruler who lacked military talent it fell. Natural calamities, such as drought or disease, and the heavy costs of ransoming important prisoners, at times produced general distress. But in the intervals its citizens and subjects enjoyed just under a century not merely of relative security, but of quite extraordinary prosperity, a prosperity which, owing to the wisdom of successive kings, was shared not only by pilgrims and churches, but by barons without honour, merchants without piety and Muslims without baptism.

The crusading states consisted, from north to south, of the county of Edessa, the principality of Antioch, the county of Tripoli and the kingdom of Jerusalem. All looked to the king at Jerusalem for military assistance, and for civil administration in cases of minority or the capture of their ruler, and so recognized a certain feudal obedience to the House of Boulogne. The special feudal system evolved to meet the new situation was generally identical in all parts. The collection known as the Assizes of Jerusalem is one of the most remarkable monuments of feudal law in existence. While in their present form its various books were composed in Cyprus after the fall of the kingdom, it rests on the customs elaborated from the time of Baldwin, and it will be convenient to give here a picture of the Latin kingdom of Jerusalem as its inhabitants knew it, for we are not concerned with its tortuous and often treacherous politics, and with the wars in which it was constantly involved.

It was in the reign of Baldwin II that the weapon was forged which was gradually to provide the equivalent of a standing army. In the reconstruction following the reign of al-Hakim the merchants of Amalfi had built and endowed a hospital at Jerusalem. Under its Master, Raymund of Puy, it added to the task of caring for sick pilgrims that of defending the Christian faith. Raymund secured permission for the creation of a military Order to be attached to the hospital, and this soon came to overshadow its former work. In this action he was following (or even anticipating) the action of a group of knights banded together under Hugh de Payne and Godfrey de St Omer to defend pilgrims on the road from Jaffa to Jerusalem. While the Hospitallers remained in their quarters south of the Church of the Holy Sepulchre (the Muristan), the other group was given quarters in the Aksa Mosque, known to the Franks as the Temple of Solomon. They thus came to be called the Templars. These two Orders captured the imagination of Europe, and gifts poured into their coffers. They were never a charge on the king of Jerusalem. On the other hand, their wealth became not only a temptation to their neighbours, but a serious cause of moral decline in themselves. The quarrels between the two arrogant Masters contributed not a little to the collapse of the kingdom, and the fatal advice of the Master of the Temple led directly to the disastrous defeat of Hattin.

The most valuable contribution of the Orders was the garrisoning of the country with a series of castles, some of which remain today as the most magnificent and complete examples of feudal military art. Their main castles were Le Krak des Chevaliers and Margat (Hospitallers) and Tortosa (Templars). All these were in the north, but within the kingdom the Templars guarded Gaza (Gadres), and next to them the Hospitallers held Ascalon with an outlying castle at Beit Gibelin (Beit Jibrin). Further north the Templars held Latrun (Le Thoron des Chevaliers) while the Hospitallers held the heights above it at Abu Ghosh (The Spring of Emmaus). In the northern part of the country the Templars later had a ring of castles round Athlit (Château des Pèlerins), including one on Mount Carmel (Château de Sainte Margaret), while on the Jordan the Hospitallers from their castle at Beauvoir commanded the bridge below the lake of Tiberias at Jisr al Majami, and (during its short existence) the Templars guarded the northern bridge of Jacob's Ford from the castle of Le Chatelet. After the fall of Jerusalem the German crusaders created an Order of Teutonic Knights, similar to the two Orders already existing and almost wholly French; and from their headquarters at Acre, built a ring of castles in western Galilee, of which the chief was Starkenberg (Montfort).

Because of the insecurity of overland communications with Europe through Byzantine territory, the sea ports came to assume an even greater importance than would, in any case, have been theirs. Owing to the treachery of Raymund de St Gilles before Ascalon, the Franks possessed at first only Jaffa, which they had obtained with the aid of the Pisan fleet. Their further conquests depended on the visits of fleets from various sources. Haifa fell in 1100 (Venetians), Arsuf and Caesarea in 1101 (Genoese). Acre was captured in 1104 (Genoese), and, with the aid of a Norwegian fleet, Sidon also was captured. Tyre did not fall till 1124 (Venetians). When finally Ascalon fell in 1153 the Franks possessed the

PALESTINE DURING THE CRUSADES

N

Sur(Tyre)

Montfort

Jacob's ford
Saphet

S. Jean d'Acre   S. Georges de Labeyn

Cayphas   Baldwin's Castle

Chateau Pelerin   Horns of Hattin   Thaberie

Nazareth   Mt Tabor

Cesaire   Beauvoir

Bessan

Arsuf   S. Jean de Sebaste

Naples

Joppe   S. Joseph d'Arimathea

S. Joseph & S. Habbakuk

S. George de Lydda

Ibelin   Le Thoron

Jerusalem

Escalone   Bethlehem

Beit Gibelin

Gadres

S. Abraham (Hebron)

Le Crac

Miles
0   10   20

Monreal

88

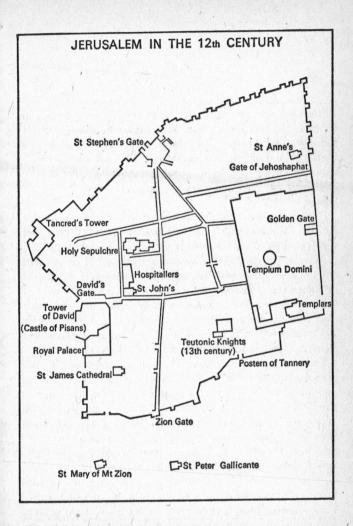

JERUSALEM IN THE 12th CENTURY

St Stephen's Gate

St Anne's

Gate of Jehoshaphat

Tancred's Tower

Golden Gate

Holy Sepulchre

Templum Domini

Hospitallers

David's
Gate

St John's

Tower
of David
(Castle of Pisans)

Templars

Royal Palace

Teutonic Knights
(13th century)

St James Cathedral

Postern of Tannery

Zion Gate

St Mary of Mt Zion

St Peter Gallicante

whole sea coast, and the Muslims had no port nearer than Egypt from which Christian shipping could be attacked. Nevertheless none of these ports was much more than a day's march from the Muslim frontier on the east. The great chain of inland cities, Aleppo, Homs, Hama and Damascus, remained impregnable; the only policy possible was therefore to seek to keep them divided and at war with each other. Only in the south did the Christian territory extend across the Jordan valley line. There the possession of the Lordship of Oultre-Jourdain assured a valuable control of the route to Egypt for both armies and caravans, and even a stretch of the pilgrim road to Mecca. The control was never complete, for the territory was large and thinly held. But it made it difficult for Syria and Egypt to help each other against the Franks.

During the whole period the Franks themselves remained a minority. This was largely due to a disaster which befell the later waves of the first crusade, which might have brought into Syria the invaluable addition of some tens of thousands of settlers. The news of the capture of Jerusalem created widespread excitement in Europe and thousands of men of all classes set out for the east in 1100 and 1101. Some bands were led by prominent barons, some were more like the poor men's crusade of 1096. But through folly and treachery all alike perished at the hands of the Turks of Asia Minor, and only a few remnants ever reached the Latin states.

The new society had, therefore, from the beginning to pay careful attention to the rights of the local population. The period in which the inhabitants of a captured city were automatically slaughtered was of short duration. It soon became necessary to assure eastern Christians, Muslims and Jews alike that they would be granted security of life and property if they surrendered peaceably. In fact the Latin states seem to have treated their peasantry, including Muslim peasants, better than they were treated in the neighbouring states. The normal tenure gave a quarter or a third to the overlord and left the tenant the rest. But in addition they were protected from bedouin raids and exempted from military service; and the general prosperity of the interior of the country exceeded anything it had known for some time previously or was to know again until modern times.

It is important to emphasize this point, because so much is said about the superiority of the Muslim culture which the Latins encountered in the country. It is true that the intellectual level of the courts of the caliphs, as well as their artistic standards and luxurious living, exceeded anything which was to be found in contemporary Europe. And this is not surprising, when it is realized that this high level was the syncretistic inheritance of the Greek, Roman, Hebrew and Persian civilizations which were far older than that of Europe. But Europe had already passed ahead in its conceptions of government, primitive though they were and still incapable of instilling loyalty and discipline into the feudal nobility itself. The ignorant Frankish baron might gape with amazement at the intellectual subtlety or artistic luxury displayed before him by a Muslim prince; when it came to dealing with his tenants or administering justice to his subjects he had nothing to learn from him. In the end the Latins took back with them to Europe the philosophical, medical, mathematical and other knowledge which they had acquired in Syria, together with many pleasant plants and stuffs. Their Mamluk successors in control of The Land spread only economic havoc, administrative decay and the destruction of all social order.

The supreme power, as we learn from the Assizes of Jerusalem, lay with the council of the greater barons, in whose hands was an elective kingship which, in fact, soon became hereditary. The kingdom contained four great baronies, Ascalon with Jaffa, Sidon, Galilee and Oultre-Jourdain (Krak and Monreal). The royal demesne consisted of the land around Jerusalem, Nablus, Acre and the port and county of Tyre. In addition to the great baronies should be mentioned the two great military Orders of the Hospitallers and Templars whose power was greater than that of the greatest baron. The service due from the barons included the normal feudal service of military aid, but for a period of a year. In addition the constant need of soldiers led to an extensive use of another form of fief already familiar in Europe. Military service was given in return for a grant by the king, not of lands, but of a rent charge in cash or kind on land. The knights were continually recruited from the richer burghers, and only so could an adequate body of heavy cavalry be maintained. For light cavalry, known as Turcopoles, extensive use was made of the native population.

The baronies, great and small, possessed their own courts with a jurisdiction commensurate with their importance, and dependent on the royal court of Jerusalem. The military Orders of the Templars and Hospitallers, however, were completely independent in their courts of both patriarch and king, and depended solely on the pope.

In addition to the baronial courts and, of course, the ecclesiastical courts, there were a variety of courts dealing with the affairs of the burgesses and citizens, whether of western or eastern origin. There were special courts to deal with commercial matters (*La Fonde*) and with maritime matters (*La Chaine*); and the native Christians had their own courts presided over by special officials called the *Rais* (head, chief). Muslims and Jews continued to exercise their own jurisdiction in religious affairs. Otherwise they enjoyed almost the same rights as native Christians, a position much more favourable than that which Jews enjoyed in feudal Europe; for it raised them to the same level as the majority of the population, and they were in no way the private property of their rulers.

The terrible losses of 1101 were never made good by subsequent mass immigration from Europe. While there was a constant trickle of men of all classes from peasants and pilgrims to merchants and knights, gradually native-born Franks came to provide the backbone of the Latin population. The first native-born ruler was Baldwin III who became king in 1144. These native-born Franks, together with those who had settled in the country permanently, soon came to consider themselves to be Syrians, and to adopt many of the habits of the country. They built their houses in the Syrian manner; they enjoyed frequent bathing; eastern dress was found more suitable to the climate than western, and they clothed themselves in long flowing robes and the head-dress covering the neck and forehead still familiar in Arab dress (it survives in western heraldry in the mantling attached to the helm in a coat of arms). Many of the chroniclers of the crusades record the speed with which French and other immigrants had acclimatized themselves; and the fact had a great importance for the social life of the country, in that it broke down the barriers between the immigrant and native groups, led to frequent intermarriage at all levels of society, and created a prosperity which all alike shared.

Even religion failed to provide a barrier; the eastern Christians, as will be discussed below, reached a *modus vivendi* with the Latins by some formal act of recognition of the patriarchs of Jerusalem and Antioch; the Muslim farmers, traders and artisans lived in complete harmony with their neighbours; and the fact that the Christian and Muslim societies shared many of the same conceptions of chivalry created a bond which tended to bring western and eastern civilizations together even in their warfare.

Finally, to increase the prosperity of a land which was itself capable of providing a good living for its agricultural and merchant citizens, a constant flow of money was brought into the country by the piety of western Europeans and the glamour of the Holy Places and the Holy War. The military Orders soon came to be fabulously wealthy; the Church of the Holy Sepulchre and other great abbeys and churches possessed property in almost every country of Europe; many of the crusaders themselves, as well as the merchant communities, were scions of rich houses, or citizens of rich cities. In a word, on a background of almost continual warfare and of the continuous threat of war, a fascinating, prosperous, and even vital society was created which had adapted itself to the country as completely as its predecessors in the days of Greece and Rome.

There was, of course, a reverse to this picture. The kingdom possessed serious weaknesses, especially in the authority of the king himself. Had there not been such an able series of monarchs on the throne, it would have fallen to pieces much earlier. King, barons, churchmen, military Orders and Italian merchant communities all came into existence at the same time, and all were capable of acting without any reference to the others. The king had the main responsibility for defence, but he was by no means the wealthiest figure in his kingdom and his constitutional authority over the different sections of the kingdom was very limited. In the thirteenth century the Orders and the merchant communities could even conduct their own negotiations with the common enemy, and make peace or war as pleased them, without reference to the wishes of the king. The absence of a strong central authority also encouraged a moral weakness and even degeneration among the Latin element of the population. Prosperity led to quarrels, and the glamour of the East and the warmth of the climate invited to a seductive luxury.

This weakness was emphasized by the unsatisfactory nature of the religious leadership. In both Antioch and Jerusalem the crusaders had taken on themselves the authority to elect new patriarchs without reference to Rome, and this meant that throughout the period of the Latin states the most important ecclesiastical dignitaries obtained their position as a result of local intrigue, and out of the clash and rivalry of local interests. Few of the patriarchs of Jerusalem were even good men; and none were great Christian leaders in any sense of the word. The most eminent Latin Christian of the whole period was William, Archbishop of Tyre, who was native-born and one of the most important historians of the crusades. Yet he was manoeuvred out of the patriarchate by a scoundrelly and ignorant cleric, Heraclius, who had already obtained the archbishopric of Caesarea because his good looks pleased the queen mother. With such conditions obtaining in the chief office, it is not surprising if there was constant complaint that the clergy were immoral and rapacious. The complaint against their rapacity was, indeed, continuous, in spite of the fact that they were the richest clergy in the world. They extended the system of tithes far beyond what it was in contemporary Europe, and were ever ready to threaten ecclesiastical penalties if they were not paid; but they also had enormous revenues from very extensive properties throughout the kingdom, from gifts from barons and pilgrims, and from property in Europe. They had, of course, considerable special expenses. They were responsible for the maintenance of poor pilgrims, and for the provision of hospitals; and it is fair to add that the care given to the sick excited the admiration of Muslim visitors. In addition they had to provide substantial levies for the defence of the kingdom. Some idea of their wealth can be seen from the fact that while the citizens of Jerusalem, Acre, Tyre, Nablus, Caesarea and the eight major towns provided between them 2,275 soldiers, the patriarch, archbishops, bishops and monasteries provided 2,750.

The patriarchate contained four archbishoprics (Tyre, Nazareth, Caesarea and Beisan), nine bishoprics and nine mitred abbacies. In Jerusalem were the canons of the Holy Sepulchre (Augustinian), and the abbeys of Mount Zion, the Valley of Josaphat and Mount Olivet. Outside Jerusalem the main abbeys were at Mount Tabor (Cluniac), St George de Labeyn between Acre and Safad (Benedictine), St Joseph of Arimathea and St Joseph with St Habbakuk, north-east of Lydda (both Premonstratensian). But in addition the patriarchal authority was accepted by a considerable number of native prelates, lauras and monasteries. One of the best sides of its work was its development of good relations with the eastern Churches. The Orthodox Church, on the whole, remained unfriendly, and a rival patriarchate was nominally maintained by Constantinople. This patriarch was not admitted in Jerusalem, as he came to be in Antioch, as the coequal of the Latin. Orthodox clergy however were readmitted to the Church of the Holy Sepulchre together with the monophysite and Nestorian Churches. The Armenians were allowed to establish themselves in the south-western corner of Jerusalem with their Church of St James, and still retain this quarter today. The Armenian catholicus took part in Church councils in both Antioch and Jerusalem. Though it may have been due to his personal distinction, Michael the Syrian, the Jacobite Patriarch of Antioch, was also held in high honour. Certain Churches returned to communion with Rome during the crusading period, and have remained in communion with her to this day. The most important group was the Maronite Church of the Lebanon which was received in 1181. In 1246 the Orthodox patriarch of Antioch also made his submission; but this and similar acts by other ecclesiastics usually only covered themselves, and possibly their immediate followers.

The policy of friendship with the native Christians was a politic act in which the clergy were following the lead of the kings. Baldwin I brought in Syrian Christians from Transjordan to populate Jerusalem, and all through there was a tendency for Christians under neighbouring Muslim rule to migrate to the Latin colonies. Nevertheless the friendship was fragile; the status of the Syrian Christians was always inferior to that of the Latin;

evil and intolerant patriarchs could do much to drive such Christians back into the hands of the Muslims; and the loyalty of the Orthodox was always uncertain. There were suspicions that the Orthodox clergy of the Holy Sepulchre were in treasonable correspondence with Saladin to deliver the city into his hands.

In dealing with the position of the Church it is impossible to omit reference to the religious military Orders. Started with the best motives and to perform the most valuable functions, their arrogance, exclusiveness and selfishness came to be a disaster for the whole community, and seriously contributed to the final downfall of the kingdom.

While the Church and the military Orders divided a great part of the wealth which came from the land, and abstracted it from the authority of the king, the wealth which came from commerce was even less in his control. The Italian cities of Genoa, Pisa and Venice, each possessed their own quarters in the ports, in which they lived completely separate lives, possessing not only complete freedom from tolls, but obeying only their own consuls and their own courts. Even their churches were independent of the patriarch of Jerusalem.

After the massacres of the early sieges, no attempt was made to displace the indigenous population – except that neither Jews nor Muslims were allowed to dwell in Jerusalem – and a substantial proportion of the subjects of the Latin states were always Muslims. What proportion this was in the kingdom of Jerusalem it is impossible to say. It is possible that many who had only adopted Islam a few generations before the arrival of the Franks returned to the Christian faith. Indeed Baldwin I on his first campaign in the southern regions is said to have been guided by local inhabitants who had recently returned to Christianity from Islam. Moreover the Arab traveller al-Maqdisi who was born in Jerusalem in the second half of the tenth century speaks of the Christians and Jews outnumbering the Muslims even in his day. But in any case the Muslim farmers and peasants must have formed a substantial proportion of the country population. What facilities they had for religious worship we do not know precisely, but there were no attempts at forcible conversion or interference with their domestic affairs. They were excluded from their sacred shrines of Jerusalem and probably from other sites on which the Christians had built churches and monasteries. But the Spanish traveller Ibn Jubair, who visited Palestine between 1183 and 1185, reports that in the old Mosque of Acre the Muslims had been left a chapel near the tomb of a Muslim prophet, though the rest had become a Christian church, and that in another mosque on the east side of the city the reverse obtained: the Muslims retained the centre and the Christians had a chapel.

The same traveller speaks highly of the prosperity of Muslim farmers in Galilee, and the fair treatment of Muslim traders in Acre. He also mentions a Muslim as mayor of one of the towns he passed through between Damascus and Acre. Even the bedouin were included in the general regulation of society, and the wealth of their flocks made them valuable 'possessions'. When the Franks first arrived, the bedouin raids on their communications, as well as on pilgrims between Jaffa and Jerusalem, were one of the main elements of insecurity. The kings of Jerusalem, however, entered into agreements with their sheikhs for the security of the roads, and the good behaviour of the tribes under their control. They were allowed to move freely to and from their pastures, and were, in their turn, protected from attacks from without.

Proportionally to their numbers, the Jews probably lost more than any other group on the conquest of the country. They had shared in the resistance offered by the Muslims, but in addition they had made the mistake of flocking into the cities for security. Actually the crusaders had spared the villages, since they needed the food that they produced, and it was the urban population which was wiped out in the first flush of conquest. In this way almost the entire Jewries of Jerusalem, Acre, Caesarea and Haifa were destroyed, and those of Ramleh and Jaffa dispersed as refugees, while the village communities of Galilee survived. In the middle of the twelfth century the community began to revive, but the numbers remained small. When the Spanish traveller Benjamin of Tudela visited the country in about 1165 he found the 'Academy of Jerusalem' established at Damascus, and the Jewish population of that city considerably larger than that of the whole of The Land. The intellectual centre during the crusading period seems to have been first at Tyre, which had the largest community

(400 families), then at Acre; and in the latter city some semblance of an academy was revived during the thirteenth century.

The main occupation of the Jews seems to have been dyeing, in which they were so expert that Jewish dyers were even allowed to return and live in Jerusalem in close proximity to the royal palace situated in the Tower of David. Other occupations were glass-making, shipping, and peddling. A few of the more prosperous Jews are mentioned as bankers or physicians to the barons. Apart from the Rabbanite Jews there were small Karaite settlements, and the Karaites were allowed to stay in Jerusalem by the Christians on the grounds that they had had no share in the guilt of the Crucifixion. Though no Latin chronicler mentions the Samaritans, Benjamin of Tudela tells us that there were at least three settlements in the country, the largest at Ascalon, the others at Caesarea and Nablus. The importance of the cities on the coast gradually caused a shift back in the Jewish population; and this was maintained in the thirteenth century when Jews who came from Europe seem on the whole to have settled in the Christian rather than the Muslim part of the country, a tribute to the status which they enjoyed in the Latin social structure.

The society created by the Franks in Syria was thus one possessing many points of interest. It was for external reasons, rather than because of the undoubted internal corruption and decadence, that it existed throughout on a curiously fragile and unstable basis, which enabled it to endure as a reality but for a century, and as a phantom for a century more. The Latin kingdoms never realized that to secure a safe land-connexion through Byzantine territory was an essential life-line for themselves; and the Byzantines in their turn never realized the extent to which their own survival depended on the Latin kingdoms. Had they made use of the military strength and vitality of the Latins to the full, the Turks would never have ruled a wide European empire from Constantinople. There were thus two essentials on which alone the Christian possession of the Syrian littoral could be permanent, and the Franks secured neither. It was not the expression of a united Christendom; for between it and its western bases lay the half-hostile and always suspicious Byzantine Empire; but also it too often failed even to present a united front, much less a united strategy, to Islam. In such circumstances its survival could be measured by the time required by a powerful Muslim prince to gather sufficient forces against it. When a brilliant soldier of Kurdish origin, Salah ed-Din (Saladin), came to rule over both Syria and Egypt, the end was inevitable. It came in 1187 with his victory at the Horns of Hattin in Galilee, though relics of the crusading enterprise survived for another century.

What permanent element was contributed to the population by the Latin kingdom and the trading cities on the coast it is impossible to state clearly. There was certainly a return to Christendom of all the leading crusaders and traders, but of the common people many may have merged themselves into the local population, Christian or Muslim. For the Jews a return or migration to Europe offered no attraction. They stayed, to share and suffer from the disorder which followed the disappearance of the crusaders' feudalism.

CHAPTER SIX

Muslim: The Mamluks

DURING the two centuries in which the main interest had been the contacts of The Land with the West, a complete change had taken place in the Christian and Islamic world around it. The last relics of Arab predominance in the political life of Islam had passed into oblivion before the last Franks left the last relics of the kingdom of Jerusalem; and the comments of European pilgrims suggest a contrast between the tolerance and urbanity of the Arabs and the roughness and cruelty of their Turkish successors. The empire of the Seljuks, which had once stretched over almost all the territories of the eastern caliphate, was reduced to the small sultanate of Rum in Asia Minor. Baghdad, the creation and seat of the Abbasid caliphs, had been sacked by the Mongol Hulagu in 1258, and the caliph al-Mustasim together with thousands of his followers murdered. During the thirteenth century even the survival of Islam in those regions appeared uncertain, for some of the Mongol conquerors professed a primitive form of Nestorian Christianity. In Egypt the Shiite caliphate of the Fatimids had passed with the collapse of the Fatimids themselves; and Syria and Egypt had been united under the Sunni orthodoxy first of the Ayyubid dynasty of Saladin and then of the Mamluks.

The word 'Mamluk' means 'slave'; and the incredible series of rulers who held Egypt and Syria intact for over two hundred and fifty years, repelled the successive invasions of the Mongols, wrote *finis* to the Latin colonies, and made of Cairo one of the most beautiful medieval cities in the world, were all foreign slaves, first mostly Turkish, then mostly Circassian. Forty-seven of them succeeded to the throne in 267 years, making an average reign of less than six. Only in the one case of the Qalaunids did power remain in one family for four generations. An-Nasir, son of Qalaun, came to the throne at the age of nine in 1293 and ruled (with two intervals of usurpation) for forty-seven years. But in the twenty-one years from 1340 to 1361 eight sons succeeded him one after another. Some of the Mamluk sultans were insane, some illiterate; among the Circassians many were figureheads set up for their own purposes by their amirs; they came to the throne by intrigue and assassination and by intrigue and assassination they perished. It has been calculated that the population of Egypt, Palestine and Syria when the Osmanli finally replaced them in 1517 may have been reduced to one third of what it was in 1250 when their rule began. And yet they held the frontiers intact and beautified their capital cities with hundreds of mosques and colleges.

The general picture is of a Mongol power stretching from the borders of China to the borders of Syria, where the Mamluks hold it at bay, while behind the scenes a new Turkish tribe, the Osmanli or Ottomans, are gathering their forces to attack, first the Seljuks of Rum, then the Mongols, and finally the Byzantines and Mamluks, and so to establish a new and secure Muslim dynasty over most of the territories of the caliphate. But if the names have changed, nothing else is new in the political picture. Turk, Mongol and Mamluk showed no greater capacity to organize and administer their territories than Arab and Seljuk. It has already been pointed out that, while Europe learnt much from her contact with the Arab world in fields where the latter was pre-eminent, the reverse is not true. In spite of the constant warfare of the Latin states, commerce and agriculture flourished; justice was administered in a hundred baronial and commercial courts; Syrian Christian, Jewish and Muslim peasants went about their business in safety. All this decayed when the Franks were expelled.

Its disappearance is all the more curious in that there is no lack of noble figures among the Mongol, Turkish and other rulers of Islam. There are many of whom it is recorded that they built and endowed schools and hospitals, that they made roads, irrigated land and provided water supplies for cities, that they favoured scholars and artists, and ruled justly and wisely. But that ever-widening decentralization of culture and responsibility which is the hallmark of a creative society they never achieved. While a sultan or an amir might by his own interests and efforts create and endow great public works, in Europe such work was being done by a thousand nameless churchmen and barons, guilds and communities; so that, whereas in Muslim lands it is necessary to go to capital cities or religious centres to see their architecture, their buildings and their planning, in Europe churches and schools and hospitals, as splendid as those of the cities of the princes, are to be found scattered through innumerable medieval towns and villages; while among the hills and dales, the forests and swamps which had covered the greater part of northern Europe at the time when Arab civilization was at its highest, now ten thousand monasteries and even manors were not only diffusing religion and education, but were draining and clearing, planting and tilling, and building up the agricultural riches of innumerable peasant communities.

The Ayyubid dynasty which Saladin founded lasted for little more than fifty years after his death. One branch ruled in Cairo, another in Damascus, and others elsewhere, and there was perpetual conflict between them. Al-Kamil, nephew of Saladin, died in 1238. His son, as-Salih Ayyab, had to meet a lightning raid of a new Turkish tribe, the Khwarizmians. Their inroad into history lasted barely forty years, but forty years of pillage and destruction. Before they were finally annihilated in 1247, after successive battles in the neighbourhood of Damascus, they sacked Jerusalem, massacring all the Christians who remained, and looting the Church of the Holy Sepulchre. When as-Salih died his widow took power into her own hands, and ruled alone until her amirs elected one of their number to the throne. Then she married and later murdered him. This amir, Aybak, was the first of the line of Mamluk sultans.

Only a few were of sufficient importance to warrant mention, and in the history of The Land there is only one, Baibars (1260–77). He began the final conquest of the Latin sea ports and the castles of the Orders. He has left a name in Muslim legend as high as that of Harun al-Rashid and Saladin, renowned for his conquests, his patronage of learning, and his piety.

Once the Latin states were disposed of by his successor Qalaun and the latter's son al-Ashraf Khalil, there were only two foreign powers with which the Mamluks had to cope: the Mongols and the Christian West. The Mongols were defeated in three successive campaigns. Their farthest penetration was to Ain Jalud, between

Nazareth and Beisan, where the forces of Hulagu were defeated
in 1260, mainly through the generalship of Baibars. Tamerlane a
hundred years later never challenged the Mamluks to battle; for
after a lightning raid on Damascus, from which he carried off
many of the best artisans of the city, he returned at once to the
East and died shortly afterwards on his way to invade China.

With the Christian West the Mamluks were only rarely involved in military activity, although Peter I, King of Cyprus
(1359-69) did attempt to arouse Europe to a new crusade. Failing
to get any adequate response he gathered enough forces to sack
Alexandria in 1365, and in 1367 he ravaged the already desolate
coasts of Syria and The Land. In revenge the Mamluks closed the
Church of the Holy Sepulchre for five years; and many Christians,
including all the Franciscans of Mount Zion, perished in prison.
Otherwise, he achieved nothing. For, with such an eventuality in
mind, the Mamluks had destroyed the coastal cities as they
captured them, and had turned the rich coastlands into a desert,
much of which remained in the same state until the end of the
nineteenth century. The real issue was not war, but trade; for a
very important part of the revenue wherewith they purchased
slaves for their armies, and built their mosques, schools, hospitals
and palaces, came from the fact that in Mamluk lands lay Alexandria and all the other ports at which European traders might
acquire the merchandise of the East, especially the pepper and
spices which were eagerly sought after to make dried, salted and
tainted meat more palatable.

For fifty years after the fall of Acre, papal policy was directed
towards the cessation of this trade. It was commonly recognized
that, unless the Mamluks could be considerably weakened, any
attempt to recover the Holy Land by force was chimerical. For the
European trade not only provided immense revenues, but many of
the deficiencies of Egypt were normally made good from Europe
and provided the basis of exchange with the produce of the East.
Egypt possessed no iron wherewith to make weapons, no wood for
ships, and needed even to import food. If these supplies could be
cut, the advantage would be obvious. For with neither iron nor
wood, nor money to buy slaves, nor adequate food, the Mamluks
would wholly lack the sinews of war. But at best the papacy

secured temporary and partial successes; the desire for wealth was too strong, and not only were the Italian cities, Venice, Pisa and Genoa, impossible permanently to coerce, but Barcelona, Marseille, Ragusa, and other ports of the Mediterranean were beginning to adventure into the field, while great merchants of the north like Jacques Coeur of Bourges were making immense fortunes from their dealings with the Levant.

When both sides were anxious, for their own advantage, to see that trade continued uninterrupted, the results are easy to foresee. The demands of the papacy met with scant regard until the popes too found that the most profitable thing to do was to license, for enormous fees, exceptions to their own prohibitions; the apostles of crusading were regarded as nuisances; Christian kings gladly made treaties with the Mamluk rulers, who in their turn extended to Christian merchants and their consuls privileges they would have scornfully refused to their own Christian subjects. Only the most ignorant and avaricious of them demanded such tolls and bribes that trade ceased to be profitable; but this began to happen with increasing frequency towards the end, when the destitution and exhaustion of their own territories after two centuries of insurrection and misrule had made the profits of Alexandria the most important part of their revenue. Unhappily for them, their increasing pressure came at a moment when improvements in navigation and ship-design made it possible for Europe to consider alternative routes to the East. Before the end of the fifteenth century Africa had been circumnavigated, and the whole balance of trade was altered. The Mediterranean lost its importance; the northern ports and northern powers inherited the affluence of Genoa and Pisa; and the Egyptian and Syrian littorals sank into the obscurity which would have long been their lot had it not been for the constant injection into their degenerate body politic of the gold of Christendom.

Against this general background the story of The Land presents a sad picture of decline. In the commercial prosperity of Egypt and the north it had no share; for its ports were in ruins and deserted. A few merchants touched at Acre for a while to buy cotton; two pilgrim ships arrived annually at Jaffa. At Ramleh there was a little activity. But this was all. Although its soil was

only once invaded by a foreign army, when the Mongols penetrated into Galilee to meet defeat at Ain Jalud, the political system
meant constant military unrest as rival amirs competed for the
uncertain joy of supreme power. Further the lack of effective
administration exposed the countryside to the depredations of the
bedouin, who on one occasion, in 1480, actually chased an amir of
Jerusalem into his palace gates, and sacked a good part of the
shops of the city in the process. For Jerusalem was again an unwalled city.

If the interest which was taken in the Haram ash-Sharif was
less than that taken in either Aleppo or Damascus, and if all three
together could not rival Cairo, yet the Mamluks did not ignore
it, and it would not be unfair to compare Jerusalem during those
centuries to an English medieval cathedral city, a famous and
ancient shrine accustomed to receive from time to time the gifts
of kings and governors for the maintenance of its religious life
and to attract the recluse and the scholar to its calm. It was also
a favourite city for exiled or semi-exiled officials and benefited
from their gifts. The Haram area was enriched by successive
Mamluk rulers and other benefactors with a number of small but
beautiful buildings, marble pulpits and fountains, while both the
Dome of the Rock and Al-Aksa Mosque were kept in repair and
received various endowments. In addition the graceful arcades
which give entrance to the platform of the Dome were built by
Mamluk sultans; some of the gates of the Haram date from the
same period; and four of that favourite creation of Seljuk and
Egyptian Muslims, the Madrasah, or mosque and school combined, were built in Jerusalem. Though it is not recorded that any
of them became famous centres of Islamic theology, they produced
a number of pious scholars. Outside Jerusalem a tower at Ramleh,
clearly based on Latin architecture, and a mosque at Khan Yunis
in the south, together with some smaller buildings elsewhere,
complete the record of architectural monuments of the period.

While the Haram and the Dome were receiving various gifts,
the Christian churches, in spite of gifts from pilgrims and rulers,
were gradually falling into decay, or being confiscated by the
Muslims. It was exceedingly difficult to effect repairs, for the
amount of bribery required to obtain permission to do so was

often more than the impoverished community could raise. The Muslim population was increasingly fanatical, and the life led by the Christians was unenviable. Whenever a Mamluk ruler had reason to be displeased with the conduct of the Christian West, he vented his indignation on his own Christian subjects. His revenge for the raids of Peter of Cyprus has already been mentioned, but such an incident was not an isolated one. In 1422 the Church of the Holy Sepulchre was again shut and many Christians imprisoned and tortured because some Catalonian ships had attacked the Egyptians; and when in 1444 Pope Eugene IV preached a new crusade, primarily against the Turks, Christian shrines were desecrated, the Holy Sepulchre was with difficulty saved from destruction, and the Christians, especially the Latins, suffered violent persecution. From this situation they were rescued, and the buildings were saved, by the king of Abyssinia, who threatened to pull down all mosques and kill all Muslims within his dominions if the Christians were not left in peace.

In the intervals between persecutions various firmans were issued from Cairo, to both Greeks and Latins, guaranteeing, or granting, rights. These are discussed in chapter nine. The basis of these firmans was the Muslim practice of regarding all property in the countries which they conquered as vested in themselves, so that it lay within their power to give it to whom they willed. It was the churches of Egypt which suffered most from this practice at this period, for it was on Cairo that the Mamluks concentrated their enthusiasm for rich and beautiful architecture, and many of their buildings were enriched with columns taken from Coptic churches. They regarded it as a normal procedure to pull down as many churches as was necessary did they wish to build a new mosque.

It was in accordance with the practice of regarding the churches as his property that Saladin, when he captured Jerusalem in 1187, shut the Church of the Holy Sepulchre until he had decided to whom to give it. His choice finally fell on the Syrian Jacobite Christians, and by what means the Orthodox patriarch returned we do not know. But for a considerable period the different Churches seem to have shared the Holy Places among themselves without conflict. The pilgrims for more than a century after

Saladin report the services of many different denominations as taking place simultaneously in the same buildings. Pilgrimages may have been less frequent than in earlier days, but they continued from both the western and eastern Churches, and they were not normally interfered with by those in control of the city, as they brought in valuable revenue.

Records of the origin of Franciscan settlement in Palestine have perished, but they certainly possessed houses in the Latin coastal cities in the thirteenth century, and some were killed in Jerusalem by the Khwarizmians in 1244. Others were martyred in Galilee by Baibars in the latter half of the century. But after the loss of Acre they appear only as pilgrims until they bought land on Mount Zion about 1335. This included the Coenaculum, the room where the Last Supper of Jesus with His disciples was reputed to have been held, and where, after the Crucifixion, they received their divine commissions to preach. This the Franciscans obtained through the good offices at Cairo of King Robert of Sicily. This convent became their headquarters, and they gradually came to be accepted as the official representatives of the Latins, and as guardians on behalf of the Western Church of the Holy Places. So far as the Latins themselves were concerned, they received the right of representation by a bull issued in 1333. But it is evident that at first this representation was accepted by both sides as implying no exclusive possession in them.

The record of the Franciscans during the following centuries is one of considerable suffering and heroism, and of a general care for the Latin pilgrims to Jerusalem. Though the brothers themselves continued their rule of poverty, they came to be an exceedingly wealthy order, and were in continual need of money since bribery was the only means of averting persecution, securing the local enforcement of firmans granted at Cairo, and sometimes even of survival at all. Once it came to countering firman with firman, neither the local Christians nor the failing Byzantines could cope with the wealth of the Franciscans or the protection which they enjoyed. For the Mamluks were indifferent to their own subjects or to the Greeks, but they cared much for the trade with the West. The Franciscans were protected by various western powers at different periods; James II of Aragon had been one of the first to seek to obtain for them the right to a settlement; Robert of Sicily had obtained it for them. But it was of particular value that they were under the protection of Venice, the wealthiest of the trading cities, and of Genoa whose traditions of commercial relations with Syria were even older than those of Venice. This connexion enabled them to care for pilgrims whether they arrived via Ramleh (from Jaffa) or Alexandria, for these cities had their special warehouses and buildings at which pilgrims could be lodged. Later the Franciscans had their own hostel at Ramleh. At all stages the pilgrims were under the protection of a western consul. There was a Venetian consul at Ramleh and a Genoese consul at Jerusalem. Later there was a Venetian consul there also.

In the middle of the fifteenth century, as a result, it is said, of a Jewish project to purchase the reputed site of the tomb of David, the Franciscans lost most of their convent on Mount Zion. For the Muslims claimed David as one of their prophets, and confiscated part of the Franciscan Church of the Coenaculum as being his tomb, and made it into a mosque. Actually David was not buried anywhere near this part of Jerusalem. It was in revenge for the supposed Jewish responsibility for this loss that for a time Jews were prevented from sailing to the Holy Land on Venetian and other ships. The Franciscans retained very narrow quarters on Zion, and in the sixteenth century succeeded in obtaining a firman ousting the Georgians from their convent actually adjoining the Church of the Holy Sepulchre. This has since been their headquarters.

During the fifteenth century their work for the sick was extended by their receiving papal permission for the Franciscan sisters, the Clares, to come and work in their hospitals at Jerusalem and Bethlehem. The life of these women must have been exceedingly difficult. One of the conditions of all the Christian houses under Muslim rule was that their doors had to be open at all times and any Muslim could enter and demand what he liked. The records of the Franciscan houses are full of descriptions of the cost this situation involved; but for the women it must have been an almost unbearable additional burden. Incidentally the Muslims also retained the right to worship in Christian shrines, particularly those associated with the Virgin Mary, whom they regarded with special reverence.

As to the various eastern Churches – Georgians, Abyssinians, Copts, Jacobites and Armenians – all continued to have some stake in the Holy Places and the Holy City together with the Greeks or Orthodox; but all alike suffered a decline during these centuries. From time to time a sultan or amir would revive the various laws of Arab days against the Christians; and Muslim fanaticism could make their lives a burden without special restrictions being added. Taxes to the sultan and the local amir, and the payment of bribes for protection, reduced the Christian peasantry to starvation or the adoption of Islam, and those who lived in the towns fared little better. The Church became a Church without a history, because there was no one with sufficient education to compile it.

In the Jewish community the tragic divisions which allowed to exist side by side in common insecurity an increasingly wealthy and intolerant Latin Franciscan community, and increasingly impoverished native Churches which they did nothing to assist, were fortunately absent. The Jews shared with their Christian, and indeed their Muslim brethren, the consequences of the general collapse of the economy of the country under the extortions of their rulers. But in compensation, it is during this period that it became the custom of the wealthier communities of the Dispersion to contribute to the maintenance of Jews in the Holy Land; and there was a small but not unimportant immigration of rabbis and others from the West which prevented any such intellectual and spiritual stagnation as seems to have befallen the native Christians.

During the period in which the country was divided between Christian and Muslim rulers, the Jews seem to have preferred to remain in the Christian cities; but it is impossible to say whether it was their commercial activity or their political system which provided the attraction. In any case the first group of immigrants from western Europe who made a substantial impact on local Jewish life seem mostly to have settled at Acre. These were rabbis and scholars from France and England – the number is usually given as three hundred – who arrived in 1211. It was the period of the controversy about the rationalism of the great Egyptian Jewish philosopher Moses Maimonides (1135–1204). The academy of Acre, led by Jewish scholars from France and England, seems to have been mystically rather than rationalistically inclined, and it was from Acre that the strongest condemnations of Maimonides were issued. Even the inscription on his grave at Tiberias was altered by them, and its laudatory phrases struck out and replaced by the simple statement that he was a heretic.

While the first western scholars settled at Acre, the next important European to arrive chose rather the impoverished and depressed community of Jerusalem. Nachmanides (1194–c. 1270) was a Jew from Spain, and one of the most important scholars of his age. His decision to go to Jerusalem may have been due to the fact that he had just been banished from Aragon after defeating Paulus Christiani in a public disputation held before James I, King of Aragon. The consequent hostility of the Dominicans, whose champion Paul was, made it safer for him to leave Christendom. Since he was an old man of seventy-three when he arrived, it is reasonable to believe that some such danger had led to his sudden change of life – for conditions in Spain and Jerusalem were very different at this time. Nachmanides managed to revive the Jewish community so successfully that there has been no gap in its history from that day to this, and his synagogue for long remained the centre of Jewish life.

During the period under review there was a constant trickle of Jewish immigrants into the country, some from Christendom and some from other Islamic territories and especially North Africa. While the persecutions in northern Europe and in Germany sent few of these immigrants, for the difficulties of travel were too great, the increasing distress of Jewish life in the Christian parts of Spain was fruitful of new settlers. After the first great persecution of 1391 many came, and still more after the final expulsion of 1492, but these latter will be considered in the following chapter. Many, however, came, not to spend the rest of their lives in the country, but as pilgrims. For to some extent the interest in Holy Places had spread from Christians to Jews, and they have left many itineraries, taking the traveller to the alleged tombs of rabbis and prophets, and illuminated with stories of myths and marvels, exactly parallel to the Christian pilgrims' guide books. They possess, moreover, one other interest in common with the comparable Christian productions. Just as we can occasionally learn something of the state of local Christianity from the Christian guides, so we learn of the existence of Jewish communities and synagogues in various cities from the Jewish guide books.

Towards the end of the period the Jerusalem community received another European rabbi whose work was comparable to that of Nachmanides at the beginning. This was the Italian scholar Obadiah de Bertinoro, who arrived in 1488, and died between 1500 and 1510. He was a learned scholar, whose character won the respect of the Muslims, and he was able to found a rabbinical college in Jerusalem which was recognized as an important authority in rabbinic matters among the Jewish communities of the Islamic world. In view of the difficulties experienced by other travellers in their contacts with Turkish rulers and officials, Bertinoro's remarks on his relations with the local Arab population are of particular interest. He records that

the Jews are not persecuted by the Arabs in those parts. I have travelled the length and breadth of the country and none of them has put an obstacle in my way. They are very kind to strangers, particularly to anyone who does not know the language; and if they see many Jews together they are not annoyed by it.

Of the organization of the community there is little that can be said. In the earliest days there is mention of a nagid in Damascus possessing authority over the Jews of the Holy Land; in the days of Bertinoro it is equally clear that this authority lay with the nagid in Cairo, and the change was probably effected early in the Mamluk period. It is likewise difficult to speak with exactitude of the sites of Jewish settlements. There was first a movement from the sea-coast back into the hill country, since the Mamluks deliberately left the coastal towns in ruins. As time went on there was another movement from the villages to the towns; for the life of the peasant – whatever his religion – had become increasingly intolerable. In Jerusalem the southern quarter, which is still a Jewish quarter, was their centre; and though two travellers in the thirteenth century speak of finding only one Jew in the city, the community numbered some hundreds by the fourteenth. Lydda and Ramleh were the only inhabited cities of the coastal plain, except for Gaza in the south and Acre in the north, where in the fourteenth century there was a community largely composed of immigrants from France and Germany. Beisan, Tiberias and Safad possessed communities, and there seems to have been continuous settlement in just a few villages, such as Nebi Samwil near Jerusalem, a few in Galilee and one or two east of the Jordan. But for the first time there is a silence (which lasts two hundred years) about most of the hill villages of Galilee. Of the Jewish sects there is even less to say. The great Samaritan colony of Caesarea perished with that city, and their centres outside Shechem itself were in Cairo and Damascus. In the former they were said to be a larger and richer community than the rabbinic Jews. The same is reported of the Karaites; few were left in The Land, including Jerusalem, but they were numerous and prosperous in the Mamluk capital.

One grievance from which both Jews and Christians suffered equally was the constant loss of their shrines and buildings on the grounds that the person commemorated was venerated also by the Muslims, or, occasionally, that their worship interfered with a Muslim mosque. The latter reason was the cause of the loss of the great Church of St Mary south of the Church of the Holy Sepulchre; but the earlier reason caused far more extensive damage. In Jerusalem the still standing Church of St Anne became a mosque when Saladin recaptured the city (and is almost unique in having been restored in the nineteenth century to Christian worship), as did the churches of Gaza, St George of Lydda and elsewhere. The Franciscan convent on Mount Zion was lost because King David was claimed as a Muslim prophet. The exquisite doorway of the cathedral at Acre was removed to Cairo to form part of the Mosque of an-Nasir Hasan. But Jewish losses were equally heavy. A thirteenth-century Jewish pilgrim, Rabbi Jacob, who came from Rabbi Jechiel of Paris on the difficult mission of collecting money from the impoverished Jerusalem Jews for the rabbinical seminary of Paris, relates, entirely without resentment, that Muslim shrines are to be found on such spots as the altar of Elijah on Carmel, the tombs of the patriarchs at Hebron, the tomb of Jethro, father-in-law of Moses, at Kfar Hittin, the tomb of Jonah at Kfar Kanah, the tomb of Samuel outside Jerusalem, and even the tomb of Rabbi Gamaliel at Jabne. In fact the only Muslim Holy Place of the period which had involved no seizure from Jews or Christians was the mythical tomb of Moses on the road from Jerusalem to Jericho, built on the spot to which, according to Muslim legend, the body of Moses had been brought by angels because he was lonely on Mount Nebo. But though the buildings on the site were set up by Baibars, the festival of Nebi Musa is of later date, and is first mentioned at the beginning of the sixteenth century.

This penetration of Islam into what had previously been Jewish or Christian sites had this justification – or at least explanation: that it is during the Mamluk period that it first becomes possible to speak of The Land as a primarily Muslim country. During the first century and a half of the Arab period the Christian and Jewish communities certainly constituted the majority of the population; if the Muslims had overtaken them before the crusades, largely through conversion under social and financial pressure, they still constituted important minorities whose presence it would have been impossible to overlook. The crusades led to a further diminution of the Jewish community, but to a more than corresponding increase of the Christian. But during the Mamluk centuries both the Jewish and Christian communities suffered tremendous losses through conditions which made life intolerable.

Yet it must not be thought that the Muslim peasant or artisan fared much better. Though in the gardens and fields around the residence of an amir cultivation may still have been flourishing, yet it is Muslim writers speaking of Muslim peasants who compare their lot unfavourably with that of slaves; and though proportionally to Christians and Jews they may have increased in numbers, their total steadily declined. The lack of ports and trading centres meant that there were few rich merchants or skilled artisans such as thronged the cities of Cairo, Damascus or Aleppo. It had become a land of peasants and of bedouin, and such it was to remain for centuries after the Mamluks had fallen.

Finally, to add to the tragedies of misrule, extortion and disorder, these centuries witnessed an exceptional number of natural calamities. In every century we hear of famines, of droughts, of plagues of locusts and of earthquakes. The Black Death which ravaged Europe from 1349 to 1352 ravaged the Mamluk dominions for seven years; and its toll of deaths was equally heavy; and there were constant lesser plagues. Exceptional rains in 1473 caused the collapse of over three hundred houses in Jerusalem, and in 1491 a disastrous winter caused still more to collapse. It is not surprising that the most frequent word in many descriptions is 'ruins'; for there can have been hardly a city in the country in which the population had not dwindled since crusading days, and many villages were entirely desolate. While medieval Europe suffered similar natural disasters, the vitality of its civilization led to the quick replacement of the losses. The same was not true under Mamluk rule. That they depended for their armies on the constant purchase of foreign slaves is enough in itself to reveal the misery and feebleness which had overcome their native subjects; and there is nothing improbable in the estimate that the two and a half centuries of their power cost the country two thirds of its population.

CHAPTER SEVEN

Muslim: The Turks

CONSTANTINOPLE fell at last in 1453. By the beginning of the sixteenth century Turkish arms had been carried to the gates of Vienna and the plains of Poland and the Ukraine; and the Mediterranean power of Venice had been humbled. But the period of Turkey's real greatness was short, and it was during the brief half-century when she was at the summit of her power that Selim I (1512–20), satisfied for the moment with what his predecessors had bequeathed him in Europe, turned the incomparable Turkish armies to the enlargement of his Asiatic empire. He conquered wide territories from the Shiite shahs of Persia, and in 1517 added to his dominions Syria, Egypt and Arabia. It is uncertain whether the story is true that he persuaded the last of the Abbasid shadow-caliphs of Cairo to hand over to him the relics of Muhammad which were the insignia of the caliphate, but from a slightly later date the sultan of the Ottoman Turks called himself also the caliph.

From the beginning of the sixteenth to the end of the eighteenth century the only military activities of the Turks in Asia against external enemies were on the northern portion of the eastern frontier of the empire where various campaigns were fought against the Persians. Syria and Egypt enjoyed complete freedom from any external invasion during the whole of the period. The campaign in which they had been won required only some minor engagements and two battles, one at Aleppo and one on the outskirts of Cairo. The Mamluk Empire was in full decay, and local chiefs and rulers were well able to see that it was the Turkish and not the Mamluk star which was in the ascendant. The important amirs Ghazali of Damascus and Khairbak of Aleppo deserted to the conquerors, and the former was rewarded by being retained in his amirate. When after the death of Selim, Ghazali revolted and tried to make himself independent, Syria was reorganized into the three pashaliks of Aleppo, Tripoli and Damascus. Later

Sidon was added. Damascus contained ten 'sanjaks', and the territory of The Land was included in those of Jerusalem, Gaza, Nablus, Sidon and Beirut. When the pashalik of Sidon was established it received Galilee. To provide himself with a strong fortress in the south of Syria, Suleiman the Magnificent (1520–66), the last of the great sultans, rebuilt the walls of Jerusalem, and it is his walls which, unchanged, surround the 'old city' today.

The government (known as 'the Sublime Porte', or 'the Porte') which had been devised by the earlier Ottoman sultans was one of the most elaborate and artificial systems ever shipwrecked by the difference between theory and practice. Designed to secure an invincible army, an incorruptible administration and a speedy and efficient system of justice, it ended by producing a byword among the nations for squalor, corruption and inefficiency. But at the time of the conquest of Syria these evil effects were not yet in existence. The empire was reaching the brief apogee of its glory, and its carefully created institutions had not yet revealed their faults. The army and administration were built on a special form of slavery. Only the judiciary, the religious hierarchy, and the local feudal estates were open to the Osmanli and other Muslims. The military and political personnel were recruited by the annual 'tribute' of Christian boys collected from all parts of the empire, but at this period primarily from Europe. Taken from their homes between the ages of twelve and twenty they were brought up in three colleges at Constantinople and educated into the Islamic faith. The system has been somewhat unjustly condemned as inhuman, but the careers open to these children offered glittering prizes they would never have known in their native mountains and villages. The sons of shepherds and peasants became ministers of state, governors of provinces and commanders of the army.

All the boys were physically fit, and those who showed little more than physical fitness became janissaries, the crack corps of the Turkish army, better trained, better disciplined, better paid, and better fed and equipped than any other forces the sixteenth century could produce. Those who showed intellectual ability passed on to a second college, and there trained for the court and the central and provincial services. The most intelligent had yet a third period of training for the highest posts of the empire. The provincial governors, the military commanders, the grand vizir himself, all were by birth Christians, by standing slaves, owing obedience only to their master, and untrammelled by ties of family or provincial influence. To such slavery there was no stigma attached. The slaves of the sultan, raised to the highest ranks of the empire, had no need to be ashamed of the fact that they were the absolute property of their imperial master. There was, however, the disability that he could, and frequently did, at a moment's notice order their execution. The conqueror of The Land, Selim I, had seven viziers decapitated in his presence during the eight years of his rule.

Such was the system the Osmanli had evolved. Its weakness was that all depended on their one master, and the sultanate itself passed by heredity, not by choice of fitness. It depended on absolute integrity at all levels, and when the sultan himself began to accept 'presents' for appointments it collapsed like a house of cards. After a brilliant series of sultans in the fifteenth and sixteenth centuries, not one single member of the family of Osman down to the nineteenth was capable of exercising either political or military leadership. That the empire did not perish earlier they owed to many reasons, not the least important being their slave vizirs, especially the unique Albanian 'dynasty' of Koprulu.

While, during the great period, the system provided for the maintenance of order and the speedy execution of justice, the function of a provincial pasha was no more than to maintain the forces allotted to him and collect the taxes due from his province; and in the course of collection he had to provide for his own salary and expenses. Apart from this the landowners of the province were left to the hereditary enjoyment of their estates in return for the provision of a fixed number of auxiliary troops. If feudal landowners in seventeenth-century Turkey chose to behave like their predecessors in fourteenth-century Europe and make war on each other for the enlargement of their estates, this left the pasha indifferent. His direct authority often extended only to his capital city and its environs, and the rest of the province was only visited once a year for the purpose of collecting taxes. It is these two factors that led to the ruin of the provinces, including Syria.

The annual progress for the collection of taxes came to be a terrifying experience for the population, as well as devastating for the country. The penalty for non-payment was often the destruction of the means by which future payments might be made. Trees were cut down, villages destroyed until whole areas passed out of cultivation, while those who managed to pay only did so at a cost which created a permanent burden of debt upon the agriculture of the country. The decline of population and the increase of waste land in its turn brought in the bedouin, accustomed to pasturing their destructive goats on any unoccupied area. Whole tracts passed back to a state in which they could only support the desert nomad instead of the rich agriculture of earlier centuries; and the tragic process of soil erosion, and the turning of rivers and streams into stagnant marshes, continued unchecked while the Turk looked on indifferent.

This recession in its turn emphasized the divisions within the settled peasantry, quarrelling for the little that was left; and the feuds between clans and villages, between northerners and southerners, became part of the regular routine of life, adding their quota to the economic destruction of their common patrimony. Nor were the feudal landowners and bedouin sheikhs idle in this situation. Private wars between families and tribes flourished, and some of the best rulers which The Land had during these troubled centuries were leaders in such conflicts who had made themselves practically independent of the local pasha.

The first of such men was Fakhr ad-Din (1583–1635), a man of uncertain origin but the hereditary amir of a Druze tribe of the Lebanon. Starting from a secure base in the Lebanese mountains, he fortified Beirut and made it his capital. Established there, he set out to attract European merchants, and allied himself with Christian princes. To the Christians of the Lebanon he showed himself favourable, hoping by their aid to establish himself as an independent prince with territories which included Galilee and Carmel. But neither the Christian powers of the West, nor the Lebanese Christians, came to his help when in 1613 the pasha of Damascus was ordered by Constantinople to suppress him. A land attack he might have resisted, but when the Turkish fleet appeared off Beirut he fled to Italy, hoping to secure help, but in vain. His son Ali

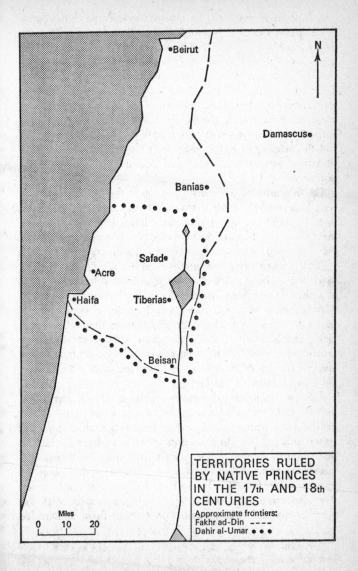

TERRITORIES RULED
BY NATIVE PRINCES
IN THE 17th AND 18th
CENTURIES
Approximate frontiers:
Fakhr ad-Din ----
Dahir al-Umar ● ● ●

took over his government and made his submission to the Porte. When peace was re-established Fakhr ad-Din returned, but to aid and not to replace his son. For fifteen years they maintained their power, but in 1633 the pasha of Damascus was again ordered to suppress them entirely. They were not strong enough to meet the Turks in a pitched battle, and Ali was killed on the field, while his father, less fortunate, was taken to Constantinople and executed. Nevertheless the family continued to exercise some authority in the Lebanon until the end of the seventeenth century, and the memory of Fakhr ad-Din was long treasured among its Christian population as the most favourable ruler they had experienced.

The insecurity of the general position of the Christians at this time is shown by the fact that the sultan Ibrahim (1640–48), the most debauched and cruel of all the sultans, decided to order the massacre of all the non-Muslim subjects of the empire, and was only prevented by the Muslim religious authorities.

During much of the seventeenth century a series of rulers of much less ability terrorized rather than ruled considerable parts of Galilee. These were the sheikhs of the bedouin tribe of the Tarabin, whose central territory was the valley of Jezreel, which they ruled from Jenin. Their authority at times stretched as far as Haifa and Safad. But during the same period there were also Druze amirs who disputed their power, and in their turn raided and sacked such cities as Safad and Tiberias, making life intolerable for the settled population.

Early in the eighteenth century another local prince appeared in Galilee, Dahir* al-Umar, sheikh of the bedouin tribe of the Beni Zaidan whose usual pasture grounds stretched from the region of Safad and Tiberias across the plain of Esdraelon. Dahir made himself master of these two towns, and after a few skirmishes the pasha of Damascus decided to leave him in peace. In 1749, when he was already a man of 64, he seized and fortified Acre and made it his capital. He secured his position with the Porte in the same manner as his predecessor, Fakhr ad-Din. He

---

*His name has several variants in the accounts of Christian travellers, for example 'Dagger'.

offered more tribute than had been paid by the pasha of Sidon from whose authority he had seized the town. Although the fortifications of Acre were an extremely primitive affair, they were sufficient to give him a secure base, and he proceeded to act as ruler of a wide territory. He gave the peasants security from bedouin raids, and acted with equal justice towards Muslims, Jews and Christians, with the result that numbers immigrated into his district from the surrounding country.

A colony of Greek Christians came from Cyprus to settle in the vicinity of Acre, and Tiberias was rebuilt by a rabbi and his followers from Smyrna. Dahir was successful also in attracting Christian merchants, and the trade of Acre began to revive. In particular he developed the growing of cotton, and an extensive trade, of which France had the monopoly, resulted. This trade continued until Mehmet Ali developed a superior cultivation in Egypt. To extend his authority he married his sons and daughters into the families of the bedouin sheikhs whose pasture lands adjoined his dominions, and gave to his sons separate governor-ships in Galilee. But this proved one of the main causes of his downfall; for the sons quarrelled among themselves and needed to extort ever larger sums from the peasants to finance their mutual conflicts. To raise more money Dahir took the desperate expedient of buying the spoils when the bedouins raided the Mecca pilgrimage as it passed east of the Sea of Galilee, and also entered into partnership with Maltese corsairs to divide the spoil taken from Turkish ships plying to Egypt.

In 1760 a new pasha, Osman, was sent to Damascus and his sons were made pashas of Tripoli and Sidon, in order that a concerted attack from all these centres should be made on Dahir. But when in 1764 Osman and his sons had gathered their forces, they suffered a disastrous defeat near Nablus. Dahir then returned to the trick of securing his position with the Porte by offering an increased tribute, and this won him a moment's respite. But Osman was only waiting to raise more troops. Unfortunately for him his only means of raising them was to increase the taxes due from various parts of his pashalik. Ramleh, Gaza and Jaffa in turn revolted; and the unsettled state of the country induced Ali Bey, the ambitious Mamluk ruler of Egypt, who had expelled the

Turkish pasha in 1770, to send his general Muhammad Bey (Abu Dahab) to invade Syria and to seek to add that country to his territories.

The moment was well chosen, for the Porte was fully occupied with one of its periodic campaigns against Russia, and a Russian fleet was actually in the Mediterranean. Ali made an alliance with Dahir, and his army advanced to Gaza. Dahir marched south while Abu Dahab occupied Jaffa and Ramleh. Osman dared not meet their combined forces, and the allies after completing their plans at Acre, marched suddenly on Damascus. The city fell into their hands with very little resistance; but then the army of Ali suddenly retired precipitately to Egypt. It was said that Abu Dahab had been bribed and intimidated by Osman. Two years later Ali was expelled from Egypt by Abu Dahab and took refuge with Dahir. Together, and with the aid of the Russian fleet, they defeated the Turks near Sidon. But on his return to Egypt in the following year, Ali was seized and killed by Abu Dahab. Osman renewed the offensive against Dahir and, after an initial defeat at Safad by Dahir's son Ali, succeeded in uniting against the old bedouin prince (Dahir was now about 85) not only the Mutawali clan of the Lebanon, but the important sheikh of the Nablus–Jaffa area. But Dahir held his enemies at bay for two more years, from 1773 to 1775, by which time the Porte was prepared to make peace with him. At this moment Abu Dahab again invaded Syria. Gaza opened its gates, Jaffa fell after a few days' siege, and Acre itself capitulated to the Mamluks. But his sudden death led to a retirement of his army, and Dahir returned to his capital.

It then appeared that the Egyptian invasion had been planned by the Porte, which had offered Dahir peace merely to lull him into a false security; for, no sooner had the Mamluks withdrawn, than Hassan, the most famous Turkish admiral of the day, seized Sidon and appeared off Acre. Dahir found himself deserted in his determination to resist, and was killed while seeking to escape from the city. He was probably the greatest and best of all the local rulers who set themselves up in different parts of the country during the Turkish period. Certainly he formed a noble contrast to his successor at Acre, al-Jazzar, 'the butcher', the builder of the large mosque in that city. A Bosnian by birth, al-Jazzar, after various adventures, was made pasha of Sidon, where his cruelty and avarice made him more hated even than most pashas.

Of the Muslim fellaheen little is recorded during this period. They shared with all other peasants in the unhappy empire the misery of constant extortion and insufficient security. It was a period in which there must have been a considerable modification of the composition of the population, a modification already begun in Mamluk days. The many travellers who visited the country tell a continual tale of lands out of cultivation and of villages destroyed. The disappearance of the settled peasants opened the doors to a continuous infiltration of bedouin tribes from the deserts and semi-deserts of the east and south into the once fertile plains of the coast, and even into the hill country of Judea and Samaria. If it is during the Mamluk period that the country can first be called a primarily Muslim country, it is not until the Turkish period that in the ethnic sense it acquired a substantial Arab population, though there were other elements as well who entered the country during these centuries.

Of Jerusalem and the Haram ash-Sharif there is nothing new to be said; it slumbered, except when it was disturbed by local disorders. But it is during this period that the festival of Nebi Musa came to play a part in the religious history of the country. First definitely mentioned about 1500, it was introduced, perhaps originally by Saladin, to balance the Christian pilgrimage to Jerusalem with a Muslim pilgrimage; to give it equal importance, it was associated with the mythical grave of Moses in the desert of Judea between Jerusalem and Jericho, over which Baibars built an extensive mosque. It served also to raise the dignity of Jerusalem by giving it an annual event comparable, though on a lesser scale, to the annual assembly of the pilgrims for Mecca at the rival city of Damascus. Curiously enough its date is fixed by the Christian, not the Muslim, calendar.

The situation of the Christians was more affected than that of the Muslims by the Turkish conquest of Constantinople; for the four Orthodox patriarchates, Constantinople, Alexandria, Antioch and Jerusalem, now lay within the territories of a single sovereign. The Turks took over the millet system from the Arabs and still further developed it. The non-Muslim citizens of the

Porte, known as 'rayahs', were divided into nations, and each nation had a single head, usually resident in Constantinople, who was responsible for the members of the nation wherever they might live. In this way the Orthodox patriarch was head of the 'Rum' millet, for the Orthodox Christians were known to the Turks as Romans. Other Christian bodies at various dates were also recognized in the same way.

The gathering of all the ancient Orthodox patriarchates within a single state might well have meant a certain increase of security as well as a strengthening of their spiritual life. That it did not do so was due to two causes. In the first place the character of the ecumenical patriarchate rapidly declined. The office came to be sold to the highest bidder, and constant intrigues led to a quick succession of men who were completely unworthy of their high position. The Orthodox Church did produce some martyrs and confessors among its patriarchs; but it produced far more rogues, charlatans and peculators. Finally, though the office was given great formal dignity and importance, the sultan could, if he so desired, regard its holder merely as another of his slaves, on whom he might inflict any humiliation he chose, and deal with as he thought fit. In so far as the Jerusalem patriarchate was concerned a further reason for decline lay in the increasing gulf between the patriarch, his officials, and especially the Brotherhood of the Holy Sepulchre on the one side, and the dwindling number of local Christians on the other. For the former came to be exclusively Greeks and the latter were wholly Arabic-speaking, and, so far as Transjordan was concerned, Arabs. The patriarch was generally a Greek of the Phanar quarter of Constantinople, elected at Constantinople under the auspices of the ecumenical patriarch, living at Constantinople, and only occasionally visiting his patriarchate.

In the second place the position of the rayahs throughout the empire was increasingly miserable. The system by which the pashas were completely free to extort what sums they could from their pashaliks exposed them to the heaviest exactions; and since the pashas and their subordinates usually changed annually, the extortion was continuous. The few worthy viziers who tried desperately to reform the administration of the provinces, and secure proper treatment for all the subjects of the Porte, passed much too quickly to effect any permanent improvement. Moreover the Christians had to suffer increasing burdens from the hostility, barbarity and avarice of the Muslim population. Islam itself decayed under the dead hand of the Turks, and the religion of the peasants, the bedouin and the urban mobs was little more than a crude, violent and intensely arrogant superstition, which took delight in robbery and murder. When the governors and officials themselves gave an example of insatiable avarice, it is not surprising if every village and tribal sheikh did the same; and there was no group who was robbed and victimized with greater delight than the unfortunate Christian population. The last *berat* or patent of office to be given to a patriarch of Jerusalem by the Turkish authorities was issued to the patriarch Damianus in 1897. It contains this astounding clause, among many which deal with the extortions of officials: 'Let there not be interference by officials when he travels in places which are dangerous; the best way to go and be saved from bandits is to disguise himself and carry arms contrary to ancient custom.' The life of the Christian peasants and townsmen in previous centuries can be imagined, when such advice is given in a solemn official document to the patriarch himself at the end of the nineteenth century, when great reforms had already taken place.

Meanwhile the Latin Christians lived just as miserable a life, made still more miserable by the violence of the religious hatred which separated them from the Orthodox and eastern Christians, a hatred which each side manifested with equal consistency. In the relations with the Porte itself the Latins were in the better position, for they were protected by European powers with which the Porte wished to remain friendly; and they were much wealthier than their rivals. The position which had been occupied by the consuls of Genoa or Venice during the Mamluk period was, from the sixteenth century, occupied by France and occasionally for brief periods by other European powers. A small group of Carmelites managed to re-establish themselves on Mount Carmel in 1631 (their predecessors had been massacred in 1291), and maintained themselves, though not without serious interruptions, from then onwards, until in 1825 they obtained security by building the present fortress-like monastery.

Apart from them the Franciscans were the only permanent residents in the Holy Land. In the sixteenth century they obtained their present buildings within the city walls in place of their old convent on Mount Zion; and outside Jerusalem and Bethlehem they maintained precarious rights in Tiberias, Nazareth, Ain Karim and at Jacob's Well near Nablus. As time went on the Franciscan Custos of the Holy Places assumed the deportment and train of a patriarch, doubtless in the belief that only so would he receive the respect of the Turks. The Order was exceedingly wealthy, but enormous sums had to be spent on bribery. A French canon, I. Doubdan, has left us the story of the attempt made in the middle of the seventeenth century to repair and restore the Franciscan convent in Jerusalem. Having obtained permission by copious bribery from the Porte for the restoration, 20,000 livres had to be spent in bribes in Jerusalem before a stone could be moved; and from then onwards extortion, riot and violence marked every step of the repairs. But it was not only for such legitimate purposes that money was spent. Where bribery could obtain a patriarchate it could as easily buy a Holy Place, and the eastern Christians could not have hoped to outbribe the wealthy and intolerant Franciscans, even had they ceased to quarrel among themselves and united to do so. The Turks favoured all these quarrels, for there was always profit to be made by setting one side against the other, and favouring those who could make the largest present in any particular incident. In fact a considerable proportion of the revenues of the governorship of Jerusalem came from the taxes on pilgrims and the money which could be made out of the disputes of the Christians.

The one outstanding event during these centuries was the council called at Jerusalem in 1672 by the patriarch Dositheus on the occasion of the repair and re-dedication of the Church of the Nativity at Bethlehem. The purpose of the council was to examine into the doctrines of one of the most interesting patriarchs of Constantinople during these centuries, Cyril Lucar (1572–1638), the donor to Charles I of the Codex Alexandrinus, now in the British Museum and one of the most important manuscripts of the Bible in the world. He was born in Crete while it was still a possession of Venice, and so came into contact with western

European thought, and particularly with the theology of Calvin and the Reformers. While he did not wholly accept any form of Protestantism, he found much in it with which he agreed, and was very anxious to reform his own Church, both in its government and its doctrine. He was killed by the Turks, on the suspicion of friendship with the Russians, and his views were condemned in successive councils. But the most important was that held under Dositheus at Jerusalem.

During this period there was a considerable change in the provenance of the pilgrims who visited the Holy Land. The Franciscans still took charge of all Latin pilgrims, but these came in decreasing numbers. They were also prepared to be hospitable to other pilgrims coming from western Europe who were members of the Protestant Churches, and who could be more accurately described as travellers than pilgrims in the old sense. They seem to have made a considerable profit out of these pilgrims, for though they charged no rent for receiving them, the pilgrim found himself obliged to make a 'present' which, according to some travellers at least, more than equalled the amount for which an equally good lodging could have been found elsewhere. But while pilgrims from the West declined in numbers, increasing quantities of the Greek Orthodox subjects of the Porte annually visited Jerusalem. In the eighteenth century their numbers amounted to several thousand a year. Towards the end of this period occurs the first mention of pilgrims from Russia, the main source of pilgrimages in the following century; for it is during the eighteenth century that Russia began to make tentative claims to the role of protector of the Greek Church to balance the position of France or other western powers in relation to the Latin subjects of the Porte.

In the beginning at any rate the change to a Turkish government involved greater opportunities for the Jewish than for the Christian population. But to get the full story of the main changes we need to go back a century to the establishment of a firm Turkish foothold in Europe. The condition of European Jews in the fifteenth century was one of steadily increasing poverty and insecurity. In Spain the persecutions and mass-baptisms of the end of the fourteenth century created for the first time a large class of 'Marranos', Jews who nominally professed the Christian religion but in their hearts remained loyal to Judaism. In Germany and central Europe persecutions and expulsions had followed each other until many ancient Jewish centres were almost denuded of population. In these circumstances, some fifty years after the Turks had established their capital at Adrianople in 1366, the rabbi of that city, Isaac Zarfatti, sent a letter to the Jewries of western Europe inviting them to settle under Turkish rule, where they would suffer neither persecution nor restriction, and could live in freedom and practise their religion openly.

Only a trickle answered the call; for the route was long, dangerous and expensive. Marranos from Spain were among the first; but Jews from Germany followed, and new Jewish centres grew up in the Balkans. In 1492 came the great expulsion from Spain, and the expulsion from Portugal followed four years later. Sephardic Jews fled mostly by sea, for the French frontier was closed to them, and many settled in Italy and throughout North Africa and the Levant. In the middle of the sixteenth century the Jews of Italy in their turn fell on evil days, when the intolerance of the counter-reformation deprived them of the protection they had hitherto enjoyed in the Papal States. But before this last calamity, the Turks had conquered Syria, and The Land was open to those who could reach it. That more did not come was due to the difficulties of travel, not to lack of desire.

The conquest of Syria and Egypt involved a change in the administration of the local Jewry. The Turks, following the example they had set with regard to the Christians, established a chief rabbi – the Haham Bashi – in Constantinople, and made him supreme over the whole Jewish millet of the empire. The Jews of The Land were no longer in any way subject to Egypt, and the last nagid of the Egyptian Jews, Isaac Solal, actually settled in Jerusalem in the very year of Selim's conquest. The great advantage of the millet system to both Christians and Jews was that it left them complete management of their own affairs, their own schools and law-courts, once they had paid the special poll tax levied on all non-Muslims.

The Jewish community under the Turks passed from a period of very rapid and brilliant expansion, during which The Land became for a brief while again the centre of the whole Jewish world, to almost as rapid and catastrophic a decline. The central cause of this expansion was the Sephardic immigration from the Iberian peninsula and from Italy. Sephardim soon came to out-number the Arabic-speaking indigenous Jews; and they were, until the eighteenth century, more numerous than the Ashkena-zic immigrants from Poland and northern Europe. The centre of the new community was in the north, where a number of Jewish villages still survived and where Safad, a seat of local government, offered a certain security. Jerusalem remained in the second place, for though its community grew in both numbers and learning, it had no Jewish hinterland to sustain it as Safad was sustained by the Galilean villages.

Jewish life in Safad was two-sided; it was an important com-mercial centre, lying between Damascus and the port of Sidon; and its industries, especially the weaving and preparation of woollen cloth, found a ready market within and outside the country. But while Safad was rich in merchants it was even richer in scholars of the Cabbala. The succession of events in Europe which marked the end of an epoch – the expulsion of the last great Jewish community; the retreat of Christendom before the advan-cing Turks; the breakdown of the religious unity of the Middle Ages – all convinced Jewry that they were living through the birth-pangs of the Messiah, and that his coming was imminent. Under the leadership of a young Ashkenazic Jew, Isaac Luria (1534–72), born in Jerusalem of German parents, the Zohar and its mysterious prophecies became the centre of study; and it was natural that Galilee should have attracted the Cabbalists, since it was in Galilee that Simeon ben Jochai, the reputed founder of Jewish mysticism, lived and was buried. His tomb at Meron on the spurs of Jebal Jarmaq is still the centre of an annual pilgrimage from Safad.

The Jewish population of the latter town rose to something like 15,000 by the middle of the century, possibly the most extra-ordinary community in Jewish history, as it passed its time in almost continuous religious excitement, dancing and ceremonial. To the weekly festival for welcoming the Sabbath Judaism owes its most familiar Sabbath hymn, Lekha Dodi, written by Solomon Halevy al-Kabbez, who came to Safad from Constantinople. But

Safad had not merely three thousand looms for weaving wool, and several times that number of mystics; one of the mystics, Joseph Caro, a Spanish Jew who had been brought to Turkey at the age of four, combined his studies of the Cabbala with so profound a knowledge of the Talmud – usually rather ignored by mystics – that he produced in the *Shulhan Arukh* what has remained to this day the standard codification of Talmudic law for Orthodox Jews throughout the world.

While Safad was reaching its zenith, Tiberias lying below it on the shores of the lake was still an unpopulated ruin. But it was to Tiberias that the attention of Dona Gracia Mendes, one of the most remarkable, wealthy and influential refugees from Spain at the court of Suleiman the Magnificent, was directed. Possibly Dona Gracia was attracted by the healing springs near the town; but for some reason, about the middle of the century, she extended her charities to the community of The Land. In 1561 she created a settlement and college in Tiberias, and announced her own intention of retiring there. This scheme was taken up by her son-in-law and nephew, Don Joseph Nasi, and a charter was obtained from Suleiman granting him Tiberias and seven villages surrounding it, with permission to rebuild the walls and settle the town and the land with Jews whether immigrant or native. Don Joseph, who became Duke of Naxos, was a practical man, and began by having the walls rebuilt. He then invited Jews to settle in the town, extending his invitation to the Jews of Europe, especially those of Italy who were feeling the full weight of the intolerance of Popes Paul IV (1555–9) and Pius V (1566–72).

Though he was able to offer transport in his own ships, yet few seem to have been able to come, and of those who did some were seized at sea by the Knights Hospitallers and sold as slaves. Don Joseph planted mulberry trees to encourage a silk industry, imported the finest wools from Spain for weaving, and hoped to develop the fishing industry on the lake. But the plan fell far short in its realization of the semi-independent refuge he had hoped to provide for the distressed Jewry of Europe. The intrigues of the court kept him at Constantinople, and he never visited his estate, though Dona Gracia may have lived there for a year or more before her death in 1569. The opposition of the Custos of the Franciscans, working through the French ambassador, and the hostility and brigandage of the local inhabitants and the bedouins all combined to wreck his hopes, and when he died in 1579 his ambitious scheme was abandoned. Nevertheless it was revived by another powerful Jewish courtier, Solomon ibn Ayesh (Alvaro Mendes), who had become Duke of Mitylene. He secured the concession for his son Jacob, who actually resided in Tiberias; but he was more interested in scholars than in commerce, and when he died in 1603 it had already become necessary for the community of Safad to rescue the scholars of Tiberias from starvation.

The development of Jerusalem, though less ambitious than that of Safad and Tiberias, was nevertheless striking, and when in the seventeenth century, Galilee became insecure, it regained its primacy. There also Sephardic Jews came to outnumber the indigenous and Ashkenazic communities; and the Jerusalem academy enjoyed a great reputation. The smallest of the four cities regarded as 'Holy Cities' was Hebron. There a community struggled with isolation and with the constant repression of local rulers and bedouin tribes. Though never wholly wiped out, it never succeeded in becoming prosperous, and the only flourishing community in the south was in the commercial city of Gaza.

All the prosperity of the sixteenth century had vanished by the beginning of the seventeenth. Both Safad and Tiberias were sacked by bedouins and Druzes in succession; and the latter was not rebuilt until eighty years later in the time of Dahir, when it was settled, at his invitation, by Hayim Abulafia of Smyrna and a new Jewish community. They managed to restore something of the prosperous agriculture of earlier days, and when the settlers were joined by some Chassidim from Poland, Tiberias became again one of the four Holy Cities. Other immigrants came from Poland and settled in Jerusalem, Safad and elsewhere during the eighteenth century, but it was impossible to restore the ground which had been lost. The insecurity created by the complete indifference of the Turkish pashas to the local wars and raids of local amirs, bedouin tribes, Druzes and others, was reducing not only the Jewish community, but the whole country to a degree of poverty and desolation even greater than it had known under the

Mamluks. Traveller after traveller reports desert and marsh where there had been fertile fields, and ruins where there had been towns and villages. But even so, the country had not yet sunk to its lowest level. It was in the early part of the nineteenth century that the cumulative effect of centuries of neglect and destruction reached its culmination.

PART TWO

Its Meaning to Three Religions

CHAPTER EIGHT

The Promised Land of Judaism

ALL through its history The Land has been the home of different peoples and of different religions. In this fact there is nothing unusual. What gives it its unique position is that members of three religions, Judaism, Christianity and Islam, who do not dwell in the country, are yet for religious reasons concerned in its destiny. This interest, though it exists for all of these religions, has in each case special characteristics. For Muslims the issue is not Palestine as a Holy Land, but Jerusalem as a Holy City. For, according to Muslim belief, the Temple of Solomon was miraculously built, and it was to and from Jerusalem that Muhammad was transported in order to make his ascent into heaven where his vocation was recognized by his prophetic predecessors. Jerusalem is therefore the third holiest shrine in Islam. For Christians, The Land as a whole is the Holy Land, as the scene of the earthly life of Jesus Christ. In this sense it is unique and pre-eminent, and has no rival. The Christian Church has never sought to make the land the religious centre of the Christian religion; neither, with small exceptions, have Christians desired to live in the country as a religious obligation. All through history Christian actions have been directed to securing access to the country for pilgrims, and control over the particular Holy Places associated with the Christian religion; and, apart from the crusades, if this access is secured they have been satisfied. For Jews The Land is a Holy Land in the sense of being a Promised Land, and the word indicates an intensity of relationship going beyond that of either of the other two religions. As it is for the Christians, The Land is unique; but the nature of its unique appeal goes further, and has throughout the centuries involved the idea of settlement and return, and an all-pervading religious centrality possessed by no other land.

To understand the full implications of this fact for the history of the Jews we must know something of the nature of Judaism; for much misunderstanding has arisen in relation to all three religions from the failure to realize that in spite of a common monotheism, with its inevitable implications of universalism, they are in their emphases three different kinds of religion. The central emphasis in Islam is on the submission of the individual to the will of Allah, and it recognizes the equality of all Muslims, whatever their colour, nationality or country. The central emphasis in Christianity is on salvation in Christ, and as such it cannot be tied either to any particular geographical area, or to any particular people. But the central emphasis in Judaism is on the divine revelation of a way of life to be lived by men in community; and it is therefore revealed to a special community. Moreover while it shares the belief in a future life with the two other religions, this belief has played a smaller role in Judaism than in either of the other two, and the concern with the life of men in community in this world has played a correspondingly larger role. Comparisons between religions are at all times difficult, and it is natural to avoid them where possible. But without some such statement of fundamentals it is impossible to get a true perspective of the relation of the three religions to the past and present history of The Land.

The intimate connexion of Judaism with the whole life of a people, with its domestic, commercial, social and public relations as much as with its religion and its relations with its God, has historically involved an emphasis on roots in physical existence and geographical actuality, such as is to be found in neither of the other religions. The Koran is not the history of the Arab people; the New Testament contains the history of no country; it passes freely from the landscape of the Gospels to the hellenistic and Roman landscape of the later books; and in both it records the story of a group of individuals within a larger environment. But the whole religious significance of the Jewish Bible – the 'Old Testament' – ties it to the history of a single people and the geographical actuality of a single land. The long religious development which it records, its law-givers and prophets, all emerge out of, and are merged into, the day-to-day life of an actual people with its political fortunes and its social environment. Its laws and customs are based on the land and climate of The Land; its agricultural festivals follow its seasons; its historical festivals are linked to events in its history – the joyful rededication of the Temple at the feast of Hanukkah, the mourning for its destruction on the ninth of Ab, and above all the commemoration of the original divine gift of the land in the feast of the Passover. The opening words of the Passover ritual conclude with the phrase: 'Now we are here, but next year may we be in the land of Israel. Now we are slaves, but next year may we be free men'. And the final blessing is followed by the single sentence 'next year in Jerusalem'.

Confusion can also result from identifying the Jewish and Christian views of the Messiah, or the Jewish view of his coming with the Christian view of his second coming. The Christian believes in a second coming of Jesus Christ to mark the end of the world and the final judgment. The function of the Jewish Messiah, as conceived in the period with which we are now dealing, was the restoration of the Jewish people from all the lands of the Dispersion to the land of Israel. Ideas of judgment, of world redemption and of eternal life, were not wholly absent; but the restoration of the Jewish people occupied the foreground of the picture.

Finally it is important to realize that such a hope of restoration was inevitably kept alive and strengthened by the impossibility of obtaining a substitute in any other land. The belief which had come to be accepted as normal by Christendom, that it was only possible to have civic unity on the basis of uniformity of belief, made it absolutely impossible for a Jewish group to be anything except second-class subjects. The same was true within Islam, and there the status of second-class subject was, of course, shared by the Christians. Neither within Christendom nor within Islam could Jewish destiny be fulfilled; and the whole world, as the Jewish people knew it, was occupied by the one religion or the other.

It is correct to say 'the Jewish people' and not 'Jews'; for even when they were scattered in a thousand ghettoes in innumerable different Christian and Muslim countries, the Jews recognized themselves as, and were universally recognized by others to be, a single people. The conception of Englishmen, Poles or Americans of the Jewish persuasion is a wholly modern one, a product of emancipation, and has never been applicable to more than a minority of Jewry. During this period, from the second century to the eighteenth, nobody would have challenged the truth of the idea that it was just as accurate to compare Jews with Turks or Frenchmen, as to compare them with Christians or Muslims. They were recognized as both a religion and a nation, and it occurred to no one that there was anything inconsistent in the dual attribution. This recognition by themselves and others that they were still a single people reinforces the naturalness of their continued association with the landscape of their independent history and of their law-givers and prophets. Moreover their restoration to the land of Israel was an article of Christian as well as of Jewish belief, even though the Christian associated it with their acceptance of Jesus Christ as their Messiah.

In following out the relationship between the Jewish people and the land of Israel, we are involved in three separate aspects of the subject. First there is the place of The Land in the general religious life of Jews in dispersion; second there is the story of messianic expectation and the appearance of false messiahs; thirdly there is the story of the actual Jewish inhabitants and of Jewish immigration into The Land. An atheist may reject any claims arising out of the first two factors. The third remains valid from any point of view.

During the centuries of their dispersion Jews built up a double religious life. Their loyalty in the lands of their sojourn was governed by the general principle that 'the law of the land is law'; and each community was entitled to build up its own ordinances for its own religious government. A wide latitude was allowed for the adjustment of Biblical and Talmudic law to the actualities of life under different rulers; and a continuous correspondence took place between communities and outstanding rabbis as to the steps to be taken when new developments made new regulations desirable. But, side by side with this, as it were, *ad hoc* legislation the central study and religious interest of Jewry lay in the great codes of the Bible, the Mishnah and the Talmud whose integral fulfilment could only take place in the land of Israel. Neither in sanctity nor in interest did the great corpus of diaspora legislation ever supplant the legislation concerned with the land of Israel;

the history of the Jewish people remained their history in that land, and it was not until late that any Jewish chronicler concerned himself with their life in Spain, or France or elsewhere. And it was never conceived to be possible that any essential new revelation could come to them anywhere save in their own Homeland.

While thus it remained central in the whole religious interest of the Jewish people in dispersion, the subject was especially focused onto their messianic expectations. All through the centuries under consideration false messiahs succeeded each other, and sudden rumours sprang up, now from the east, now from the west, that the Messiah had actually manifested himself. Rabbinical scholars, even the most eminent, gave themselves to calculations of the time of his coming, though there were some few scholars, equally eminent, who resisted the temptation. Three times, in the eleventh, the sixteenth and the seventeenth centuries, messianic excitement swelled to a climax which swept all through Jewry, from the furthest communities of the west, to North Africa, Arabia and Tartary.

The first of such waves of excitement came in 1096, the year of the first crusade. It seems to have arisen in Abydos, opposite Constantinople, at the time when the German crusaders were still milling round the capital, pillaging and looting, uncertain whither to proceed. The rumours reached France and Germany that the Messiah had appeared in the east; men in Turkey said that they had met Elijah, returned in the flesh, and that he had promised that the Messiah was on the way. In the land of the Khazars seventeen communities abandoned their possessions and set out to meet the lost tribes who were said to be coming from the east to join him. Jews from all countries began to gather at Salonika to take ship to the land of Israel to meet him. In both west and east the more responsible leaders seem to have kept their heads; but twenty years later, when Benjamin of Tudela visited Germany, he found the Jews still in a ferment at the Messiah's expected coming. But by then most knew the reality; no Messiah had come; instead thousands of Jews had been massacred by the crusaders in the Rhineland, and hundreds had been burnt in their synagogue when the Christian armies reached Jerusalem. But soon the rumours began again. A proselyte, Obadiah, had spoken with him on the road to Damascus. He had been seen in Cordova; men had heard that in Fez he had declared himself. Then in Persia. Then in the Yemen. Always the Messiah was coming; and when hope died the calculations began afresh; fresh figures, fresh dates were examined; and, unheeded, the cautious warned against the belief that the time could be known.

In the thirteenth century Nachmanides, taking the analogy of the demand of Moses to Pharaoh that he would release the children of Israel, proclaimed that when the Messiah really came it would be known because he would appear before the pope and demand the freeing of his people; and in 1280 the Spanish mystic, Abraham Abulafia, convinced that he was the Messiah or his forerunner, sought to visit Nicholas III. The pope gave orders that, if he came, he should be seized and burnt at the stake. But on the very night that Abraham arrived, the pope died suddenly, and Abraham was saved. Then for two hundred years the ferment died down; the sordid miseries of the later Middle Ages contained none of that dramatic element of high tragedy which could seem the prelude to great events.

As the sixteenth century dawned the ferment welled up again with even greater strength. The expulsion from Spain, the breakdown of medieval Christian unity, the conquering advances of the Turk, all convinced men that some great dramatic change was coming. For the first time there was a faint breath of Christian speculation accompanying the Jewish excitement. Millenarian sects arose, awaiting the speedy End of the World. As it was believed that before this could take place all the tribes of Israel would have to be gathered together, a new interest arose in 'the lost ten tribes'. In those days, when voyages of discovery were taking place almost every year, rumours were constant that they had been found, now in Africa, now in some hidden part of Asia, even in America.

In this atmosphere there appeared in Istria a German Jew, Asher Lammlein, who travelled through central Europe, giving himself out to be the Messiah, and then vanished (*c.* 1502). Twenty years later appeared a much more flamboyant character, David Reubeni, self-styled brother of Joseph, Davidic king of a Jewish kingdom of Khaibar in Arabia. He did not give himself out as Messiah; he promised no immediate deliverance to his fellow Jews. But he was able to say where, in Africa and Asia, the lost tribes were to be found; and his mission had the messianic flavour of the deliverance of Jerusalem from the Turks. But it was a military deliverance he proposed, and he offered the princes of Europe an alliance with his imaginary brother's forces to this end. He was received by the pope; his offer was favourably considered by the king of Portugal; other princes followed suit, and he set out to see the Emperor Charles V at Ratisbon. But by this time men had come to judge him an impostor, and he was arrested by the emperor and sent to Portugal, where he disappeared in the prisons of the Inquisition. During the same years a gentle Spanish mystic and visionary, Solomon Molcho, gave himself out as Messiah. He was a Marrano by birth, and this in the end caused his death. But his attractive character and deep religious sincerity made a great impression on Christians as well as Jews. He was received by the pope and by Christian princes, and he accompanied David Reubeni on his fateful visit to the emperor. He also was arrested, and was burnt at the stake as an apostate.

For a hundred years the excitement died down again in Europe; but a change was taking place in The Land. Under the influence of Isaac Luria, cabbalistic interest passed from the gnostic and theosophist contemplation and examination of the Divine Nature, to the practical question of the coming of the Messiah; and the influence of the mystics of Safad, armed as they were with the first printing press in Asia, spread all through the Jewries of Europe, particularly of eastern Europe. Dates and times were calculated again; but this time the Christian interest equalled, if it did not even outweigh, the Jewish. Everywhere – in France, in Germany, but especially in England – there was religious disorder, and new Protestant sects, each with wilder ideas than its predecessors, were to be found on all sides. Again the lost ten tribes were proclaimed to have been discovered; so that nothing was lacking but their conversion to belief in Jesus as Messiah, and His return could not be delayed.

The year 1648 was believed to be the appointed time. It was a period of immense distress in Europe. For thirty years Germany had been ravaged by a religious civil war which utterly destroyed whole cities and provinces, and reduced the population from sixteen to six million. England was in the throes of a bitter conflict between king and parliament. And in the east the cruel bands of the Cossack Chmielnitzki, aided by Tartar allies, had spread havoc and desolation through all the Polish Ukraine, massacring Poles and Jews by tens of thousands. Jews and Christians were equally oppressed by the evil of the age, equally looking for deliverance. When 1648 passed and nothing was revealed, Christians accepted the date of Jewish expectation, 1666; and waited with a painful intensity equal to that of Jewry.

This time it seemed to many thousands that their hopes were to be answered. There was born in 1626 in Smyrna, son of the agent of an English merchant, Shabbetai Zevi. From his early years Shabbetai devoted himself to the Cabbala and practised rigorous austerities. In 1648 he confided to the intimate circle of his friends that he was the expected Messiah; but the knowledge did not pass beyond Smyrna. Nevertheless in 1651 he was banished from the synagogue of the city for his pretensions, and for ten years he led a wandering life. In 1660 he settled at Cairo under the patronage of a wealthy Jewish tax-farmer and mint-master, Raphael Joseph Halabi. Thence in 1663 he went to Jerusalem, still making no open claims, but seeking to make himself popular with the Jews there. On their behalf he returned to Cairo to seek financial help from Joseph. In Cairo he heard of a young woman, Sarah, refugee from the massacres of Chmielnitzki, who had announced that she was to be the bride of the Messiah. Shabbetai sent for her, married her and with her returned to Jerusalem. On the way he found a certain Nathan at Gaza who was to be his prophet. Nathan wrote to Jewish communities throughout the world, announcing that his Master, the Messiah, had revealed himself. But Jerusalem would have none of him and, fearing to make an open announcement there, Shabbetai returned to Smyrna, arousing wild excitement on the way. There in 1665 he openly proclaimed himself Messiah.

The news spread like wildfire. Businessmen in London and Amsterdam discussed it seriously; Jews everywhere prepared for their departure for the Homeland. Shabbetai went to Constantinople, perhaps expecting that some miracle would intervene to establish him with the sultan. Instead he was put into honourable confinement and, after several months' imprisonment, he was brought one day before the sovereign and brusquely given the alternatives of Islam or death. No miracle occurred, and he chose Islam. Nevertheless, men still believed in him. When he died some years later, an obscure prisoner at Dulcigno in Albania, he still had enthusiastic followers in many countries, especially in Poland. The Shabbetaian controversy troubled the Synagogue for another century; it produced curious sects like the Frankists in Poland; and one survived in Turkey as a mixed Jewish-Muslim sect known as the Donmeh until the twentieth century.

Jewry could not easily recover from the blow of the apostasy of the man on whom so many hopes were set. There set in a bitter reaction and nowhere was it felt more than in The Land itself. The local Jewry, oppressed by Turkish misgovernment and crushed by the weight of taxes and exactions, sank to its lowest level of physical and intellectual misery. After Shabbetai no messianic ripples disturbed its stagnant waters. The long centuries of alternate messianic hope and despair were succeeded by an apathy which was not broken until the nineteenth century.

Though it was only at the coming of the Messiah that the rabbis expected a mass movement, it was held at all times to be a meritorious action to settle and live in the land of Israel. But just as there is a natural connexion between messianic expectation and the pressure of external events, so also those who came of their own will did so mostly as a result of pressure in the land of origin. The voyage was exceedingly expensive and fraught with many dangers; the conditions of The Land were well known from the reports of travellers, and men knew that they could expect only the most miserable poverty to await them. It is not surprising if in the more prosperous communities most Jews found that their contributions to the fund for the relief of captives who had fallen into the hands of the Knights Hospitallers or the Barbary corsairs on their way to The Land, and to the fund for the maintenance of those who lived in The Land itself, excused them from considering their own removal from their familiar surroundings before it was perfectly clear that the Messiah had

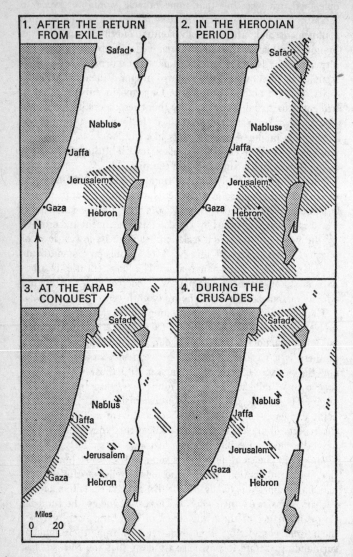

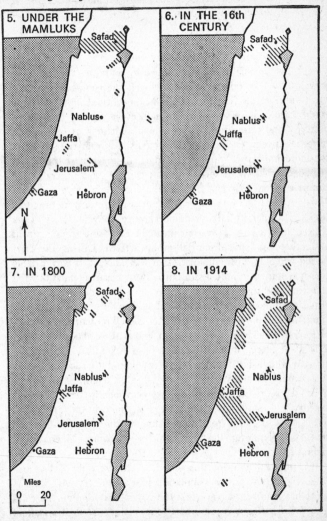

5. UNDER THE MAMLUKS

6. IN THE 16th CENTURY

7. IN 1800

8. IN 1914

come. At times a Jehudah Halevy or an Obadiah of Bertinoro would be moved by purely religious emotions; but most came like the refugees from Spain, because they were refugees.

It is interesting that the Muslim rulers seem at no period to have refused to allow Jews from foreign countries to enter and settle. This was not a permission accorded to western Christians; for the Franciscan Custos was obliged to guarantee that pilgrims stayed only a certain time and then left the country. It was of great value to the Jewish population, for without immigration it could scarcely have survived. Through every century there came a steady and unrecorded trickle which at least kept a few communities in existence, and made it possible, from time to time, for more important numbers to come. In the period before the crusades we know of several groups coming from other Islamic countries, from Babylon, from Arabia and the Yemen, and from North Africa. The first important European group were the three hundred scholars from England and France who came early in the thirteenth century. It was not until the expulsion from Spain in 1492 that another substantial group arrived. During the brief period when Turkish administration was efficient, it was possible for the country to hold a substantially increased population, and this time the immigrants amounted to some thousands. But the situation quickly deteriorated, and it was only a trickle which came in the following century. After the Ukrainian massacres of 1648–9 the trickle grew to a stream, and at the end of the century a band of fifteen hundred set out from Poland and a thousand actually reached Palestine; but many found themselves unable to maintain themselves and sorrowfully left again. Small groups of students came from Italy on two occasions in the eighteenth century and established their colleges in the country; and larger groups of Chassidim from Poland came in the second half of the century, rebuilding the communities of Safad, Tiberias and Hebron.

It is impossible during this period to estimate what was, at any time, the actual Jewish population of the country. At times it must have sunk to a very few thousands; but though the community of indigenous Jews, who could claim that their ancestors had never known exile, dwindled to a single village by the nineteenth century, there had grown up in its place a community, accepting hardship and poverty, insecurity and danger, which represented almost all the Jewries of the world, eastern, Sephardic and Ashkenazic, which was supported in its need by all the Jewries of the world, and which was regarded by Jews everywhere as peculiarly blessed because it lived upon the holy soil itself.

CHAPTER NINE

The Holy Land of Christianity

SOMETHING has already been said in the previous chapter of the differences between the Jewish concept of a 'promised' land and the Christian concept of a 'holy' land. The Christian association rests on its being the scene of the earthly life of Jesus Christ, and not on any subsequent primacy of the country in the institutional hierarchy or religious thought of the Christian Church. That this unique characteristic has resulted in a tragic conflict for the ownership of various Holy Places is due to some extent to the chequered political history of the country, but owes something also to the evolution of the Church of Jerusalem in relation to the rest of Christendom.

After the separation of Christianity from Judaism had been consummated in the early decades of the second Christian century, the centre of the former passed very rapidly into the Gentile world, and in the following century the bishopric of Jerusalem lost all but local interest. The destruction by Hadrian even of the name of the city in which Jesus had lived, taught and died, and the building of a new city with a new name on the site, doubtless accelerated the process; but we must also consider the probability that until the fourth century Christians had not that veneration for sites and relics which afterwards came to invest the Holy Land with a special significance.

A change came in the days of Constantine, under whom the sacred land and its capital city were turned into a central religious shrine for Christendom. Not only in Jerusalem but all through the country, in Galilee and Samaria as well as in Judea, churches and monasteries sprang up associated with incidents in the life of Jesus Christ. The result was inevitably a stimulation of religious and intellectual life; but even then Jerusalem had neither ecclesiastical nor intellectual pre-eminence. Its bishop was still a suffragan of the archbishop of Caesarea, himself subordinate to the patriarch of Antioch; in the great religious discussions of the time it played but a secondary role. But this was of no importance, for it was not a rival or competitive eminence with other bishoprics that Jerusalem and the Holy Land were accorded, but a peculiar primacy which made it the common property of the whole Church. Such a shrine as that created by Constantine to embrace the accepted sites of the Crucifixion and Resurrection of Jesus Christ had as intimate and direct a relationship to the furthest parish in the premier patriarchate of Rome, as it had to the nearest parish of the local suffragan bishop of Jerusalem in the patriarchate of Antioch.

It is not unnatural that, when such universal veneration was poured out upon the church in which their episcopal throne was established, it should seem improper to the bishops of Jerusalem that their office should occupy so subordinate a position in the ecclesiastical hierarchy; and they set out to secure the recognition of patriarchal dignity for the Church of Jerusalem. They achieved it in 451, and they thereby unconsciously altered the whole standing of the Holy Places under their guardianship. It would have been better if they had sought some title equal to a patriarchate in dignity, but in itself unique.

The position of the patriarch of Jerusalem was still further affected when the eastern Church was rent by schisms which were never healed. The patriarchate of Jerusalem remained faithful to the creed of Chalcedon, and the Orthodoxy which is henceforth, for convenience, called Greek; so that the shrines which were equally venerated by all Christians now came to be the exclusive possession of one section of the Christian body and, so far as we know of this period, closed to other sections. Justinian certainly would have been unlikely to tolerate the presence in them of those he judged heretics. With the Arab conquest a still further break took place. The patriarchates of Antioch, Alexandria and Jerusalem all fell within the Arab dominion and were shut off from their customary contact not only with the premier patriarchate of Rome but with what had come to be accepted as the premier eastern patriarchate of Constantinople. Relations continued, but of a different kind; and they were liable to interruption. However, during this period the special and universal character of the Holy Places came again to the fore, while the significance of their possession by the local patriarchate of Jerusalem fell into the background. The Land became a centre of pilgrimage from all parts of the Christian Church, from outside as much as from within the political dominions of the caliphs. As Islam itself venerated certain shrines of Christians and Jews, and tolerated the religions of both, and as the pilgrimages were profitable, the Muslim rulers of Jerusalem encouraged them, and on two occasions gave explicit recognition to the universal Christian interest in the Holy Land of Christianity.

In 797 Harun al-Rashid recognized the interest of Charlemagne by permitting him to endow and maintain centres for pilgrims from the West, and this action not only did not offend the patriarch of Jerusalem but was, partially at least, inspired by him. In 1036 the Fatimid caliph, al-Mustansir, in permitting the Christians to rebuild their shrines, recognized the right of the Greek emperor Constantine Monomachus to nominate the patriarch of Jerusalem and to rebuild the Church of the Holy Sepulchre, destroyed with other churches by his predecessor al-Hakim. It is doubtful whether any inference can be drawn from the fact that Charlemagne was a 'Latin' and the Byzantine emperor a 'Greek'. The reason for the Muslim choice may well have been in each case purely political; and though both 797 and 1036 fell in periods of great tension, the eastern and western Churches were not yet divided. Harun al-Rashid may well have preferred the western emperor simply because he was at war with the eastern one, whereas al-Mustansir preferred to conciliate the ruler of Byzantium because both alike were in fear of the same enemy on their eastern and northern frontiers.

The action of Charlemagne and Constantine restored the distinction between the universal significance of the Holy Places and the local significance of the Jerusalem patriarchate; and it seems to have been restored during this period in a second sphere also. The Orthodox patriarch of Jerusalem himself came to recognize the interest of eastern schismatic or heretical Christians in the Holy Places, and they began to be admitted to what after the rebuilding by Constantine Monomachus was a single church embracing the sites of the Crucifixion (Golgotha) and the Resurrection (the Holy Sepulchre). This was probably a natural consequence of the drawing together of the scattered Christian populations under Muslim rule; but in any case there is the fact that the first head of the Christian community recognized by Islam was the Nestorian catholicus in Mesopotamia, and that their subsequent recognitions of other Christian ecclesiastics were based on their own convenience and not on the orthodoxy of the ecclesiastic concerned.

This action of the Orthodox patriarch was therefore the natural consequence of his recognition by the caliphs as the head of the whole Christian community in Jerusalem, but it corresponded also to a tendency among the eastern Churches to create for themselves a special position in the Holy City. In most cases we cannot date exactly when such an interest developed. In some it goes back to Byzantine times; in some it took place during the Middle Ages. One of the earliest Churches to establish a special centre in Jerusalem was that of Georgia, a mountain kingdom in the Caucasus. As early as the time of Justinian the Georgians established in Jerusalem the Monastery of the Cross, covering the site where the tree was supposed to have grown from which the Cross was made. During the period in which Nestorianism and monophysitism flourished in the east the Georgians remained strictly Orthodox. In the time of the Mamluks they obtained special favours from the conquerors, probably because they were famous warriors, and their kingdom lay on the frontiers of Islam and Byzantium, where their friendship was valuable to both sides. They came to possess a number of other monasteries in Jerusalem and they are the first Church of whom we hear as sole custodians of special portions of the Church of the Holy Sepulchre.

It was during the crusading period that the Jacobite Syrians created a special bishopric in Jerusalem in order to counter the attempt of the Latin patriarch to assume authority over the native Christians; and there has been a continuous line of bishops since the middle of the twelfth century, some of whom have assumed the title of patriarch. In the middle of the twelfth century the Copts, who had hitherto accepted the authority of the Jacobite patriarch of Antioch over Coptic Christians outside Egypt, also consecrated a special bishop for Jerusalem, and have likewise maintained their bishopric. It is the only see outside Egypt. Two other Churches which had taken similar steps at some period before the thirteenth century were the Nubians, or Abyssinians, and the Armenians. They also early established claims to special places in the Church of the Holy Sepulchre. The former do not seem to have established a special bishopric, being content with monasteries; but the latter created a bishopric which in the eighteenth century assumed patriarchal dignity. Except the Georgians all these Churches were monophysite. The Nestorians appointed a bishop of Jerusalem as early as 893, whose function was to care for Nestorian pilgrims, rather than for any settled Nestorian congregation. After 1065 their bishops in Jerusalem ranked as metropolitans, and continued to be appointed up to the beginning of the seventeenth century.

While such was the situation of the eastern Churches, relations with the West followed a different pattern. In the middle of the eleventh century the final break took place between Rome and Constantinople. This did not appear to have any immediate effect on the treatment of western – or as we now call them, Latin – pilgrims to Jerusalem; and what might have developed subsequently was interrupted by the crusades. According to the western tradition the Orthodox patriarch died just at the time of the arrival of the Latins, so that the consequences of appointing a Latin patriarch may not have been fully worked out. The eastern tradition maintains that he lived until 1106, so that the appointment of a Latin patriarch was definitely an act of schism; but the step was itself inevitable during the Latin occupation. The Latin Christians would not have accepted the jurisdiction of a 'Greek' patriarch whom they in their turn regarded as schismatic. But, *mutatis mutandis*, the same applied to the local Christian population, and still more to the Greek Orthodox population of Byzantium. A successor to the Orthodox patriarch was, therefore, consecrated at Constantinople, and seems to have resided there during the crusading period.

Nevertheless the distinction between the patriarchal see and the Holy Places was recognized. The Orthodox and other eastern Christians were not excluded from worship in the Church of the Holy Sepulchre. The monk Theodoric in 1172 found Greeks, Syrians, Armenians, Jacobites and Abyssinians possessing altars;

and the Latin kings were even prepared to attend Orthodox ceremonies. Moreover the Orthodox reached some *modus vivendi* with the Latin ecclesiastics, though it would probably be anachronistic to attempt to define its implications too clearly. It did not amount to reunion. While some of the Latin patriarchs showed themselves intolerant and oppressive to the local 'Greeks' and Syrians, no fundamental change was made in the situation during the period of the Latin patriarchs. The Orthodox and Syrians continued to use the church. When the Latins were expelled, the Orthodox patriarch automatically assumed his previous rights, though he did not expel the Latin Christians from the shrines.

The humiliating and disastrous failure of the crusades led to a widespread heart-searching throughout the Western Church. While some still thought out strategic plans by which an armed attempt might be made to recapture what had been lost, the more spiritually minded, especially the newly constituted Franciscan and Dominican Orders, turned to a religious rather than a military solution of the problem. They were influenced in this attitude not only by a desire to convert the Muslims themselves, but by the increasing knowledge which the crusades had brought them of the existence of very widespread Christian congregations in the East which were not in communion with the West, but which were not felt, as was the Orthodox Church, to have deliberately and consciously broken off contact with the papacy.

It was soon found that missions to the Muslims were impossible. Even such men as Francis of Assisi himself, or the saintly Dominican, Raymund Lull, were unable to make any impression on the adherents of Islam; and as death was the penalty both for the missionary who sought to turn a Muslim from his faith, and for his convert, did he succeed in making one, the attempt was soon abandoned. There were always a few fanatics from both western and eastern Churches who sought deliberate martyrdom by proclaiming their faith in the mosques of Islam, but the conversion of Muslims at this period was not regarded officially as practicable. A more hopeful line seemed the rallying and strengthening of the Christian forces which existed throughout the wide dominions claimed by Islam. Something has already been said of the sterile hope that the Mongols might permanently adopt Christianity – though had they done so at that stage of their development they might well have been as much a liability to Christendom as the Ottoman Turks were later to Islam – and many missions, half religious, half diplomatic, were sent to the Mongol khans. But there were also hundreds of thousands of descendants of pre-Islamic Christian communities in Persia, Armenia, Georgia and other lands, as well as in Syria and Asia Minor, who might be strengthened by the presence and assistance of western clergy and missionary stations.

The ending of the crusades, then, imposed a double task on the western Church, and it was entrusted by Pope Innocent IV to the two great preaching Orders. To the Dominicans was given the missionary task throughout the East, and to the Franciscans that of safeguarding the access of the West to the Holy Land. It may be said at once that it proved impossible for the Dominicans to get any foothold whatsoever in what had been the kingdom of Jerusalem as, section by section, it passed back into Muslim hands. The Franciscans, on the other hand, did succeed in establishing themselves in Jerusalem and, to some extent, other towns, and in caring for the pilgrims who still came from Europe to visit the Holy Places. But the manner in which they conducted the struggle to establish themselves in these Holy Places made them so hated by almost all the eastern Christians that they could not hope to combine their guardianship with any missionary work among native Christians who regarded them as more deadly and insidious enemies than the Muslims themselves. In Syria and further afield the Dominicans succeeded in establishing good relations with native Christian groups, and some, through their work, were reunited with Rome. To such work the Franciscans themselves had closed the door, so that an eastern Christian, as the fourteenth-century pilgrim Burchard reports, would rather have become a Muslim than a Latin.

As the rest of the story is, from all standpoints, tragic, and to many must seem highly unedifying, it is well to remember three facts without which a real understanding of the problem is impossible. In the first place, all through the centuries the Holy Places were visited with deep and sincere devotion by tens of thousands of simple Christians of all Churches who were concerned with a genuine and humble adoration of the Master in whose earthly footsteps they believed themselves to be following as they visited the various shrines shown to them; and who viewed the variety of language and devotion which they witnessed at those shrines as evidence of the universal nature of their religion, rather than as the assertion of the rival rights and claims of different ecclesiastical institutions. Their thoughts dwelt only on the sinless life and redeeming death of their Saviour. In their pilgrimages they underwent great hardship and passed through many dangers in order to express a religious faith which was wholly sincere; and many of them died in the course of their pilgrimage.

In the second place those Churches and ecclesiastics themselves which became involved in unworthy acts of bribery, and even in bloody conflicts, were led originally into these mournful courses, not by any personal ambition but by an extreme, and even fanatical sense of the importance of the sites which they conceived it to be their duty to guard for the innumerable members of their respective faiths. They fought in order that simple pilgrims might not be excluded from shrines which they regarded with the utmost veneration; and in order that the spiritual benefits which they believed to accrue from the pious visitation of such sites should not be lost to members of their own Church.

Finally, when we consider the bitter and contemptuous terms in which each tended to condemn the activities and ceremonies of the other, especially the Latin descriptions of the devotions of the Orthodox and the Syrians which are mentioned later in the chapter, we must remember that these authors did not belong to a period in which the study of religious psychology would have enabled them to understand the underlying reality in actions which, if performed by themselves, might have been frivolous and unseemly. The members of the eastern Churches, living in the oriental environment of Islam, naturally tended to express their religious emotions in the manner familiar to them from their environment, but the faith and devotion which they sought to express was the same as that of their more restrained western brethren.

The problem which faced the Latin Church when its patriarch

and clergy were compelled to quit Jerusalem, and still more when they were compelled to quit the country, was a difficult one. The Orthodox patriarch had already become accustomed to making some accommodation with schismatic or heretical eastern Churches as to the use of the Holy Places. The Latins themselves had not wholly excluded them during the crusading period. But no such accommodation had been formally made during the brief decades between the split between East and West and the crusaders' capture of Jerusalem, and no such accommodation could easily be made at the time of the collapse of the Latin kingdom in view of the hostility between the Churches at that moment. In consequence, as they ceased to be residents in the Holy Land, the Latins, alone of all Christian bodies, gradually found themselves with no status in the Holy Places. At the very beginning of this stage the step was taken of obtaining rights, not from their fellow Christian, the Orthodox patriarch, but from Saladin.

The step itself was possible, as has been already said, because of the Muslim conception of the legal ownership of such places. Muslim rulers held themselves to be the owners of all religious buildings within their dominions, to whatever religion they were devoted, and therefore claimed the right to allocate them, confiscate them or close them. No such buildings could be repaired or rebuilt without their permission. No protest could lie, if they decided that they should be turned into mosques. Such is the background of a situation of which we can find many examples in Jerusalem in every century down to the end of Turkish rule. At the very moment of the re-conquest there was a discussion as to whether the Church of the Holy Sepulchre should not be again destroyed, as it had been by al-Hakim. It would be unfair to say of Saladin that his motives for deciding to allow the building to stand were financial; but such were certainly the motives of his successors. The Muslim governors of Jerusalem and all their hangers-on made immense profits out of the Christian shrines. For the pilgrim was taxed on entering not only into Jerusalem, but also into the Church of the Holy Sepulchre, which was open free only on certain days during Easter and the festival of the Invention of the Cross. And yet, when the pilgrim Thietmar visited Jerusalem in 1217, he found the church closed, empty and deserted.

It was a reminder to all Christian sects that they held their rights only by the goodwill of their rulers, and other occasions on which the church was closed have already been mentioned.

For the understanding of the subsequent story some account of the Church of the Holy Sepulchre is essential. At the west is a large rotunda, covered by a dome, often rebuilt and usually open to the sky in the centre, and surrounded by a two-storied aisle. In the centre of the rotunda is the Holy Sepulchre, with a chapel around and over it. To the east of this rotunda are the transepts and choir of the crusaders' cathedral. North of the north transept is a large chapel: the Chapel of the Apparition, where Jesus was supposed to have revealed Himself after His resurrection (Matthew xxviii, 9). In the south transept, which contains the main entrance to the Church, is the Stone of Anointing, on which the body of Jesus was believed to have been prepared for burial; and east of the south transept is a two-storied building containing the rock of Golgotha above and the chapel of Adam below. Apart from the crusading period, the choir has always been the seat of the Orthodox patriarch, but around its apse are the usual series of chapels, each of which has come to be allotted an incident from the Passion story. Still further east, and at a lower level, is the Chapel of the Empress Helena, and beyond and below that lies the chapel of the Invention (i.e. 'discovery': Latin *inventio*) of the Cross. The church is surrounded by monastic buildings in the possession of various Christian bodies.

From 1239 the keys of the Church of the Holy Sepulchre have been kept by a Muslim family; since 1517 order has been maintained by Turkish soldiers, and the very heavy tax on entrance (until the end of Turkish rule) was collected by Muslim officials from every Christian resident or pilgrim.

The official re-establishment of the Latins was originally due to an interview in 1192 between the bishop of Salisbury and Saladin, as a result of which they received permission for two priests and two deacons to be attached to the churches at Jerusalem, Nazareth and Bethlehem, and for Latins to visit the Holy Land on pilgrimage. How long this permission lasted we do not know, but there is no mention of these priests in the accounts of pilgrimages from the beginning of the thirteenth century. The significance of this new departure was not immediately visible; for a brief period certain Latin bodies still continued to exist in the Holy Places apart from this permission, and many eastern Churches continued, throughout the Mamluk period, to enjoy rights in the Church of the Holy Sepulchre and elsewhere which they had received from the Orthodox patriarch without any payment to the Muslim rulers. Of these at the beginning of the period the Georgians were the most powerful group. They had more shrines than the Latins or any other community except, of course, the Orthodox, and they had the privilege of keeping the keys of the Sepulchre itself. Mention is made by medieval pilgrims of special shrines of the Abyssinians, the Armenians and the Syrians; but doubtless the Copts and Nestorians also possessed some special centres, though it is only mentioned that they were to be found in the church.

By a bull of 1333 the authority of the Latin Church in relation to the Holy Places was given to the Franciscans, and the head of their Order in Palestine had episcopal dignity and the title of Guardian, or Custos, of the Holy Places. They gave the first sign of their increasing power when in the middle of the fifteenth century (a period when, after the Council of Florence, reunion with the East was in the air) they were able to outbid the Georgians for the keys of the Sepulchre, the first example of the policy they were to pursue with increasing single-mindedness during the succeeding centuries, of displacing other Christian groups by bribing the Muslim authorities. But at the end of the Mamluk period they still had no more than four altars, though these included the exclusive possession of an altar on Golgotha and the right to celebrate mass in the Holy Sepulchre – the two principal shrines of the whole building.

The Turkish conquest introduced a new factor into the position of the Latins by substituting the power of France for that of individual princes and the Italian cities. The French Church had for long regarded with pride the historic connexion between France and The Land. The relations between Harun al-Rashid and Charlemagne were magnified until it came to be believed that Charlemagne was admitted by the caliph to be his overlord for the Holy Land. The predominant part that France had taken in the whole crusading movement was proudly emphasized. When therefore France received the most favourable privileges for her trade and consular activities in Turkish territory, the effect was immediately seen in an intensification of the activity of the Latins in regard to the Holy Places. The main feature of the period which runs from 1517 to 1740, when the Franciscans secured the most complete recognition of their claims, is the partial disappearance of the lesser Churches. The lavish scale on which the Franciscans could buy rights and the vigour of the political pressure which France was prepared to apply compelled them to drop out. They had no influence and no money.

A French traveller, Canon Morison, visiting Jerusalem in 1698, records the unhappy situation of the Copts. There was but one priest left in a dark corner of the aisle of the rotunda. He was unable to go out, and his people could not pay the fees demanded for the opening of the doors to come in. They could only visit him twice a year when the doors were opened free. If the Franciscans had not occasionally given him food he would have starved. Only one eastern group had been able to improve its position. This was the Nestorian Church which had been taken under the wing of the Dominicans and Franciscans in the hope of reunion. In consequence they had been given definite possession of a tiny alcove off one of the Franciscan chapels 'big enough for four people to enter'. The Armenians, however, though at their weakest at this time, managed to restore their influence later, and during the nineteenth century and today their patriarch enjoys an equal status with the Orthodox and Latin patriarchs in relation to the Holy Places.

Politically the position of France rested on the capitulations which had been agreed between Suleiman the Magnificent and Francis I in 1535. While they involved no diminution of Turkish sovereignty (as did later European 'capitulations' with Asiatic powers) they gave France complete pre-eminence over other European powers, who might only trade with Turkey in ships bearing the French flag, and whose European residents depended for their protection on the French consuls. While these capitulations made no reference to the Holy Places, they gave a handle for subsequent claims on behalf of the Franciscans in that they allowed France the protection of the western pilgrims and the Franciscan residents. The fact, however, that the Franciscans themselves came from all the Roman Catholic countries of Europe, and especially from Italy and Spain, brought in the interest of other European powers, so that even when there was tension between France and the Porte, the Franciscans were not without protectors.

After the Reformation the Franciscans still remained responsible to the Turkish authorities for all western pilgrims, who now included Lutherans, Calvinists and other Protestants. On the whole they seem to have acquitted themselves fairly of what must have been a difficult task. If up to the end of the eighteenth century the pilgrims sometimes complained that the Franciscans expected considerable payments for their hospitality, it may well be that they were unaware of the fees which had to be paid by their hosts to the Turks. Nor was it unnatural that the Franciscans should feel that sums given them by faithful pilgrims of their own flock, or by the princes of Europe, should not be expended on the care of heretics. They were therefore careful to see, when a Protestant pilgrim arrived at Jaffa, whether he had adequate money for all his expenses. If he appeared to be insolvent he was liable to be sent home again. During the eighteenth century the wealth of the Franciscans diminished considerably; the number of pilgrims was much reduced, and the exactions of the Turks increased. They were compelled by circumstances to exercise every economy and, even so, lived a sufficiently miserable existence. In the nineteenth century their situation gradually improved, and almost every Protestant pilgrim records his gratitude to them for their care and attention.

The pressure they exercised from the sixteenth century onwards led to a reaction on the part of the Orthodox, whose power, though less than that of their rivals, was increased by the political reunion of the Jerusalem patriarchate with the ecumenical patriarchate of Constantinople. The intensity of the struggle was increased by the mutual antipathy of the antagonists. The Latins held the eastern Christians, whether Orthodox or schismatic, in ever increasing contempt; and it has to be admitted that the descriptions of western travellers go far to explain this feeling. While the members of the patriarchal staff and the Brotherhood of the Holy Sepulchre were Greeks, there was no difference in cultural level between the laity of the Orthodox, the Syrian, or the other eastern Churches; and all alike had become thoroughly 'orientalized'. The combination of a wildly emotional devotion to the Holy Places with all the physical gyrations, contortions and extravagances normal to a congress of dervishes did not predispose western visitors, whether Roman Catholic or Protestant, in favour of the rights – or rites – of eastern Christians. And in addition to the religious exercises of the easterners they must have suffered considerably from the dirt and smell of a shrine in which one of them gravely raised the question whether it were possible that the marble pavement spontaneously generated fleas.

As one of the great assets in establishing possession was that the party in question had been permitted to effect a repair or rebuilding, the Latins scored a triumph when in 1555, at the request of the Franciscan Custos, the Emperor Charles V and his son, Philip II of Spain, secured permission to rebuild the dilapidated chapel over the Sepulchre itself. This made it a Latin possession, and from then onwards they exercised the right not merely to say mass in the tomb, but to prevent any other Church from doing the same. With the permission of the Franciscans an eastern Christian might enter this, the holiest shrine of the whole building, to say his private prayers; but he was not allowed to do more. Such was the curious position of this church that if he did, a fine of 500 piastres had to be paid to the Turks. The securing of so exclusive a right in such a place as the Sepulchre itself meant war to the knife on the part of the Orthodox, and it is not surprising that deaths and severe bodily wounding became a feature of the Latin–Orthodox conflict from then on.

During the seventeenth century the Franciscans – according to their later claims – increased their holdings; but it is uncertain what shrines they actually had occupied to produce the edicts in favour of the Orthodox of 1634, 1644 and 1676, cancelling their 'encroachments'. For the Turks with perfect indifference described as 'encroachments' in an edict to the Orthodox what they had recognized as 'rights' in capitulations made with the French, or edicts issued to the Latins. In 1634 the Orthodox for a time ousted the Latins from Golgotha, and in 1676 scored a further triumph in ousting them from the Sepulchre, and proceeded to celebrate their victory by giving the maximum offence to their opponents. But their triumph was short lived, for in 1691 the Latins recovered the Sepulchre, and their position on Golgotha, and held them until a disastrous fire in 1808. In 1740 the French negotiated new capitulations with sultan Mahmoud I, and Article 33 guaranteed the Franciscans in the possession of 'the Holy Places of pilgrimage which they have, in the same manner as they have possessed them in the past'. At no time were the Turks anxious to define more exactly the privileges which they granted; so that when in 1757 the sultan Osman guaranteed the Orthodox against any further encroachments of the Latins, he left it happily vague as to what was encroachment and what was ancient possession. That there had been encroachment can be seen from the fact that in 1850, when the Latins were claiming to be put in possession of the shrines to which they had secured rights by the capitulation of 1740, they claimed, instead of the four which they had possessed since the Middle Ages and which still remained the whole of their claims in 1621, almost the whole of the building except the actual choir of the crusader church which was the cathedral of the Orthodox patriarch.

They claimed the whole of the rotunda and the transepts with all their Holy Places, practically the whole of the ambulatory around the Orthodox choir with its Holy Places, the crypt of the Invention of the Cross, all except one altar of the two-storied building of Golgotha, and the whole of the quadrangle on the south side of the building by which alone it was possible for anyone to enter it from outside. That they had ever, in practice, exercised the exclusive possession of these fantastic claims for more than brief periods they were of course unable to show; but the subtle nature of the privileges granted by the Turks made it equally impossible to prove that they had not. While the main interest of the Churches centred in the Church of the Holy Sepulchre, similar conflicts existed over Holy Places in the Church of the Nativity in Bethlehem and elsewhere.

In 1808 a fresh situation was created in the Church of the Holy Sepulchre by a fire which started in the gallery of the rotunda. It destroyed the whole rotunda, including the shrine of the Sepulchre, and severely damaged the rest of the building. In spite of protests from the Latins, the Orthodox managed to secure the exclusive right to execute all the necessary repairs; and put such haste into it that the church was ready for rededication in 1810. In doing the work some £200,000 was expended, of which £125,000 was accounted for by bribery at Constantinople, and of the remaining £75,000 much went on similar expenses at Jerusalem. The result can be easily foreseen; the building lost what dignity it had possessed; the architecture was poor, the reconstruction clumsy and slipshod, and the execution shoddy. In the course of the work the Orthodox managed to oust the Latins from many of the shrines of which they were actually in possession, and even vented their spite in destroying the tombs of the Latin kings of Jerusalem.

For some decades the Latins were not in a position to attempt to counter this increasing influence of their opponents, or to recover the altars which they had lost. It was only in 1850 that the French ambassador to the Porte, supported by the ambassadors of the Roman Catholic kingdoms of Sardinia, Spain, Belgium and Austria, made a formal demand for the restoration to the Latins of all the places which they claimed to have possessed in 1740. These demands were, of course, opposed by Russia, and for two years an extraordinary battle raged between the embassies at Constantinople. The actual issue was in itself trifling and concerned the Church of the Nativity in Bethlehem. The Orthodox had stolen a silver star which the Latins had placed over the actual spot marking the Nativity, and had secured the keys of the church itself. The negotiations made it clear that neither France nor Russia intended a settlement. The star and the key being disposed of by a new star and key being provided by the sultan, an issue was found in the decayed state of the dome of the rotunda of the Church of the Holy Sepulchre. When that was disposed of by an agreement that a new dome should be built by the rulers of Turkey, France and Russia, the Latin rights in the Church of the Tomb of the Virgin proved impossible of settlement; and when the difficult matter had been dealt with as to whether the Latins could be expected to say mass on a 'schismatic' block of marble, on which stood as ornaments 'schismatic' vases, it was at last found that the position of the Russian fleet was an intolerable menace, and Britain, France and Turkey found themselves allies in a war against Russia.

Partly through the influence of Sir Stratford Canning, the British ambassador who had no claims to make for himself, the Porte resisted the attempts of either side to secure new definitions of rights; and in 1852 the sultan Abdul Mejid issued a firman in which he ordered the maintenance of the status which each Church possessed in 1757. This declaration of the *status quo* was confirmed by the Congress of Berlin in 1878, and formed the basis of the rights exercised by the different Churches when they were most carefully defined by the British in 1929 in which each lamp, picture and altar is exactly specified.

A similar story of the piety of innumerable individual pilgrims and the unhappy jealousies of Churches could be told of all the other Christian shrines in the country. In the case of those sites to which Christians regained access only in the nineteenth century, the usual habit has been for different Churches to select different spots as the authentic holy place; and this has obvious advantages, so long as they are unable to go back to the early medieval system of sharing them without quarrel or question of precedence. There are thus two gardens of Gethsemane, two Mounts of Temptation, two scenes of the Transfiguration, two dwellings in Cana of Galilee where the wedding feast took place, and so on. In each case one of these is in the possession of the Latins, and one belongs to the Orthodox. But with other sites such divisions were not possible, and the struggle had to be for a single site. Of these the more interesting are the Churches of the Nativity and of the Tomb of the Virgin.

The Virgin Mary enjoys such reverence among the Muslims that the Church of the Nativity at Bethlehem was the only Christian shrine spared by al-Hakim. From the days of the Arab conquest the Muslims enjoyed the right of praying in the south transept, where Umar himself prayed. They are recorded as having joined in the Christmas pilgrimages in the ninth century; and in the treaties made in 1241 and 1244 with the sultan of Damascus, this right was specifically retained. Another point of interest in regard to this church is the rare record, written by a fourteenth-century pilgrim, Jacques de Verona, of the presence of Indian

Nestorian Christians celebrating in the north transept, with other Nestorians and the Abyssinians. In the Church of the Tomb of the Virgin there is likewise evidence of Muslim interest; and they possessed a prayer recess in the southern wall between the Latin and Greek altars.

The restoration by the Orthodox of the Church of the Holy Sepulchre in 1808 was largely made possible by the extensive contributions made by the Russians; and thereby marks a new stage in the conflict over the Holy Places. In the nineteenth century the Russians stood behind the claims of the Orthodox just as the French had stood behind those of the Latins. The two powers came into open conflict in the middle of the century, and made the issue of the Holy Places the pretext for a struggle for power over the decaying body of the Turkish Empire which led to the Crimean War. Actually the war did nothing to solve the problem of the Holy Places, for at the end of it the powers agreed to maintain the *status quo* which had been drawn up by the Turks before its beginning. But the balance of power had changed, and in a later chapter the new position established by the Russians will need consideration.

CHAPTER TEN

The Third Holy City of Islam and the Arab Patrimony

THE common phrase that Palestine is the Holy Land of three faiths is not strictly accurate. It is not appropriate to the Islamic relationship, for the land which corresponds to its position in the thought of Jews and Christians is for Muslims Arabia. Moreover no particular sanctity of any kind has ever been attributed to the country as a whole. Its Biblical frontiers had no significance, and were never used to define a separate Muslim administration. The country was divided, according to convenience, between different provinces, whose frontiers were continually altered. Jerusalem also was never a Muslim capital. Even the two Umayyad caliphs who were most closely associated with the country, Muawiyah and Sulayman, showed no special regard for it. Muawiyah, who was proclaimed caliph at Jerusalem, made Damascus the seat of his government; and Sulayman, who chose The Land for his residence during the three years of his rule, built himself a new capital at Ramleh. Nor had it a paramount religious position, save for brief periods when Mecca was, for some reason, inaccessible to the Muslims of Syria. When the crusaders were approaching the city in 1098, the Abbasids were unmoved by appeals from their fellow Muslims for assistance. The Ayyubid, al-Kamil, exchanged it for a treaty of alliance against Damascus with Frederick II. On two occasions in the thirteenth century, when the Christians captured Damietta, al-Kamil and his successor as-Salih were prepared to exchange this port for the holy city of Jerusalem.

Such a situation sufficiently indicates the political difference between being the first holy city of a religion and the third. But Jerusalem remains the third holy city of Islam. Its Arabic name is al-Quds, the Sanctuary, a name which it owes to the Haram ash-Sharif with the twin shrines of the Dome of the Rock and the Aksa Mosque, and the group of colleges, libraries, tombs and other religious buildings occupying the wide area of Solomon's Temple and its courts and palaces.

From the historian's point of view there is a difficulty in the fact that the very sanctity which Islam attributes to the Haram ash-Sharif is due to the association of the spot with the other two religions involved, and not to any comparable Muslim relationship. In the earliest days of his preaching, when the contrast between the lofty monotheistic faiths of Judaism and Christianity and the primitive paganism of Arabia was still vividly impressed on his mind, Muhammad showed his preference for these older faiths by making Jerusalem the city towards which his followers should turn in prayer. But when it became obvious to him that neither Jews nor Christians were willing to accept his claims to a divine mission, entitling him to the position of the last and final authority on the revelation of God to man, he changed his mind. He had conquered Mecca, and he made its originally pagan shrine, the black stone of the Kaaba, the centre to which all Muslims should turn in prayer. But while neither Christians nor Jews were prepared to assign such claims to Muhammad as he demanded for himself, he was unable to dissociate himself from the spiritual authority attributed to Moses and to Jesus by so large a part of the world with which he was familiar. He therefore continued to demand the support of both of them for his new religion, and to claim to have more fully understood their contribution to revelation than the adherents to the faiths of Judaism and Christianity themselves who had hitherto accepted their respective revelations as final.

It was to emphasize this claim that he had been recognized by his two predecessors that he placed the scene of his ascent to Heaven on the site of the Jewish Temple in Jerusalem, even after he had moved the direction of prayer from Jerusalem to Mecca; and in their commemoration of this event, the Muslims have attempted to parallel not merely Jewish but Christian Holy Places. For as there was once the Jewish Holy of Holies on the spot whereon the ladder stood by which Muhammad climbed, so on leaving earth he left the imprint of his foot upon the rock, to equate the imprint of the foot of Christ shown on the Mount of Olives in the Church (now the Mosque) of the Ascension.

The difficulty of the historian is still further emphasized by the fact that the nature of the ascension of Muhammad is such that it is entirely useless as historical evidence. The association of Jews with The Land is a historical fact, whether one believes that association to be the result of a divine decision or not. The association of the Founder of Christianity with Galilee and Judea is a historical fact, whether or not one accepts the Christian theological claim as to His nature, or even the ecclesiastical claim of authenticity for the Holy Places. But the association of Muhammad with the country rests on willingness to believe that in a single night, and on a winged horse, Muhammad flew to and from Arabia in order that he might then mount by a ladder for a personal view of the heavens; while his remarkable mount, al-Burak, remained tied near to that point in the whole area which stood above the only remaining Jewish Holy Place, the Wailing Wall. The event is not the poetical or theological dramatization of an incident which, stripped of the miraculous element, rests on solid historical foundations. It has to be accepted as it stands, or there remains no evidence whatever associating Muhammad with Jerusalem other than the early choice and quick rejection of that city as the direction towards which Muslims should pray; and this choice, in any case, rested on a veneration for Judaism and Christianity and not on a personal experience of Muhammad.

What is true of Jerusalem turns out also to be true of the other sites in the country on the basis of which the claim is made that Palestine is the 'Holy Land of three faiths'. The shrines are either Jewish or Christian; and in any historical consideration a prior claim to their enjoyment would rest with one or the other, or both, of those two religions. The two holiest of these shrines are the Tomb of the Patriarchs at Hebron, and the 'Tomb of Moses' in the wilderness between Jerusalem and Jericho. The former of these is an ancient Jewish shrine, which was also venerated by Christians, to the extent that the name of the town in crusading days was 'Saint Abraham'; and the Muslim sanctuary is largely of crusading or earlier Jewish construction. The latter is not an ancient shrine, but rests on a Muslim legend about the Jewish leader. The present group of buildings was not erected before the thirteenth century, and it did not become an important place of

Muslim pilgrimage until the sixteenth. And, as with the footsteps of Muhammad, so here, the Holy Place did not arise out of Muslim autonomous tradition, but from the desire to provide for Muslims an attraction which gave Jerusalem an importance for Islam similar to that which it received for Christianity from the constant stream of Christian pilgrims.

Of the other shrines, we can sometimes trace the actual date and circumstances in which the Muslims seized them from either Jewish or Christian possessors, and all alike relate to Jewish or Christian and not to Islamic history. Such are the Jewish Holy Places of the tombs of Rachel, Samuel, David, Gamaliel and others, or the well of Jacob; or such Christian Holy Places as the tomb and the house of Lazarus, and the reputed scene of the Ascension. The Cenacle and Franciscan convent on Mount Zion were taken as late as the sixteenth century. In addition to these shrines, from which in most cases Jews and Christians were wholly or largely excluded after their seizure by the Muslims, Muslims always demanded access to the shrines still left to Jews and Christians.

One of the most interesting cases of this concerns the great autocephalous convent of Saint Catherine at the foot of Mount Sinai. The convent is built as a fortress against the depredations of raiding bedouins; but such was the Muslim veneration for St Catherine, of whose life incidentally they knew absolutely nothing, that during the Mamluk period a mosque with minaret was built within the actual walls of the fortress. The monks who, in accordance with the tradition established by the Church of the Holy Sepulchre, had provided chapels for all the different eastern Churches, had to maintain also this mosque in case any important Muslim desired to worship there.

We must, however, recognize that, from the Muslim point of view, the appropriation of Jewish and Christian shrines followed naturally from the belief of Muhammad that Islam had superseded and fulfilled what were genuine previous revelations given by God to Jews and Christians. In this belief he was, to some extent, following the precedent already set by the Christian Church, which similarly appropriated to itself the Jewish Scriptures, and spoke of the Jews and their understanding of the Scriptures in terms considerably more opprobrious than those used by Muhammad. There was, however, this important difference. Christians considered the text of the Old Testament to have divine authority and left it unaltered (though they sometimes accused Jews of falsifying particular passages) so that they embodied in their religious faith the moral and ethical teaching of the Law and the prophets, and the personal religion of the Psalms. But Muhammad, while expressing high respect for Moses and Jesus, considered the Old and New Testaments full of error, and provided in the Koran, especially in the second and third Suras, his own version of the sacred history of both Jews and Christians. In doing this he omitted almost everything of independent value in their teaching.

From the historical point of view the version of Muhammad has no special significance. It rests on no independent tradition, but is based on verbal communications from Jews and Christians; for the Bible did not exist in Arabic in his days, and there is no evidence that he could read it in any of the languages in which it did exist. But from the point of view of a Muslim, the version of Muhammad rested on an independent divine revelation, and was ample authority for the appropriation of any shrines of the earlier religions if the Koran showed that the Prophet had venerated the personality with whom the shrine was associated. While this remains true of particular sites, it does not constitute the country as a whole an Islamic Holy Land. For Muhammad in the third Sura declared an association between Abraham and Mecca. The land which was promised by God to Abraham was made to be not the land of Canaan but Arabia. The pilgrimage to Mecca was given a high antiquity by being attributed to a divine command given by God to Abraham, and his footprint was shown within the sacred enclosure of the Kaaba itself.

But even if the claims of Islam to a place alongside of Judaism and Christianity in their relationships to The Land be based on appropriations from those religions, rather than on any genuine historical association proper to itself, two things still remain true. The majority of the inhabitants of The Land have for many centuries been Muslims; and in such matters as religious veneration it is necessary to take into account the emotional as well as the historical aspect of the question. Even if the Muslim Holy Places of Palestine have been appropriated from other religions, the veneration paid to them by Muslim believers is a historical factor of importance.

As the previous chapters will have shown, the Muslim inhabitants of the country are, to a large extent, the previous inhabitants, converted to Islam from either Christianity or Judaism during the centuries which preceded or followed the crusades. There has been a constant addition from other stocks, as was inevitable in a country which changed masters so often, and which was always something of a corridor; but the basic Muslim stock remains ex-Christians and ex-Jews who have entirely forgotten their previous language and religion and who feel themselves to be successors of the original Muslim conquerors of the country.

There is in Islam a very strong sentiment of the inalienability of territory conferred by Allah on true believers; and while this sentiment was not deeply affected by the loss of the European possessions of the Turks, the land won by the original wave of the Arab conquests of the seventh century is felt to be peculiarly a Muslim patrimony. Damascus prides itself enormously on the fact that the unbeliever has never held the city since its first conquest by the soldiers of Umar; and it is felt to be a stigma in the history of Jerusalem that it has been lost to Islam for periods in its history. Though the Abbasids did nothing to prevent its conquest in the eleventh century, some at least of the enthusiasm which inspired Nur ad-Din and Saladin for its reconquest in the twelfth was religious, the duty to recover from the pollution of Christian ownership what had been Islamic territory and what had been Islamic shrines, especially of course the Haram ash-Sharif. To what extent this remained a conscious feeling it is impossible to estimate, for the occasion never arose subsequently for its exercise. The Land remained in the heart of the Islamic world until the First World War.

During that period the possession of the Haram ash-Sharif was never questioned, and it continued to enjoy great prestige. It did not rank with Mecca in holiness, or indeed, with Damascus, Baghdad, Cairo or Constantinople in the wealth that was poured out on it; it was something that was there, and it never occurred to a Muslim that it would not always be there. The pilgrimages to the Haram, to the Tomb of Moses, to the Tomb of the Patriarchs

at Hebron, were pilgrimages of great local significance, and
attracted a certain number from distant Islamic territories.
Jerusalem has already been compared to one of those cathedral
cities of Europe, remote from the world's affairs, whose sanctity
was commonly accepted but whose paths were rarely trodden by
men busy with more mundane matters; and this is indeed a fair
parallel. For the sanctity of Jerusalem in Islam does not stand
apart in splendid isolation, as it does in the traditions of Judaism
and Christianity. Thus both Judaism and Christianity saw it as
the scene of the final judgment. But Islam, which accepted Jesus
as the final Judge, and believed that this judgment would take
place in Jerusalem, believed that it would be preceded by the
appearance of the Messiah on the minaret of a mosque in Damascus, and followed by his burial at the side of the Prophet at
Medina.

As a centre of scholarship or spiritual life Muslim and Christian
Jerusalem present close parallels. For it was never an important
centre of Islamic studies, though it had its schools, and was often
visited by famous scholars from more celebrated centres of learning
and piety. Its own scholars were mostly associated with the
'Shafiite' school of interpretation, which lies half way between the
liberalism of Iraq and the conservatism of Medina. Muhammad
ibn Idris al-Shafii, its founder, was born in Gaza in 767, but his
teaching was mostly given at Baghdad or Fustat in Egypt. Most
Palestinian Muslims still belong to this school of thought. Several
Jerusalem scholars became martyrs to their faith. One was Abul
Kasim ar-Ruwaili, who was murdered by the crusaders on their
entry into the city in 1099. Perhaps the most famous Islamic
writer which Jerusalem produced was the geographer al-Maqdisi
(al-Mukaddasi) who flourished in the second half of the tenth
century, and wrote a famous account of his travels in all Islamic
countries except Spain.

The Islamic veneration for Jerusalem has been greatly increased
in modern times by association with the growth of Arab nationalism but this aspect of the question must be reserved for a
subsequent chapter. It is, however, pertinent to observe that from
the political standpoint it is impossible to base political treatment
on the actual *authenticity* or historical validity of a religious and

emotional veneration. The Jewish sentiment attached to the Wailing Wall, the Christian devotion to the Churches of the Holy Sepulchre and the Nativity, and the Muslim veneration for the Haram ash-Sharif and the sanctuary at Hebron, are political facts of high importance, and can only be violated by a political authority at the cost of a great deal of violence and bloody repression. This was recognized as early as the thirteenth century, when Frederick II guaranteed Muslim access to and authority over the Haram ash-Sharif; and it was maintained by the Turks in their attitude to the Jewish and Christian shrines in their possession.

There is one further point of interest. While the increasing fanaticism both of Islam and of the local Muslim population led in many cases to the complete exclusion of non-believers from sites regarded by Islam as holy, this principle allowed of exceptions. In the days before the Arab conquest the normal procedure was for both churches and synagogues to be open to all who desired to enter them, except during special services. The Muslims, of course, claimed the right of access for themselves to all Christian shrines; but there still remained one or two places where the old tradition survived, and where members of all faiths were allowed either equal rights or at any rate some right of access. Examples have already been quoted from the crusading period; there was the curious situation at the convent of St Catherine at Sinai. Other cases were the Church of the Tomb of the Virgin and the Mosque of the Ascension. The fact that such cases survived the increasing bitterness, ignorance and fanaticism of the centuries under review is not without importance.

In dealing with the relations between Islam and The Land there are important aspects of the question which cannot be covered by a discussion of actual Holy Places. In such a discussion Islam inevitably appears at a disadvantage as compared with Judaism and Christianity. But on the other side must be set the fact that the main cultural and religious influence to which the population has been exposed for more than a thousand years, apart from the crusading period, has come from Islam. It is inevitable that we should condemn the Muslim rulers, Arab, Mamluk and Turk, for having turned a fruitful land into a desert by their avarice and misgovernment. But it is unjust to forget their positive contribution also. In all centuries we get evidence from western travellers, Christian and Jewish, not only of robbery and extortion, but also of courtesy and hospitality, tolerance and sympathy; and if Islam must bear the blame for the one it is right that it should have the credit for the other. Moreover, there has always been a small cultured class of clergy, merchants and landowners whose rational philosophy and religious tolerance have been in favourable contrast to the fierce intolerance of the Christian sects, or the narrowness and misery of the Jews.

And it remains true that in the Dome of the Rock Islam has created, albeit with a Greek architect and fragments of Roman and Christian masonry, one of the most exquisite and spacious sanctuaries in the world. This very quality of an intensely individual creation out of elements which were neither Arab nor Muslim is indeed the essential quality of the Islamic civilization at its greatest period, when it gathered together under the Umayyads and Abbasids the passing greatness of the Hellenic, the Persian and the eastern Christian cultures. The Land was never the country in which this harvest was shown in philosophy, mysticism or literature. But in marble and mosaic, in column and arch and dome, as well as in spacious planning and gracious approach, there is no Islamic monument in the Middle East whose beauty excels that of the Dome of the Rock and the area of the Haram.

PART THREE

Modern Re-adjustment

CHAPTER ELEVEN

Political History from Napoleon to 1914

DURING the eighteenth century Turkey had maintained the integrity of her territory not by the power of her armies but by the mutual jealousies of the European powers. None of them were willing to see a rival enriched at her expense, and this situation continued through the nineteenth century down to the First World War. Nevertheless the most significant factor in the eighteenth century had been the gradual expansion of Russia southwards, and this movement continued during much of the nineteenth century. The expansion of European interests through trade, colonization and conquest, which marks the eighteenth century, brought to an end the period in which European interest in the Middle East had been academic or religious. But this change involved a reversion, not to the type of interest of Rome or Byzantium, or even of the crusades, but to that of an earlier period. It was not Palestine as part of the Mediterranean littoral which drew would-be conquerors, but Palestine the bridge between great possessions. As once those had been expressed in the empires of the valleys of the Nile and the Euphrates, now they were expressed in the relations of European political and commercial powers with the wealth of India, China, the Far East and Australasia. And European powers were determined that a strong Russia should not bestride this bridge.

It was just over five hundred years after the last European forces of the crusaders had been driven out that a new European army, under the command of Napoleon Bonaparte, crossed its frontiers. He had just concluded a successful campaign in Italy, and considered the time ripe to strike a blow at England's eastern empire by conquering Egypt and Syria. On 1 July 1798 the army landed at Alexandria and captured the city on the following day. By the battle of the Pyramids on 26 July he obtained control of Egypt; but a week later his whole plan was seriously endangered – if not shattered – by the complete destruction of his fleet by

Nelson at the Battle of the Nile. Return to Europe thus cut off, Napoleon settled down for the winter in Egypt, and introduced considerable reforms into the corrupt Mamluk government of the country, besides setting on foot important scientific and archaeological projects. But the time for such activities was short. The sultan had declared war on France on 1 September, and two expeditions were being organized against him, one by land through Syria, one by sea from Rhodes. Napoleon decided to meet the first before preparations for the second could be completed, and then to return to Egypt to meet it. In the latter task he succeeded, but not in the former.

He seized Suez in December and advanced with 13,000 men; al-Arish was reached in February 1799, and on 6 March, after a brief resistance, Jaffa fell. Twelve hundred soldiers of the garrison were barbarously executed after their surrender, on the grounds that many of them had been previously taken prisoner at al-Arish and released on condition that they took no further part in the fighting. Twelve days after the fall of Jaffa, he was encamped before Acre, and expected the town to fall after the first assault. It was here that, for the second time, his plans went wrong. In spite of the destruction of his fleet, he had sent his siege guns from Jaffa by sea along the coast, and they were detected and captured by a British squadron under Sir Sidney Smith. Smith then had time to return to Acre, where he found not only a resolute pasha – the infamous al-Jazzar – but a brilliant French royalist engineer, Colonel Phelippeaux. Working together the three set out to make something of the ruinous defences of the city.

They succeeded so well that on 18 May Napoleon decided to retreat, writing to the French government in his dispatches that the town was not worth the effort to capture it. On 20 May the camp was secretly evacuated, and in the beginning of June he recrossed the Egyptian frontier without having had to fight any rearguard actions. Jerusalem he never attacked, but it had been put into a position of defence by the combined efforts of the Muslims, Christians and Jews, none of whom were deceived by Napoleon's proclamation to each that he had come as their special protector. On 23 August he left secretly for Europe, leaving behind him his army and his dreams of eastern conquest. Once or twice during the long drawn out war which ended at Waterloo he attempted to replan his eastern policy, but without success; and for thirty years after his departure The Land sank back into obscurity. Al-Jazzar died in 1804, and a new chief appeared in the Lebanon; but the greater part of the country passed back into the hands of pashas appointed annually from Constantinople, who provided with scarcely relieved monotony the traditional misgovernment.

In Turkey itself, however, events were slowly moving towards some elementary measures of reform. The sultan Mahmoud II, though not particularly able or, indeed, forceful, possessed a patient tenacity, and in a reign which lasted from 1808 to 1839 was able to lay certain foundations. His most important achievement was the destruction of the janissaries. For more than a century this once famous corps had been entirely without military value; but it dominated the capital and the palace, and made and unmade sultans at will. After waiting patiently for eighteen years, in 1826 he suddenly turned on them and mowed them down in the streets of Constantinople and in their barracks. But it was too late for him to reap the benefit of this action himself. Largely encouraged by Russia, but with the support of other European countries also, all his Christian European provinces were in a ferment, and in Greece he was involved in a long and costly war.

That was not his only difficulty; his pashas, profiting from the weakness of the central authority, made themselves practically independent in their provinces and robbed him of both the military and the financial resources of his empire. In Syria and Egypt the Christian minorities were too weak to think of revolting; but in the race between Christian rayahs and Turkish pashas to dismember the empire, one of the ablest of the latter class was the Albanian, Mehmet Ali (1769–1849), pasha of Egypt.

In 1801 he had made himself pasha with the support of the Mamluks. In 1805 the sultan confirmed him in his pashalik, and he set out to organize his dominion. Strongly favouring the French, he drove the British out when they staged a rather ill-planned invasion in 1807, and invited all kinds of French experts to reorganize first his army, then the industry of his country;

and finally, with their help, he built himself a navy. He organized a curious kind of totalitarian state, half barbarous, half highly civilized for his day. Land was ruthlessly nationalized; all profitable raw materials or industries were made state monopolies; conscription was introduced to provide an army of 100,000 and forced labour was employed on large public works. These projects led to a great increase of taxation, and the lot of the fellaheen became even more unendurable than under the Mamluks. The possible hostility of the latter he eliminated by a treacherous and wholesale massacre in 1811.

In the next eighteen years Mehmet was occupied with wars nominally at least on behalf, and at the request, of the sultan Mahmoud. He planned to obtain as a reward the pashalik of the Peloponnese (Morea) for his son, and of Crete for himself. When this failed he demanded Syria; and on being refused satisfaction, he sent an army to invade it in 1831 under his son Ibrahim, whose ability equalled his own. Gaza, Jaffa and Jerusalem were occupied with little opposition, for Turkish rule had few admirers even among the Muslim peasants. Acre and Damascus fell in May and June of 1832, and Ibrahim marched rapidly northwards. The army which the sultan sent against him was easily destroyed, and Ibrahim was soon master of the whole of Syria and threatening Asia Minor. At this moment Mahmoud appealed to Europe for help, and Ibrahim captured Konieh and advanced towards Constantinople.

The moment was a bad one for European intervention. In 1832 England was fully preoccupied with reform at home; France, which half-supported Mehmet, was also preoccupied with domestic troubles. It was Russia's opportunity, and she took it, to crown a half-century of slow but successful penetration. Moreover she had no intention of allowing a new and vigorous dynasty to occupy the seat of the decadent Ottoman sultans. She sent three successive contingents, both naval and military, to Constantinople, and the Bosphorus and Dardanelles were fortified at the orders of the 'Russian Commander in Chief and Ambassador Extraordinary in the Turkish Empire'. Europe took alarm. Russia refused to withdraw until Mehmet Ali also withdrew his forces; and this Ibrahim refused to do. Finally the powers forced Mehmet and Ibrahim to be content with the whole of Syria, and the Russian forces withdrew from Constantinople. So matters remained for six years. But in 1839 Mahmoud decided to reconquer Syria, and his troops were disastrously defeated.

Again the powers intervened; and though France half-heartedly supported Mehmet, Britain sent a fleet to bombard the Syrian coast. Beirut, Sidon and Acre were occupied, and Mehmet was compelled to content himself with the hereditary pashalik of Egypt. Those who had readily welcomed Ibrahim ten years previously, as readily saw him driven out. For conscription, high taxation and a crude efficiency had proved more intolerable than the slipshod exploitation of the Turks. Nevertheless the period of Egyptian rule had important consequences for the future. Mehmet and Ibrahim readily opened The Land to western visitors, and it was under their rule that the first western schools and hospitals were introduced by British and American missionary societies. In addition the increased security of their government made it possible to travel with relative safety throughout The Land, and this possibility has left permanent results in Biblical research and in the series of exquisitely illustrated books on the Holy Land, which provide the most illuminating, if not always the most pedantically accurate, pictures of the country, its conditions and its natives. The first half of the nineteenth century was a great period of book illustration, and the steel engravings of Finden, Bartlett and others, and the lithographs of Roberts, illustrate almost every corner of The Land. One event of this period, which had nothing to do with politics, must be mentioned. On 1 January 1837 a terrible earthquake devastated Galilee, especially Safad and Tiberias. In the former town more than 5,000 perished out of a population of 10,000, and in the latter 700 out of 2,500.

The period between the restoration of The Land to Turkish rule and the Crimean War was one of considerable importance. It witnessed many changes – changes which, however, still left it possible to say of Turkish rule *plus ça change, plus c'est la même chose*. The successor to Mahmoud II, Abdul Mejid (1839–61), was a man of totally different character. Weak and debauched, he was yet mild and benevolent, and accepted, without resistance, the passage of effective authority to the European ambassadors at his court, and in particular to the British ambassador, Sir Stratford Canning, later Lord Stratford de Redcliffe, who 'reigned' at Constantinople from 1842 to 1858.

Following advice left by his father, Abdul Mejid at the very beginning of his reign proclaimed with great solemnity the Hatti-Sherif of Gulhané, in which he granted various important reforms to his subjects. All, without distinction of race or creed, were promised security of life, honour and property, just incidence of taxes, and the public trial of prisoners. But the vizir who inspired and drew up these generous promises, Reshid Pasha, was immediately violently attacked by all the reactionary forces of the empire, and their implementation was left to his successor, a man of so appropriate a temperament that he would admit to the administration no one who could even speak or understand a Christian language. Naturally they were ineffective. Sixteen years later, at the close of the Crimean War, the measures of the Hatti-Sherif of Gulhané were repeated and enlarged in the Hatti-Humayoun of 1856 which gave non-Muslims legal equality and access to the army and the civil service. It remained, however, an even deader letter than its predecessor.

Nevertheless certain measures were inevitably taken, and this was particularly the case in The Land, where the rule of the ambassadors at Constantinople was paralleled by the rule of the consuls at Jerusalem. The first of the consuls was actually appointed by Great Britain in 1838, during the rule of Ibrahim. This was followed in 1843 by the appointment of consuls by France, Prussia and Sardinia. In the next year an American consul arrived; and in 1849 Austria replaced Sardinia. Spain followed suit in 1854. The Russians, however, were content to possess an agent in Jerusalem dependent on Beirut, where they had maintained a consulate-general since 1839. In addition to the consuls there were various officials with special interests in different classes of the local population, particularly the non-Muslims, who possessed another nationality than the Turkish, or required some special protection. There was a rabbi with authority over Jews who were Russian or Austrian subjects; an English bishop was sent out jointly by England and Prussia in 1842; a Latin patriarch arrived with authority over Latin Christians in 1847.

While all these officials together could not amend the basic venality and incompetence of Turkish rule, or indeed exercise much influence over the affairs of the Muslim population, they could, and did, secure that some of the reforms of Gulhané were carried out in the interest of Jews and Christians. Such international protection was very necessary at the period in which the consulates were established. In 1840, partly at least owing to the denunciations of an antisemitic Frenchman, the Jews of Damascus were involved in an accusation of ritual murder, and feelings against the Jewish population became dangerously high. During the whole decade there was unrest in the Lebanon, and sometimes open civil war between the Latin, Orthodox and other Christians and the Druzes.

It would have been easy for such troubles to have spread southwards but the protection afforded by the presence of the consuls proved adequate. The Christians turned to the French or Russian officials for assistance; and the British consuls, as one of their official duties, exercised a general protection over the Jewish subjects of the sultan and over Jewish residents who possessed no other protector. This work, often difficult and delicate, took up a good deal of the time of the first two consuls, Mr Young (1839–45) and Mr James Finn (1845–62). Later it was considerably reduced. And yet the most interesting story of the protection of one people by another during this period comes not from the work of the European consuls, but as an act of reparation in the long story of Jewish-Samaritan relations. In 1841 the Muslims of Nablus, always among the most fanatical of the inhabitants of the country, planned the extermination of the last remnants of the Samaritan people. They were saved by the chief rabbi of Jerusalem, who gave them a certificate attesting that 'the Samaritan people is a branch of the Children of Israel, who acknowledge the truth of Torah' and so were entitled to protection as one of the 'Peoples of the Book'. In 1854, as a result of the appeals of Joseph esh-Shaleby, a Samaritan leader, they were taken under the protection of the British consul.

While the security of the rayahs and foreign visitors and pilgrims steadily increased, until not merely travel but residence in the country became relatively safe for Europeans, there was little basic change in the position of the Muslim population. As has been said, the consuls could not alter the system of government, nor could they normally interfere in any matter concerning Muslims. To remind them that they had no authority where 'true believers' were concerned, each consul had to be accompanied by an armed Muslim Kawass, for it would have been dangerous for a Christian to strike a Muslim, even in self-defence. But even on this subject some changes took place. Up to the middle of the nineteenth century no Christian had been permitted to enter openly the area of the Haram; one or two did so disguised as Muslims, or by bribery and under extraordinary precautions. But in 1855 the government of an exceptionally enlightened pasha happened to coincide with the visit of the Duke and Duchess of Brabant, later King and Queen of the Belgians, and the royal guests expressed a wish to visit the area. The pasha, after taking the utmost precautions, consented, and a large party of Christians was rapidly shown over the more important sites. The visit having passed off successfully, it was not long before it was repeated, each time with fewer precautions, until the Muslim population became accustomed to the idea of Christians entering the area without fear.

Pashas were appointed annually, and some of them were men of over eighty. They were surrounded by a council of local Arab notables; but this contributed little to their efficiency, for the notables were both corrupt and themselves involved in the constant feuds which disturbed the country. These feuds the pashas lacked the power to put down, and often the will. For it had been a regular principle of Turkish government to sow discord among the subject populations, lest they should unite against their Turkish masters; and the most corrupt and inefficient pasha was, by very instinct, a master of the art of encouraging jealousy and discord. In the north of the country the two families of Abdul Hadi and Tukan perpetually disputed control over the Tulkarm, Nablus and Jenin areas. West of Jerusalem the powerful clan of Abu Ghosh divided its time between mutual rivalries and the plundering of travellers on the road to Jerusalem. In the south the sheikhs of Hebron and Beit Jibrin copied the example of their peers in the north. And, profiting from all this rivalry and conflict, the bedouin sheikhs and their tribes sold their aid to one side or the other, robbed and murdered sometimes at will, and increased both the poverty and insecurity of the unhappy peasant. While such a picture is warranted by the facts, yet such is human nature that, in spite of it, many villages lived tranquilly and prosperously, under competent and humane local rulers. Taxation, where it was justly exacted, was light, the land was fertile, there was an ample market for their produce, and in normal times the evils of conscription only lightly affected them.

The Crimean War had singularly little effect on the local situation. The claims about the Holy Places made on behalf of the Latins by Napoleon III had been no more than an indication to Turkey and to Europe that France had recovered the determination to re-establish herself after the loss of influence which had followed the defeat of Napoleon I and the disregard for her views at the time of Mehmet Ali. She was no longer unwilling to challenge Russia who had reached the high-water mark of her power in the treaty of Unkiar Skelesi in 1833. This situation was expressed locally in the increasing hostility between the Orthodox, under Russian protection, and the Latins. The removal of the Latin star at the scene of the Nativity in Bethlehem took place during this period of Russian ascendancy, and was one of the principal subjects of grievance brought forward by France in 1850. The issue of the Holy Places was settled by the sultan issuing, on his own authority, an edict establishing the *status quo* at the shrines, which, without entering into details, prescribed that the actual situation at the time of the edict (1852) was to be maintained; and this, in the end, prevailed against all the intrigues and counter-intrigues of the embassies in Constantinople and the Churches in Jerusalem. The real issue was elsewhere, in the balance of power in the eastern Mediterranean, and it left The Land untouched. Strangely enough, the defeat of Russia by England, France and Turkey, also left the Russian influence in The Land intact, and it was in the decades following the Crimean defeat that Russia secured an immense increase in her prestige by the Turkish surrender of the Maidan, the great public recreation and parade ground outside the city walls, for the erection of the huge Russian compound, with cathedral, hospital, and hostels for pilgrims, which is still a conspicuous part of the landscape of modern Jerusalem.

The shifts in the balance of power led to the French temporary occupation of the Lebanon in 1860 to protect the Christian population, and the British long-term occupation of Egypt twenty years later led likewise to further wars and rebellions in the Balkans and a fresh conflict between Russia and Turkey. But all this, which fills the pages of the history of the eastern Mediterranean in the sixties and seventies, had singularly little effect on the situation in The Land. The death of Abdul Mejid, the brief reign of his amiable but drunken and extravagant successor, Abdul Aziz, likewise produced no change. But in 1876, on the accession of Abdul Hamid II, a new and important stage in the reform of the empire was announced, with the proclamation of a National Assembly, in which all sections of the population should equally take part. This measure was the work of a great reforming vizir, Midhat Pasha, who had already tried to reorganize the provincial system ten years earlier. But in Abdul Hamid a sultan had ascended the throne who had no intention of favouring reform but who, unlike his predecessors, had the skill and tenacity to defeat both the pressures of the European powers and the desires of his own subjects. The Turkish parliament survived only a matter of months, and then the unhappy country found itself in the toils of a subtle and evil tyrant, whose long reign effectively prevented any further amelioration of the conditions of his subjects until the twentieth century.

There was, however, one branch of his administration which it was in his own interest for Abdul Hamid to reform. During his reign Turkey pressed forward the modernization of her army; and this involved a certain tightening up of the provincial administration, both in order to obtain finance and to enforce conscription. The hatred of conscription among the fellaheen explains the fact that most of the figures for the population of the country in the later nineteenth century err on the side of under-estimates, since the villagers cheerfully rendered false returns in order to avoid the permanent loss of their children.

In the tightening up of the administration various changes took place in the provincial boundaries. At the beginning of the cen-

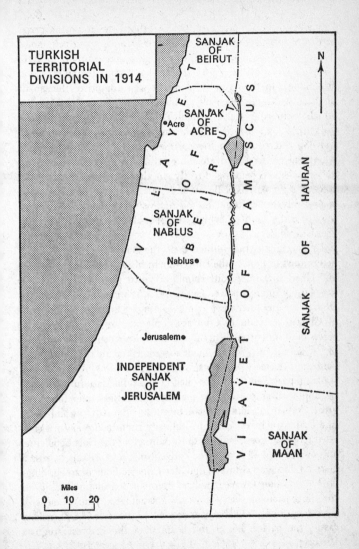

TURKISH
TERRITORIAL
DIVISIONS IN 1914

N

SANJAK
OF
BEIRUT

SANJAK
OF
ACRE

•Acre

VILAYET OF BEIRUT

SANJAK
OF
NABLUS

Nablus•

Jerusalem•

INDEPENDENT
SANJAK
OF
JERUSALEM

VILAYET OF DAMASCUS

HAURAN

SANJAK OF

SANJAK
OF
MAAN

Miles
0   10   20

tury there had been a pashalik of Acre which covered the coastal region as far south as Jaffa. Below that the pashalik of Gaza extended to the Egyptian frontier. All the hinterland formed part of the large and important pashalik of Damascus. Abdul Hamid created a new pashalik of Beirut and gave new frontiers to Syria (or Damascus, for the Arab name for both province and capital is ash-Shams). In the pashalik of Beirut were comprised the sanjak of Acre which included all of Galilee, and the sanjak of Balqa which included Samaria. All of Transjordan right down to the gulf of Akaba fell into different sanjaks of the pashalik of Syria. In 1889 a territory roughly corresponding to the ancient Judea was turned into a separate mutesarifat (or independent sanjak) of Jerusalem, depending directly on the Porte, and outside the control of the pashas of Beirut and Syria. The need for this change is probably to be found in the increasing European population drawn to the country, which, in 1889, already included the first Zionist colonies.

To checkmate the influence of the powers previously most determined to protect their interests in his empire, Russia, France and Great Britain, Abdul Hamid accepted the friendship of the new European great power, Germany. In 1889, the Kaiser Wilhelm II, after visiting Athens for the wedding of his sister to the king of Greece, went on to Constantinople and was the first of the rulers of an important Christian country to accept the hospitality of the sultan. In 1898 he made a second tour in the Levant and paid an extremely theatrical state visit to the Holy Land. The walls of Jerusalem were breached at the Jaffa Gate in order that he might enter the city in mounted procession, and forthwith great German buildings began to out-top the Russian and other European structures which had already risen in the modern city. At the nearest possible point to the Church of the Holy Sepulchre, and on the site of part of the convent of the Hospitallers, rose a German Lutheran church. High above the old Franciscan buildings on Mount Zion towered the vast German Benedictine basilica of the Dormition of the Virgin. And dominating the whole city from the Mount of Olives, was erected, in the style of a Rhineland castle, the palace, hostel and hospital of the Empress Augusta Victoria.

In 1908, after more than thirty years of the oppression and misgovernment of Abdul Hamid, the Turks themselves revolted. He was deposed by the Committee of Union and Progress, led by a group of army officers known as the 'Young Turks'. But the course of the revolt revealed only too clearly the limitation of the Turkish understanding of the contemporary world. The officers represented almost the only class which had been effectively westernized since, as already said, even Abdul Hamid had realized that without a modernized and Europeanized army, the state could not hold together. But the military mind and military interests are both limited. The Young Turks believed themselves to be liberal in offering the non-Muslim and non-Turkish population equal participation in a Turkish constitutional assembly, under strongly Turkish influences. It was rejected as hopelessly inadequate by peoples who desired national independence, and the Young Turks found it no easier to handle their Christian subjects in Europe than had the sultans. They made the same mistake with the Arabs in the eastern half of their empire. The old council of the Arab notables desired no constitutional changes. They had been useless from the standpoint of government, and indifferent to the rights of their own tenants; but they had enjoyed both personal power and considerable profit out of the Turkish system, and had been left largely to manage their own affairs. In consequence they were hostile not only to conscription in the interests of a Turkish imperialism, but even more to forms of government and education which were designed to create an artificial unity on the basis of a deliberate turcification of the non-Turkish population. In view of the general situation at the beginning of the twentieth century, the Young Turks found that they had stimulated, more than the old Turks had ever done, the rise of an Arab national feeling, and the consciousness of a separate Arab destiny.

In consequence, when the First World War broke out, the loyalty of the Arab sections of the empire was, for the first time, in doubt. In The Land itself Arab nationalism had hardly come into existence; the centres of the new movement were in Damascus and Beirut; but it was affected as much as any other Arab country in the struggle for Arab support waged between the main antagonists, Britain and Germany. The Germans hoped that the war would be proclaimed a *jihad*, a holy war, and that this would involve Britain in unrest or rebellion among her many million Muslim subjects. But a Holy War would need to be supported by the Arab prince Hussain, a descendant of the Prophet and Guardian of the Muslim Holy Places of Mecca and Medina. Hussain was therefore arduously courted not only by the Turks and Germans in the interests of Turkey, but also by the British, once Turkey, in November 1914, had thrown in her lot with Germany. The success of the British, and particularly of Colonel Lawrence, in raising and maintaining a bedouin Arab force commanded by Hussain's son Faisal played an important part in the later phases of the campaign which led to the capture of Jerusalem and Damascus.

It was obvious from the beginning that one of the objectives which Germany would set her Turkish ally was the cutting of British communications at the Suez canal; and considerable forces were concentrated in Syria. Nevertheless in 1916 the British crossed the canal; and in December they crossed the desert and occupied al-Arish. While the British were still establishing their position at al-Arish, the revolt of the desert Arabs had begun to cause some embarrassment to the Turkish left front; and, to prevent the Arabs or Jews of The Land from showing sympathy with the enemy, the Turks adopted a ruthless policy of oppression, which resulted in the deliberate destruction of houses, roads, fruit trees and crops, and the execution or imprisonment of considerable numbers of the population. In consequence few took part with the British in their campaign. The general effect of the war on the inhabitants is described in chapter fifteen.

In March 1917 the British made an unsuccessful attack on the Turkish line at Gaza, and for six months no further move was made. In the summer General Allenby replaced General Sir Archibald Murray as commander-in-chief, and the Arabs reached Akaba, where they were within possible communication with the British army to the west of them. By the end of October Allenby's plans were ready and, making a feint on Gaza, he heavily attacked and routed the Turkish left flank at Beersheba. The Turks retired to a line from Jerusalem westwards to south of Jaffa, and there Allenby attacked again on 16 November. Jaffa was taken, and he detached a considerable force to march directly eastwards on Jerusalem. On 21 November Nebi Samwil was occupied, but there were not enough men to take the city. It fell without resistance on 11 December, and both sides prepared for the final battle, which took place on 19 September 1918, on a line across the Judean hills south of Nablus and Tulkarm. This time Allenby feinted against the Turkish left stretching beyond the Jordan valley and covering the railway from Damascus southwards, and delivered his main attack in the coastal plain. British desert forces and the Arabs together held the left occupied, while Allenby annihilated the forces in the plain, and with a swift cavalry movement reached Nazareth, Jenin and Beisan in less than forty-eight hours. Thereby he completely cut off the Turkish retreat, save across the Jordan where the Arabs were waiting for them. After the rout of 19 September, there was little more to be done. Damascus was occupied both by the Amir Faisal and the British on 1 October, and the armies swept northwards. The armistice was signed on 31 October 1918, and four hundred years of Turkish misrule came to an end.

CHAPTER TWELVE

Christian Interests between 1815 and 1914

THE changes which took place during the nineteenth century in the world situation and in the political history of Turkey not only had a general effect on the position in The Land, but also had special effects on the three communities within its frontiers, the Muslims, the Christians and the Jews. The motives which led to these effects were in each case largely different and independent of each other. In this situation it is logical to take first the position of the Christians; for it was in the relationship to the country of Christians that changes first took place, and the new Christian interest, while primarily concerned with religious matters, did, in fact, have a considerable influence on subsequent developments affecting the general population and the Jews.

In so far as Christians are concerned the nineteenth century witnessed a revolution in two fields: in the position of the indigenous Christian population and in the relations of Christendom to a common Christian Holy Land. While in the main the two movements were distinct, they met in the field of education, and in the offering by other Churches, Orthodox, Catholic and Protestant, of new educational opportunities to the indigenous population. While in most cases this education was offered to the whole population, it was the Christians who most frequently took advantage of it. For, in spite of the fact that Sir Stratford Canning had, in 1844, secured the right of the Muslim to change his religion without incurring the death penalty prescribed by the Koran, the Muslims were afraid of Christian influence; and in 1854 they returned to a policy of open hostility, from which the Christian schools and mission stations throughout the empire had to suffer, and which caused many of them to be closed. The Turkish attitude was clearly expressed in four points:

1. The Turkish Government will not allow any attempts, public or private, to assail Islam.

2. They will not allow the missionaries or their agents to speak publicly against Islam.

3. All attempts to convince Muslims that their religion is not of God must be regarded by the Turkish authorities as insults to the national faith.

4. They will not allow the sale or distribution, in public or private, of any controversial works.

While it is perfectly correct to speak of a 'new' Christian interest in the country in this century, and while this is as true of the Roman Catholic as of other Churches, in the case of the Roman Catholics this new interest was additional to an established policy which had been continued with but little interruption since the break between the eastern and western Churches, and had been consolidated in 1622 by the establishment of the Congregation, and later of the College, of Propaganda in Rome. The papacy aimed always at a restoration of relations with the members of eastern communions and had, in the course of the centuries, made considerable progress in parts of the eastern world. Hence arose uniate Churches, representing sections of the various Churches of the east which retained their own language, together with many of their customs, but were in communion with Rome and accepted the doctrines of the Roman Church.

In the case of the Maronites the whole body accepted reunion with Rome, and the Maronite Uniate Church dates from the crusading period. In all other cases it was only a section which was reunited, so that two bodies, and often two patriarchs, are to be found in the subsequent period. A uniate Church was formed from Syrian Jacobites about the end of the seventeenth century; in 1724 one was formed from the Orthodox in the patriarchate of Antioch, and to this Church is given the name of Melkite, a name which in the controversies of the fifth century had applied to all Christians who accepted the decrees of Chalcedon. There is a long and tangled history of relationships with Rome in the stories of the Armenian, Nestorian, Coptic and Abyssinian Churches, in each of which uniate bodies ultimately came into existence and had their position regularized during the nineteenth century. Most of these Churches possessed no members in The Land, but

Maronites and Melkites had small congregations which had their part in Latin ceremonies in the Church of the Holy Sepulchre.

The motives which led the first Protestant Christians to settle in the country were twofold: the reformation of the eastern Christian Churches and the conversion of the Jews. The English Church Missionary Society and the American Board of Commissioners for Foreign Missions seem to have arrived almost simultaneously at the idea that the time was ripe for a friendly approach to eastern Christendom from the Protestant world. Between 1816 and 1819 the Rev. W. Jowett travelled through the Asiatic provinces of Turkey, making contacts both with the Orthodox and with other eastern Christians on behalf of the Church Missionary Society. In 1821 he returned, and in Syria encountered an American, Pliny Fisk. Together they visited Jerusalem, but neither was able to remain in the country, owing to the hostility of the Turks. But in the same year another American, Levi Parsons, attempted to set up a permanent station in Jerusalem. His main desire was to circulate the Bible, believing it would lead to a revivification and reform of the Churches, and he was well received by many of the eastern clergy. But his health broke down, and he died the following year in Alexandria.

In fact death took a heavy toll of the pioneers in this field from Britain, Europe and America. The Americans then decided to make Beirut their centre. There they became firmly established, in spite of the violent hostility of the Maronite clergy to their distribution of the Bible to the Maronite laity. So violent was the opposition of the Maronite patriarch that in 1824 he secured a firman from the sultan, forbidding the giving of the Bible to Turkish subjects, and in 1826 the first Protestant convert, Asaad esh-Shidiak, was starved to death by his orders in a cell of the Maronite monastery of Kannobin. Nevertheless the translation of the whole Bible into Arabic, and its printing on well-cut Arabic type, was one of the most important works of the Americans at Beirut. In 1828 there was another violent persecution, and most of the missionaries had to retire temporarily to Malta.

Meanwhile the second interest of the western Churches, the conversion of the Jews, was also leading to action. The earliest society directly concerned with that object was the London Society for Promoting Christianity among the Jews, which was founded, under the royal patronage of the Duke of Kent, in 1808. It began work in England, and only gradually spread through Europe (where it encountered Swiss and German societies with the same objects) to The Land. In 1820 it sent out a young Swiss pastor, M. Tschudi, but he encountered violent opposition among the Jews of Jerusalem, and was not able to establish a permanent post. It was not until 1833 that this was created for the society by Dr Nicholayson, a Danish minister in the service of the London Society, and it was not until 1849 that the first Protestant church was dedicated in Jerusalem. But in the meantime medical work on a substantial scale had been undertaken, and gradually a number of medical units were established throughout the country by doctors and nurses from various European countries.

In 1841 a much more grandiose step was taken, the establishment, under British and Prussian auspices, of a Protestant bishopric to stand beside the Latin, Orthodox and other Churches at the central shrine of Christendom. The action had many contributory causes. One, which had nothing to do with Jerusalem, was the desire of the Prussian king, by securing Anglican episcopal ordination for a Prussian Protestant minister, to re-insert the thin end of the wedge of episcopacy into the State Church of Prussia and to unite German Calvinists and Lutherans into a single episcopal church; another was the desire of England to signify its position as a Christian power *vis-à-vis* the Porte. A third was a desire on the part of the Anglican Church to establish relations with the Orthodox patriarchate, and the first bishop, Dr S. Alexander, took with him letters to the patriarch which were warmly received. The bishop had not the title of 'Bishop of Jerusalem', but 'Bishop in Jerusalem', in order to make it clear that there was no intention to deny the authority of the Orthodox patriarch. Dr Alexander, who was an English Jewish convert, died in 1845, and was succeeded, on the king of Prussia's nomination, by Dr Gobat, a Swiss who had previously served the Church Missionary Society in Abyssinia. He held the see from 1846 until 1879 and during that period undertook extensive educational and medical work, as well as building several churches for English congregations. With the death of his successor in 1881, the dual arrangement lapsed.

Prussia refused to nominate, and in 1887 the Church of England re-established the bishopric, so that succeeding bishops were representatives of the Anglican Church only.

In 1851 the Church Missionary Society of London also began educational work in the country, and towards the end of Dr Gobat's episcopate they took over many of his schools. The result of these different efforts was that, whereas when Dr Gobat opened his first school the only other western establishment was a Roman Catholic school with twenty boys, at the end of his period there were over a hundred schools in the country conducted by a number of different societies, representing different Churches and countries. The fact that educational work inevitably led to a desire among the pupils to join the Church of the teachers led to complicated relations later with the Orthodox Church; and, in spite of their desire not to offend the Orthodox, Arab Christian congregations attached to the western Churches came into existence.

The activities of the Protestant Churches did not leave the Roman Catholics unmoved. In 1847 the Latin patriarchate of Jerusalem was revived, and at the same time efforts were made throughout the east to bring order and conformity into the various eastern Churches in union with Rome. In 1848 a Greek uniate patriarchate was established on a firm footing at Damascus, and in 1865 a seminary for Melkite Uniates was established in Jerusalem at the ancient crusading church of St Anne, which had been presented to France by the sultan at the conclusion of the Crimean War. While it was not difficult to secure friendly relations through the Latin patriarchate with the native Christians of the Uniate Churches, it was more difficult to fit a new patriarchate into the ancient pattern of authority spun by the Franciscan Guardian of the Holy Places; and the patriarch was in the somewhat embarrassing position of being very much poorer, and possessed of very much larger responsibilities, than the Franciscan Guardian who remained firmly outside his jurisdiction.

The third Christian power to establish itself impressively in the Holy Land was Russia. In the 1820s Russian Orthodox circles had become interested in the distribution of Bibles to the eastern Christians, and Russian pilgrims had been coming in numbers which increased in every decade. At first many had come overland through the Caucasus, and only half ever expected to return, so heavy were the losses at the hands of Arab brigands, and so severe the physical strain. Others came in sailing ships, taking a month or more to make the journey from the Black Sea. After the Crimean War steamers ran special services for the pilgrims, and they began to come by thousands. Their maintenance in Jerusalem laid a heavy responsibility on the Orthodox patriarch and the Brotherhood of the Holy Sepulchre, and this involved many complaints on both sides. The Russians complained that the pilgrims were ruthlessly fleeced by the monks, and the monks that the pilgrims constituted an unjust drain on the finances of the patriarchate. The Russian government was at first uncertain whether it desired officially to encourage these pilgrims or no, and in 1859 the Grand Duke Constantine came at the time of the pilgrimage, apparently in order to report on it to the government. The result of his visit was the purchase in the following year of the Maidan, an area of ten acres north-west of the Jaffa Gate, though it was the only flat area in the neighbourhood of the city, and as such used for all ceremonies and reviews.

The evangelical revival which marked the first half of the nineteenth century throughout the Protestant world, and which was productive of much of the work already described, produced also a revival of various forms of millenarianism. This led certain groups to settle in the Holy Land in expectation of the return of the Messiah. These movements can be traced as far back as the 1840s, but it was twenty years later, in 1866, that a group of colonists actually arrived at Jaffa from the United States. They called themselves the 'Church of the Messiah' and brought prefabricated houses with them which they erected in Jaffa. The following year the movement collapsed, and the survivors of the colony departed. But in the meantime a Lutheran group of pietists from Württemberg, known as 'the Temple' and led by Doctors Hardegg and Hoffmann, had been exploring the possibility of settling in the country. They encountered every kind of obstacle from the Porte, but in 1867 twelve of them established themselves near Nazareth. They all died of fever within a year; but, undeterred, the Templars bought the houses of the departing Americans and in 1868 established two colonies, one at Sarona near

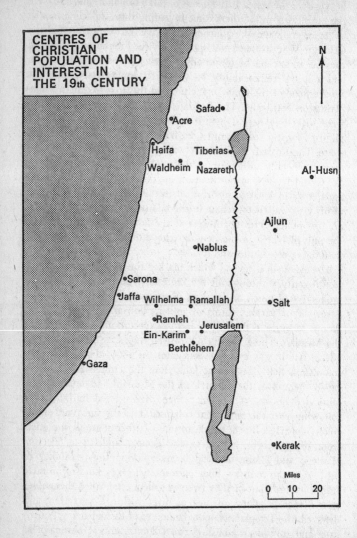

CENTRES OF CHRISTIAN POPULATION AND INTEREST IN THE 19th CENTURY

N

Safad

Acre

Haifa   Tiberias

Waldheim   Nazareth

Al-Husn

Ajlun

Nablus

Sarona

Jaffa   Wilhelma Ramallah

Salt

Ramleh

Ein-Karim   Jerusalem

Bethlehem

Gaza

Kerak

Miles

0   10   20

Jaffa and one at Haifa, while individual settlers established themselves in other parts of the country. The movement prospered, and soon had additional settlements near Jerusalem, at Wilhelma near Jaffa and at Waldheim in Galilee. At its height it included over a thousand members, who had been carefully chosen for their physical fitness and training before they were allowed to come.

The settlers encountered continual difficulties from the Turkish authorities and from their neighbours, who trespassed freely on their land. In Haifa they had also to encounter the hostility of the Carmelites whose lands adjoined theirs. Nevertheless they persisted, and their craftsmanship and good farming gradually led the more intelligent of their neighbours to copy their example and improve the fertility and cropping of their land. They were able to show both that it was possible for Europeans to work the soil and that its fertility could be increased by proper developments. They were also the first modern settlers to introduce wheeled vehicles, and to make roads on which such vehicles could operate. Though they had their internal difficulties and divisions, they survived until 1939 when the colonies were closed. They had never forgotten their German origin, and from 1933 onwards were sedulously worked by Nazi agents, with the result that they were regarded as suspect by the British authorities. And with some reason, for a number of Nazi leaders in the Middle East were drawn from these colonies which had once been composed exclusively of Lutheran pietists expecting the return of the Messiah.

To complete the picture of the changes wrought during this period, one other aspect of the interest of the Christian world needs to be described. While the establishment of the missions, the Anglo-Prussian bishopric, the Latin patriarchate and the Russian compound were all directly concerned with religious and ecclesiastical questions, and the Templars with their own affairs, the country was 'invaded' simultaneously by Christian scholars whose interest was in Biblical and Christian archaeology, and who revolutionized the study of the land, its peoples, its ancient sites and its historical geography. While earlier travellers engaged on such studies had to encounter considerable dangers and difficulties in their task, by the middle of the century it had become relatively safe to wander over the whole land, provided adequate financial precautions were taken to secure the approval and assistance of the village and tribal chiefs in whose territories travel was intended.

The travellers came from nearly every country of western Europe and from the United States. A German, Dr U. J. Seetzen, explored the eastern and southern area between 1805 and 1807. In 1809 a Swiss, J. L. Burckhardt, discovered Petra. Thirty years later an American expedition, led by Lieutenant Lynch, revealed the true depth and nature of the Jordan rift. The identification of Biblical sites was immensely advanced by Dr Edward Robinson of the Union Theological Seminary, New York, who recognized that many names were still preserved by the fellaheen, and that their identifications were much more reliable than those of Christian 'archaeologists' of the crusading or earlier periods. In 1858 Dr W. M. Thomson, an American stationed at Beirut, published *The Land and the Book*, in which he related the customs and folklore of the existing fellaheen to hitherto unexplained, or wrongly explained, Biblical narratives, and created a new type of Biblical study and illustration in which the 'stained glass window' types of early Christians were replaced by real local characters.

In 1865 another immense step forward was taken by the founding in London of the Palestine Exploration Fund, though the idea had older roots – a Palestine Society founded in London at the beginning of the century, and the Jerusalem Literary Society established by the British consul, James Finn, in 1849. The first task of the Fund was a survey map of the whole area west of the Jordan on which distinguished members of the Royal Engineers were working for a dozen years. Claude Regnier Conder carried through most of it, and Lieutenant (later Lord) Kitchener completed it in 1878. Meanwhile the excavation of sites was also being developed, and in this task as well as in architectural studies French scholars, especially the de Vogüés and Ernest Renan, took an important part. In 1887 the accidental discovery by Egyptian fellaheen of some clay tablets at Tell el-Amarna in Egypt threw a new light on early Israelite history and relations with Egypt in the fourteenth century B.C.E.; and three years later, Flinders Petrie, the interpreter of the tablets, was invited by the Palestine Exploration

Fund to start the excavation of Tell el-Hesi, which was ultimately revealed as the site of eight successive cities of Eglon. The scientific dating of its pottery introduced a new era in the excavation of many other cities. The year after the excavations at Tell el-Hesi, George Adam Smith published his *Historical Geography of the Holy Land*, in which the unity and interdependence of history and geography in the long millennia of its story were shown in a book which is still a delight to all Biblical students and travellers.

During the period between the end of the Crimean War and 1914, there was a general extension of all the religious interests whose establishment has already been mentioned. In this they were aided by the continued presence of the European consuls, which gave them the security of a certain political dignity; and when Abdul Hamid came to the throne in 1876 he made genuine efforts – if largely from self-interested motives – both to see that the officials sent to govern the country were reasonably efficient and presentable, and that the administration of the affairs of the Christian minorities gave no excuses for the intervention of Christian governments. The unreality of the Crimean War, in so far as Christian Holy Places were concerned, has already been shown in the facts that the war only resulted in the re-statement of the position about Holy Places as it had existed previously, and that the defeated power, Russia, within less than ten years of its termination, was able to erect the vast Russian compound overlooking the walls of Jerusalem.

The increase of Russian influence in relation to the Orthodox Christians was balanced by a steady increase of French influence among the Latins and Uniates. At the beginning of the century the Franciscans had been alone as representatives of the Latin West, and their tenure of certain of their monasteries outside Jerusalem and Bethlehem was still uncertain. Then came the re-establishment of the Carmelites on Mount Carmel, and the restoration of the Latin patriarchate. After the Crimean War there was a general advance all along the line and new foundations were established such as the Institute of the brothers Ratisbonne, the houses of the Sisters of Our Lady of Zion, the Sisters of Nazareth, the seminary of the Algerian Fathers in the Church of Saint Anne, and many others. The work of these institutes and convents was very varied. Many were educational, many medical, some cared for orphans, some for women, some concentrated on Jews, some on Uniates, some on eastern Christians, and some on western pilgrims. Many of the Holy Places from which Christians had been for centuries excluded, were reoccupied.

At the same time the great and established Orders, with the assistance of different Roman Catholic powers, established centres in the country. The Jesuits concentrated on a Bible Institute in Jerusalem and the Catholic University of St Joseph at Beirut. This was founded a year after the American Protestant College, and headed up all the educational work done in the many different institutes in the area. The Dominicans established a convent on the site of the Church of St Stephen, north of the Damascus Gate, which became an important centre of scholarship. In all, at the end of the century, the Roman Catholic Church had established in the country thirty Orders, Brotherhoods and associations, with twenty convents, eighteen hospices, six higher schools, forty-six day schools, sixteen orphanages, four industrial schools and five

---

Key for map on opposite page.

1 Syrian Orphanage and School
2 St George's Cathedral and School
3 American Colony
4 German Hospice
5 Abyssinian Church
6 Italian Hospital
7 St Stephen (Benedictine)
8 German Hospital
9 Anglican Girls' School
10 Ratisbonne School
11 School and Orphanage of the Rosary
12 Russian Compound
13 French Hospital
14 Notre Dame de France Hospice (Dominican)
15 Latin Church of Gethsemane
16 Russian Church of Gethsemane
17 Viri Galilaei
18 Carmelite Convent
19 Terra Santa College
20 YMCA
21 Jesuit Bible Institute
22 Latin Patriarchate
23 Greek Patriarchate
24 Armenian Patriarchate
25 Church of the Holy Sepulchre
26 Coptic Patriarchate
27 Austrian Hospice
28 Convent of Soeurs de Sion
29 St Anne's Church (Pères Blancs)
30 Lutheran Church
31 Bishop Gobat's School
32 Church of the Dormition

hospitals. It is a remarkable record of activity in which France, Austria, Spain, Italy, Germany and other countries cooperated.

Some of the work done by these institutions was made possible by the financial support they received from different governments, interested to maintain their prestige in the Holy Land. On the whole the Protestant Churches had to depend on voluntary contributions, and the only substantial creations by a government were the original Prussian gift towards the Anglo-Prussian bishopric, and the German emperor's acquisition of a site in the Muristan for a Lutheran church. The work was done by many different societies, representing Churches in different countries. The main difficulty involved was, as already mentioned, the dilemma created by the desire of the Anglican Church and others for cordial relations with the Orthodox and other eastern patriarchates, and the desire of the more Protestant bodies for the acceptance of proselytes from these Churches into what they believed to be a purer form of Christianity.

When the replacement of the Anglo-Prussian by an Anglican bishopric was being discussed in 1887, the proposal was made that it should be set up at Beirut, in order to avoid the clash of interests in Jerusalem; and it was the direct request of the Orthodox patriarch which led to its return to the latter city, still with the

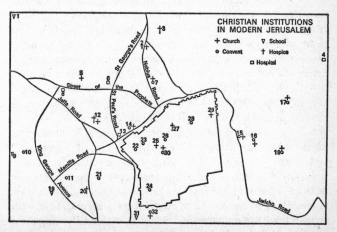

title of 'Bishop in Jerusalem'. These friendly relations led to interesting breaches with the ancient and unhappy tradition by which Christian bodies outbid each other for rights in Holy Places, and violently opposed the extension of rights of any Church other than their own. It became the habit of the Armenian patriarch to invite the Anglican bishop to give the blessing at the conclusion of one of the great ceremonies of the Armenian Holy Week. Even more interesting was the invitation of the Orthodox patriarch to hold services in a chapel of the Church of the Holy Sepulchre itself. This invitation was originally made in an individual case in 1885 to Dr C. Hale, an American Episcopalian. When the Anglican bishopric was established in 1887 it was extended to all those on whose behalf the Anglican bishop asked for the courtesy. The chapel selected is the chapel of Abraham, situated above the site of Golgotha; the use of it lies wholly in the hands of the patriarch; the service is prepared for by him; and it is understood to convey no legal rights which would create an alteration in the *status quo*. During the mandatory period the interchange of courtesies between the two communions was considerably extended.

At the same time, the position of the bishop and the Protestant societies was not easy. The latter were alarmed, and even hostile, at an attitude which appeared to them to ignore the practical difficulties they encountered when individuals, clergy and laity, from the eastern Churches affirmed to them their inability to remain within their previous communities. Though the situation was less difficult than that which confronted the Americans in the Lebanon dealing with the Maronite Church, it was a problem neither the bishop nor the Church Missionary Society found easy to resolve. Dr Gobat had at times been in a very embarrassing position as representative of both Prussia and England, both the Anglican and the Lutheran Churches. Dr Popham Blyth, the first bishop on the Anglican establishment, found himself in an equally embarrassing position as bishop without any diocesan clergy, since the many Anglican workers in the area covered by his bishopric were all servants of different missionary societies and under their orders. He therefore set out to establish the bishopric itself, with its own funds, headquarters and activities, without allowing these to appear in competition with the existing societies. The result was the creation of a new society, the Jerusalem and the East Mission, through which he built St George's Close and cathedral church, together with other churches in the country, and a series of schools for boys and girls directly under his jurisdiction.

The activities of the Roman Catholics and Protestants were paralleled by those of the Russians. Having established their centre at Jerusalem, they extended their work to cover other sites visited by their pilgrims, and gradually came to be extensive owners of land throughout the country. Two of their main establishments were at Nazareth and at Ain Karim outside Jerusalem. They also started schools for native eastern Christians, and, while the work of all the Churches also contributed to a renewal of life within native Christianity, it was through Russian action that a new and critical issue arose within the Orthodox patriarchate.

While in the struggle of European powers over the body of Turkey Russia naturally stood as the defender of Orthodoxy against the pretensions of the Latins, within the Orthodox Church she engaged in a parallel struggle to lessen the influence of the Greeks, by forwarding the interests not only of her own Moscow patriarchate, but of all movements for independence or recognition among non-Greek elements in the Balkans and elsewhere. This inevitably involved her in a struggle in Jerusalem where the peculiar nature of the patriarchate made it one of the most important centres of purely Greek interest within the Orthodox Church.

In eastern Churches there has often been a much closer connexion between the monastic and episcopal hierarchies than has ever been common in the West. But the Jerusalem patriarchate was unusual for being wholly in the hands of the monastic Brotherhood of the Holy Sepulchre. From its ranks were chosen not only the patriarch but all the higher clergy, most of whom continued to be resident members of the court of the patriarch in Jerusalem, even while enjoying metropolitan and episcopal titles from centres where there were Arabic-speaking Christian congregations. This would have been a serious matter in any case, but the situation was made worse by the fact that the Brotherhood in the nineteenth century was an exclusively and fanatically Greek body, to which access was almost wholly impossible for the native Christians of the patriarchate; and the fact that Patriarch Cyril II (1845–72) moved his regular residence from Constantinople to Jerusalem did not make any difference.

It was the old dilemma of the patriarchate in a new form, the issue as to whether it existed because of the Holy Places or because of the presence of a body of Christians – though they amounted to considerably less than fifty thousand – within the geographical area over which it held sway. The situation had been gradually developing ever since the return of the Orthodox patriarch after the crusades. During the Mamluk period, though the links with the ecumenical patriarch at Constantinople were never broken, and though the liturgical language continued to be mainly Greek, there had always been a strong local influence in the Holy Places, and many of the patriarchs were Arabic-speaking local Christians. But after the Turkish conquest the ecclesiastical hierarchy tended to become more and more exclusively Greek in origin. In the nineteenth century, when Greek nationalism had been fanned to a flame by the War of Independence, it became wholly so. The Brotherhood, which was exceedingly wealthy, regarded itself as an outpost of Greek culture, guarding on behalf of the Greek Church and nation Holy Places largely erected by emperors they considered Greek.

In 1875 conflicts between the local Christians and the Greeks, largely fomented by the Russians, led to an intervention by the Porte. By a new constitution, natives were to be admitted to the Brotherhood, schools were to be established and governed by a mixed council of equal numbers of clergy and laity, and bishops of dioceses where there were congregations (Nazareth and Acre) were to be chosen from men able to speak Arabic and to spend a suitable part of their time in their dioceses. None of these reforms were carried out, and matters simmered until the Turkish revolution of 1908. Under the new Turkish constitution the patriarchate was obliged to set up a mixed council of clergy and laity for its government. The local Christians proceeded at once to demand such a council, even before the law for its establishment had been ratified. The Patriarch Damianus refused to agree; but the Brotherhood believed that he was sympathetic to some of their demands (especially admission to the Brotherhood) and demanded his resignation. When he refused, they deposed him; but he refused to accept this, as being wholly uncanonical. Nevertheless the new Turkish government recognized his deposition. But when there were riots of the local Christians in Jerusalem, Jaffa and Bethlehem, and the local pasha had assured the government that his deposition could not be effected except by bloodshed and the display of a considerable force, the Brotherhood climbed down.

Unhappily at this point the new policy of turcification caused the government to maintain the deposition, as they had no intention of supporting what appeared – and was – an Arab demonstration. There were more riots and the tension continued for several years. In 1910 it was ordained that a mixed council should be set up with control, in the interest of the local Christians, of one third of the patriarchal revenues or £30,000 annually, whichever sum should be the larger. But this was not put into effect and nothing had been finally put into practice when in 1917 both the patriarch and his synod were removed by the Turks to Damascus. The affairs of the patriarchate were left in the hands of a committee of the Brotherhood. This committee showed that its attitude was unchanged by immediately placing its affairs in the hands of the Greek government.

The indifference of the Brotherhood to the needs of the Arabic-speaking congregations led to a considerable decline in numbers during the nineteenth century. At the beginning of the century nine tenths of the local Christians were members of the Orthodox Church; at the end of it they amounted only to two thirds. The main congregations outside Jerusalem were to be found in fairly compact groups. Around that city there were Orthodox Christians in Ramallah and some villages in the north-east corner of the Judean hills to the north, and in Bethlehem, Beit Jala and Beit Sahur to the south. In the southern district were substantial communities at Jaffa, Gaza and Ramleh. In Galilee they were to be found at Acre and Nazareth; and in the central hills were smaller communities at or around Tulkarm, Nablus and Jenin. Across the Jordan were three main centres; Salt, Kerak and al-Husn. For a time the Monastery of the Cross outside Jerusalem was maintained as a theological college for local clergy; but in spite of this, many of them were almost entirely uneducated, and those of their congregations who rejected the schools of the Protestants or Roman Catholics had to rely on the Russians who maintained about a hundred schools in connexion with their properties and convents. Schools maintained by the patriarchate were non-existent outside of Jerusalem.

As a result of this century of activity The Land, at the outbreak of the First World War, presented a curiously contradictory spectacle. It possessed more schools, hospitals, orphanages and similar institutions than any other country of the east. It was visited annually by large numbers of Christians from all over the world, and though they lacked comfort in their travels they enjoyed almost complete security. And yet almost nothing had changed in the government of the country; it remained wholly indifferent to health, education and social welfare, and concerned itself almost exclusively with the collection of taxes from the local population and the exploitation for its own advantage of the interest of other countries in the area. In so far as the local population itself was concerned it was only the small Christian minority which was able to enjoy the benefits conferred by the work of other Churches. The Muslims were largely afraid or indifferent; the fellaheen remained ignorant and downtrodden, and the bedouins continued their millennial ways. The only sign of indigenous life had been the revolt of the Arab Orthodox Christians against the Greek policy of the patriarchate and even that had not produced any effect by 1914.

CHAPTER THIRTEEN

The Birth of Arab Nationalism
and the Local Population

THE increased security and protection which Christian interests obtained during the nineteenth century was by no means immediately reflected in parallel improvements in the lot of the local population. Neither Egyptian nor Turkish rulers were vitally concerned with the lot of their own subjects and warfare between the different clans and tribes was endemic until the despotism of Abdul Hamid managed to secure a certain authority over the local sheikhs and their followers. Movements towards a national revival and ambitions towards independence only affected narrow circles of the intelligentsia, and that in the years immediately preceding the First World War.

Up to that time it is not possible to speak of the existence of any general sentiment of nationality, and the word 'Arab' needs to be used with care. It is applicable to the bedouin and to a section of the urban and effendi classes; it is inappropriate as a description of the rural mass of the population, the fellaheen. The whole population spoke Arabic, usually corrupted by dialects bearing traces of words of other origin, but it was only the bedouin who habitually thought of themselves as Arabs. Western travellers from the sixteenth century onwards make the same distinction, and the word 'Arab' almost always refers to them exclusively.

During the nineteenth century many European scholars visited the country for long periods, and some took up their permanent residence there. It was these scholars, some working as missionaries, doctors and educators, some in the consulates, who first made independent studies of the fellaheen, and gathered reliable information about their customs, religion and origin. Gradually it was realized that there remained a substantial stratum of the pre-Israelite peasantry, and that the oldest element among the peasants were not 'Arabs' in the sense of having entered the country with or after the conquerors of the seventh century, but had been there already when the Arabs came. One of the clearest proofs of this arose from the attempt of men like Doctors Thomson or Robinson, and above all the makers of the Palestine survey, to identify the various sites mentioned in the Old Testament. The identifications made by the crusaders or later Christian travellers were often found to be obviously wrong, and then some spot or heap of ruins in the neighbourhood was found to be called by the local peasantry by a name which was founded on the Biblical Hebrew.

Gezer was identified in Tel-Jezer, Ai in Haiyan, Gibeon in al-Jib, and so on in hundreds of examples. In many cases Greek and Roman and later names had been discarded, and the old Biblical name recalled, as when Bethshan, which had been Scythopolis, reverted to Beisan. In fact almost the only classical names which have survived are Nablus (Neapolis) and Sebastiyah (Samaria-Sebaste). This could only have happened if there had been continuity in the villages, independent of successive conquests. Yet further evidence was provided by the presence of customs which were not the product of Islam, but which recalled in some cases pre-Israelite religion and in some the laws of the Mosaic code. Perhaps the most striking survival is the local 'high place' or *mukam* which neither the centralizing tendency of early Judaism, nor the stern monotheism of Islam sufficed to destroy. The customs and religious traditions which centre in the mukam, as the mukam in turn occupies the real centre of peasant religion, owe little to the three great monotheistic faiths which in succession have controlled the country.

The Land's many changes of master have, in fact, not been accompanied by wholesale alterations of the population. There have been cases in which new masters meant only the addition of a new official class. There were, for example, few Roman or Turkish settlers. But even when new masters meant new settlements, as with the original Israelites, the Greeks, the Arabs or the crusaders, the newcomers were never sufficiently numerous to displace the existing population. There are, therefore, to be found among the fellaheen traces of all the strata from neolithic to modern times. On a foundation of Canaanite, which in itself is a name possibly covering many settlements, Israelite, Syrian, Greek,

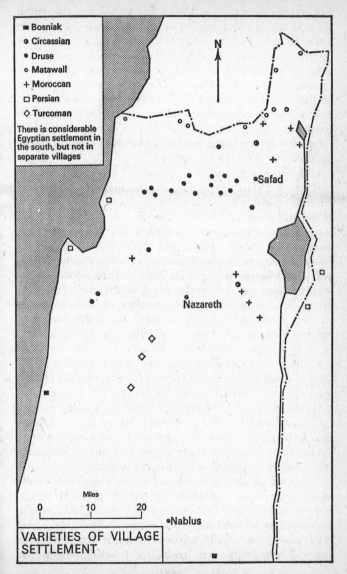

Legend:
- ■ Bosniak
- ◉ Circassian
- ● Druse
- ○ Matawall
- + Moroccan
- □ Persian
- ◇ Turcoman

There is considerable Egyptian settlement in the south, but not in separate villages

N

● Safad

● Nazareth

Miles

0   10   20

● Nablus

VARIETIES OF VILLAGE SETTLEMENT

Arab, Latin, Egyptian and Balkan peoples have all contributed elements to the present population. Some are completely absorbed; some still show distinct origins. In some cases villages are wholly populated by settlers from other portions of the Turkish Empire within the nineteenth century. There are villages of Bosnians, Druzes, Circassians and Egyptians. The proportion in which these different elements are present is, of course, impossible to define. But the long period of Islamic rule, community in the use of the Arabic language, and a sense of kinship have made it easy for a thoroughly diverse population to find its unity in modern Arab nationalism.

In the towns the situation is somewhat different. It is probable that each successive conquest displaced the previous population to a considerable extent, and in many cases towns have been wholly sacked and repeopled. Moreover townsmen have shallower roots. Arab landowners and ex-soldiers, Greek and Syrian merchants, slaves and ex-slaves from all parts of the Turkish Empire and beyond, Armenian refugees, Christians drawn by the Holy Places, Jews drawn by the appeal of the Promised Land, all can show a long residence in the different towns of Palestine. They have always been cosmopolitan; they have always contained different quarters where different races and tongues lived their own lives, sometimes unimpeded, sometimes all alike crushed under the heel of a master, alien to all or most of them.

But townsmen and peasants have never been the only inhabitants of a country containing wide areas lacking adequate rainfall, and with the desert on its eastern and southern frontiers. The antiquity of nomad life was referred to in the opening pages of the book. Throughout there have been references to the presence – usually hostile – of nomad peoples. In the nineteenth century systematic study of both their life and their history was undertaken, largely by English and American travellers.

It was soon realized that bedouins are not a single community or of a single origin. Not only are the customs of the tribes singularly diverse, but they are far more fluid than had been thought. Bedouins have become villagers and *vice versa*. The rich village of Abu Ghosh on the road from Jaffa to Jerusalem, or of Abu Dis on the road from Jerusalem to Jericho, are of bedouin origin. Both settled because they controlled pilgrim routes, and were licensed to provide those pilgrims who paid them with appropriate escorts. Those who refused to pay them suffered accordingly, for, once the bedouins had a settled base, it was impossible to avoid them. There are bedouins today who trace their origin to Muslim villages, or to Jewish or Christian ancestors. Among the most interesting of the last group are the tinkers (the Salabyin) who, in small groups, are found working in the whole bedouin world. They use a cross (*salib*) to mark various possessions, claiming to be descended from the crusaders. Their names are taken almost exclusively from the Old Testament suggesting that they also have a Jewish link.

There is a hierarchy of bedouin life as complex as the courts of nineteenth-century Spain or Austria. At the peak come the camel breeders, of which the chief tribes in Jordan are the Beni Sakr and the Howeitat. The breeders of sheep and goats are still regarded as inferior. Then there are tribes, such as the Terrabin, who pass some months of the year cultivating their tribal ground, and who travel only after the harvest. Right into the twentieth century, there were also tribes heavily involved in slave-trading. The slaves were primarily unwanted daughters of the fellaheen, and were not necessarily reluctant to exchange life in a Palestinian village for the richer households of Arabia which could afford to buy them.

There are great differences too in the range of their nomadism. Many traditional routes pay scant attention to modern political frontiers. Those breeding camels naturally penetrate further into the desert than those breeding sheep or goats. Every tribe has its recognized route, though these may change as a result of tribal wars or shifts of allegiance.

The impossibility of making clear-cut distinctions in the field of ethnology applies also in that of religion. Of the Muslim peasant stock of today it is possible to say that its oldest elements are composed in the main of ex-Jews and ex-Christians. For if it be true that in the days of the Hebrew kingdom the Mosaic religion may not have reached many of the villages which, even today, show signs of pre-Israelitish customs, yet in the time of the Maccabees and the Herods, it is probable that most of the country-side, nominally at least, practised Judaism. It is likewise true of the Christian period that at first the religion spread mostly in the towns; and it is as well to remember that in many parts of the country Greek religion and Greek mysteries prevailed; but in the last centuries before the Islamic conquest most of the villages were probably reached by the Church, and Justinian in the sixth century disfranchised all who did not accept the religion of the state.

After the Arab conquest we have already seen that the country remained for some time predominantly Christian and Jewish. But it is equally important to remember that the process of Islamization is one which has been going on throughout the whole period, right into modern times. There are villages which today are Muslim which were Christian or Jewish within the last couple of centuries. Nor can we always identify the word 'Arab' as used in its pre-war sense with the word 'Muslim'. Of those Arabs who lived in the eastern and southern parts of the country before the Arab conquest many professed Christianity and there are pure Arabs east of the Jordan who are still Christian. The situation of these groups has already been discussed in the previous chapter; and the situation of those Jews who are Arabic-speaking, and can consider themselves as much 'indigenous' as any other section of the population, will be discussed in the following chapter. Here we are concerned with two groups who are today both 'Muslim' and 'Arab'. On the one hand there are those who are descended from the Arab conquerors and settlers of the seventh and succeeding centuries, and on the other are the majority of the population who have come to speak Arabic and profess Islam at various dates, but who only began to think of themselves as 'Arabs' in the present century.

Dealing, as we are in this chapter, with the period before 1914, we have to recognize that the mass of the population had no real feeling of belonging to any wider unit than their village, clan or possibly confederation of clans. The extent to which warfare went on between tribes and villages right into the second half of the nineteenth century exceeded anything that was known in the most turbulent centuries of early feudal Europe. The units were constantly changing. Sometimes they were grouped around the traditional contrast between 'northern' and 'southern' (Qais and Yemen) for which all historical reason (in so far as any ever existed) had been forgotten; sometimes they were attracted by personal leaders such as Abu Ghosh of Kuriat al-Anab, Akhil Aga, the Egyptian fellah leader from Galilee, or many others who appeared in each generation. The Turkish governors were not averse to a continuation of this state of affairs, since they had no desire to see the power of any of the local landowning families consolidated on the permanent basis which peace and security would have ensured; and governors were even known to have been ready to lend (for a suitable fee) the forces of the government to aid a warring sheikh to overcome his more powerful neighbours. In such circumstances it was impossible for the ordinary villager to extend his loyalty beyond that of the sheikh or clan to which he belonged. If people the other side of his own hill could (with the connivance of the government) be regarded as his permanent enemies, the material was lacking by which he might have been led to the understanding that all the population were his brothers within a national unity.

Actually the Turkish Empire itself was anonymous. It had no name other than 'the realm of the sultan', so that there was nothing concrete to make the peasant, who was not conscious of his local or national affiliation, conscious even of the nature of his political affiliation. He had no idea of the extent or nature of the empire to which he belonged, and the Turkish official did nothing to enlighten him. On the contrary, the censorship constantly showed the most absurd fears when western educators tried to make it clear to their students what and where 'Turkey' and the 'Turkish Empire' were. One of the founders of the American university at Beirut relates that when they had painstakingly produced a map of the Turkish dominions they were forced to destroy it because it distinguished the provinces by different colours and this implied 'inequality' in the eyes of the censorship. And in one case a cookery book was forbidden because it contained recipes for cooking turkey – to the censors an obvious political plot!

It might be thought that Islam could take the place of the state as the centre of unity. But this also did not prove to be so in practice, save for limited and not always desirable purposes. Common membership of the religion of Muhammad never prevented inter-tribal wars between Muslims, and in these wars few of the merciful practices recommended by Abu Bakr against enemies outside of the fold were observed towards brothers within it. To a large extent the loyalty of the people to Islam was a formal and even superstitious loyalty, and they were little affected by the ethical and philosophic toleration and spirituality which were to be found in other centres of Muslim orthodoxy. Jerusalem was almost negligible as a centre of Muslim study; the dervish orders who were to be found in the country were on the whole an element of superstition and not of mystical devotion; and the mosque had long ceased to be a centre whence radiated an effective religious education.

In fact much of the actual religion and ethic of the population owed nothing to Islam at all. It was pre-Islamic or independent in its origin. This is particularly true of the one characteristic which is almost universally commended by travellers of all nations – the hospitality of the Arab and his loyalty to the laws of hospitality. Though there were strict and even narrow limits to the exercise of this virtue, there is no doubt of its reality, and of the contempt which any Arab or Muslim would have incurred who violated its rules. But the idea of sanctuary and the exercise and definition of hospitality is an essential of nomadic life in a semi-desert country and is to be found wherever such conditions of life exist apart from Islam. All that Islam needed to do was to consecrate already existing laws with the sanction of its authority.

Of more questionable value is the Muslim acceptance of the worship of the 'high places' which antedated not merely Islam but both Christianity and Judaism, and which might entitle local peasantry to claim to be the most tenacious in the world. The religion of Israel had to compromise with this local worship, and Christianity, as in pagan Europe, turned many local deities into Christian saints in order to purify the ineradicable practices of the rural population. Christianity did, in fact, effect a considerable purification of such local worship, because the cult of local saints was accepted and incorporated into general worship. Islam made no such concession to 'idolatry' as to try to reform it, but did wink at its survival, with the result that the worship retained untrammelled the superstitious features of antiquity. The village mukam contained provisions for hospitality, it is true, but beyond that it contained little which could elevate the villager. Many of the 'saints' to which such shrines were dedicated were wholly non-existent; some were brigand sheikhs; many had the names of Jewish or Christian characters – Elijah and St George being the most popular – but without any knowledge whatever of the lives or virtues of those characters. In fact the stories told of the local 'saints' in absurdity and meaninglessness make many of the lives of saints in eastern monasticism appear the moral lessons of a Puritan Sunday School.

It was, and still is, the tragedy of Islam that all movements of reform suffer from a nostalgia for the simple life of the desert in which the faith was originally proclaimed, and have not found the way to make the teaching of its saints and mystics available for the life of the peasant and the townsman. The eighteenth-century revival of the Wahhabi and the nineteenth-century revival of the Sanussi both partake of the same nostalgia for the desert, and both have found their following in the desert – in Saudi Arabia and in the oases of the deserts of North Africa.

During the nineteenth century Islam produced two great figures who preached reform apart from these movements back to the desert. Jamaluddin al-Afghani propounded the doctrines of Pan-Islam as a basis for the revival of Asia, and al-Kawakebi fought valiantly against injustice in Syria and Egypt. But in fact the extent of the idea of reform in Islam at this period could be compared only to the state of Christianity in the time of Wiclif. There was nothing suggesting a pulsation of new life such as was to be found in the period of the sixteenth-century Christian reformers. Nationalism has taken the place of religion and not acted as a servant of it, and there has been no religious revival which might affect the daily lives of Muslim peasants and townsmen anywhere.

One movement which needs mention in this connexion is the Bahai; for in view of its numerous adherents in Europe and America it might be thought that it should have played a beneficent part in the revival of religion in The Land. The story of the Bahai movement goes back to 1835 when a young Persian Shiite proclaimed himself the Bab, the Doorway by which alone might

God be approached. Later he advanced his claim to be the last
Imam or successor to Ali, founder of the Shiite schism, and an
incarnation of Divinity. He proclaimed the need for reform in
Islam with such vigour that, in spite of the lofty ethical character
of his preaching, he was executed in 1849. Before he died he
appointed a successor who, with his half-brother (who later took
the name of Baha-ullah) was exiled from Persia. The sultan of
Turkey kept them as state prisoners in Adrianople, where a schism
took place. One was sent to Famagusta, and his following gradually dwindled. Baha-ullah was sent to Acre where he lived in
complete retirement but in great state. He died in 1892. His son,
Abbas Effendi, dropped the claim to be a divine incarnation, but
continued the message of his predecessors. But while he attracted
many followers both in Persia and in the West, he made no
attempt to spread his teaching or attract followers locally. There
the movement consists of only a few hundreds, and has no
influence on local Muslim life.

In general, then, Islam has unhappily proved an agent for the
division and degradation of the country, as much as for its enlight-
enment. Among the Muslim clergy, the muftis, imams and leading
figures in the dervish orders, many Christian travellers in all
centuries have found men of a wider vision and tolerance than
were easily to be found among the eastern Churches. But little or
none of this genuine religious sentiment was reflected in the
religion of the peasant and townsman. The festivals and pilgrimages, such as those of Nebi Musa and of Nebi Rubin near Jaffa,
had in them little of the religious devotion which marked the
ordinary Christian pilgrim to the Holy Places; and the religion of
Islam normally expressed itself only in the intolerant and intolerable belief in his superiority which was exhibited by the most
ignorant Muslim in the presence of a Christian patriarch or a
Jewish rabbi. So ignorant was their arrogance that nineteenth-
century writers report again and again their belief that the British
sovereign, and all the other princes of Christendom, were merely
the vassals of the sultan, who fought the Crimean War or expelled
Ibrahim from Syria in execution of his orders. Fanaticism is a
natural concomitant of ignorance and arrogance; and it is unfortunate that Christians and Jews, in the hope of securing better

treatment for their fellows under Muslim rule by the flattery of the Muslim authorities, should have created out of Koranic tolerance of the Peoples of the Book the legend of the favourable treatment of Christians and Jews. It might indeed be said of the Turkish authorities that they exhibited the toleration of indifference when suitably paid to do so. But, apart from this, the legend of good treatment of the Christian and Jewish minorities has no support in the Muslim history of the last thousand years, apart from the brief period of the early Osmanli sultans.

At the same time, it is well to remember in dealing with the Muslim peasantry and townsfolk of The Land that they also were a subject people, exploited and misgoverned by Turkish rulers with no interest in them save as payers of taxes and conscripts in wars not of their seeking. That they should have become cruel, treacherous and untruthful is not surprising in the circumstances. That their good qualities should be reserved for their own circle and for their own friends and allies has been the fate of other peoples similarly oppressed. But here also Islam has been no help to them. For side by side with an absence of any effective social teaching is the fatalism of its predestinarianism, and the coldness of its Puritan monotheism. Islam may proclaim that Allah is generous and merciful. But it does not, like Judaism and Christianity, proclaim that men are His children. They are His slaves or His subjects; and in consequence Islam has provided little consolation and strengthening for the weak and oppressed.

Nevertheless both peasant and bedouin have many good qualities. There is no doubt that the peasantry are industrious and hardworking during the season of agricultural labour. They are deeply attached to their native soil, and part of their hatred of conscription arose from their hatred of leaving – often for ever – their native village. Family life is respected, and poverty makes most of them monogamous. They are loyal to their word, once it is given; and docile and obedient to their sheikhs; they are brave and willing to endure hardship. The bedouin likewise are a people with an intense admiration for courage and endurance, and a detestation of what by their traditions they consider dishonesty or disloyalty. They accept willingly the poverty which their love of freedom entails. The tragedy has been that they keep faith only with those whom they have accepted as friends or allies, and are cruel, cunning and unreliable in any dealings with those outside that charmed circle.

Peasant and bedouin alike have contributed to the ruin of the countryside on which both depend for a livelihood. In the wars between villages it was far too common a practice to cut down fruit trees and olives and to destroy crops, and this in the end caused as much loss of life through hunger as was caused by the actual casualties of fighting. Bedouins freely destroyed the crops of villages which they raided, and killed or carried off their livestock. They filled wells with stones and broke down reservoirs and cisterns. They often caused such insecurity in whole districts that wide fertile areas were for years left completely uncultivated, while streams and rivers became dammed, malaria became endemic and the unlucky peasants fled elsewhere or starved in the towns. As already related some villagers in the nineteenth century themselves took to the bedouin life because of the ruin of their agriculture.

An agriculture conducted on so precarious a basis could not hope to avoid the curse from which such an industry has suffered in every primarily agricultural country in the world – hopeless peasant indebtedness. The peasants were indebted to their landowners, to the tax farmers, and to professional moneylenders, and they paid rates of interest from fifty per cent upwards. From birth to death and from generation to generation they could never hope to escape from crippling debts. In the midst of an already ruined country the flocks of goats ably assisted the work of man, and the recurrence of earthquakes and famines and of epidemics of cholera, smallpox and other diseases, as well as the ruthless oppression of the government tax-collectors, completed the work of destruction created by the goats, the peasants themselves, the bedouin and the moneylenders.

Nor did the land-holding system in vogue in much of the country lead to agricultural improvement in areas in which security and the fertility of the soil made a precarious prosperity possible. While in some villages the individual peasant was a freeholder or an individual tenant, in many the village land was held collectively and re-distributed biennially between the cultivators.

In such a situation proper maintenance and manuring, the planting of trees and the maintenance of terraces, all suffer. For each labourer thought that in making such long-term expenditures of his labour he might only be benefiting another. An established crop-rotation continued unchanged, exhausting the soil, just because it had always been so, and the peasant, intensely conservative by nature, only slowly responded to the suggestions of change which western schools, or the agriculture of such bodies as the Templars, suggested to him. In spite of the immense fertility of the soil, it is probable that in the first half of the nineteenth century the population sank to the lowest level it had ever known in historic times.

In this situation the realization that the peasantry of today contained widespread elements of the pre-Islamic and pre-Arab population contains a seed of hope. It is unhappily true that for a picture of Palestinian prosperity we need to go back to a time when the two elements out of which the present majority and the present nationalist temper are composed were absent from the picture. But, just as it is true that the bedouin camping in the ruins of Petra or Palmyra is camping amidst the works of his ancestors, so it is true in The Land that the terraces and reservoirs which the peasants of many centuries destroyed were the work of their own ancestors; the irrigation channels which once gave the land prosperity were part of an agricultural life with which their ancestors were familiar. The ownership may have been in the hands of foreigners; the workmen were of their own blood. It is easier to hope that what they have done once they might do again, than to expect men of a different race and civilization to understand and to inherit the work of men with whom they had no link through history and tradition.

During the reign of Abdul Hamid material conditions began to improve in certain fields. Something at least was done to suppress the continual village warfare and to restrain the raids of the bedouin. During the seventies much of the great plain of Esdraelon was brought into cultivation again by a family of rich Syrian bankers, the Sursoks. The cultivation of oranges in the maritime plain proved extremely successful. Roads began to appear, and one joined Jerusalem with Jaffa. There followed a railway between these two towns and another which joined Acre with Damascus on the Hedjaz line east of the Jordan. Better security for agriculture and increased opportunities for work caused the population to begin to increase, and probably led also to some rise in the standard of living of the peasantry and the towns. There was even a certain immigration from the northern parts of Syria. But trade still remained extremely slight. Palestine had no port, and there was little exchange except of local produce. Some beginning was made in education, but here also it hardly penetrated into more than a small proportion of the villages; and more children were still educated in the foreign schools than in those run by the authorities. Nevertheless a change was slowly appearing, and providing some background for future developments.

It was, however, not in The Land but in the Lebanon that Arab nationalism was born out of the groundwork provided by the Syrian Protestant University which the Americans had founded. Even here the soil on which such a movement could grow was extremely poor. During the brief period in which Ibrahim had governed Syria for his father Mehmet Ali he had tried to bring an Arab national movement into existence as a background to the dream of an Arab empire which he shared with his father. But though he improved the administration, ensured equality before the law for Christians and Jews, and attempted to develop local education, he was unable to arouse any national feeling; and when he increased taxes and enforced conscription he had to face rebellion in many parts of the country. When the European powers forced him to abandon the country and returned it to Turkish rule, what few improvements he had introduced were lost, and the country sank back again into apathy.

It contained none of the elements out of which nationalism had risen to be a force in many countries of Europe. There was a land-owning class, but almost no middle class of merchants, professional men and officials. The Muslim and Druze peasants had not a glimmering of either national consciousness or the meaning of political nationality; the Maronites were attracted to France rather than to the idea of Arab unity; and the bedouins felt no solidarity either with the villages or the towns. There was no national literature possessing any relevance for a political revival, and the spoken dialects had departed so far from literary Arabic that the great masterpieces of the period of the Arab caliphate were unreadable by the ordinary man. The only Arab history to which they could refer with pride belonged to an age which had passed away almost a thousand years earlier. Finally, what education was available came almost wholly from the Christian schools of foreign powers. There was, however, another side to this sorry situation. From the point of view of effective political action the destiny of the Arab world lay in the hands of a very small class, and they had no need in the early stages of their movement to worry about popular support.

This was important because it brought into high relief the two historical factors into which a new Arab political nationalism could most easily be grafted: Islam and Arabic. Once the movement had passed its initial stages, stages in which the initiative had largely lain with the Christians, it had become a Muslim movement, and the unity of Islam, together with the religious primacy of the Arab in the creation of Islam and its theology, was a matter of common pride uniting the small class of educated Arabs throughout the Middle East. Likewise Arabic, though in its colloquial forms it followed a hundred dialects, was a single literary language throughout the whole area, and it was the language of the Koran and of the classical literature of Islam. In the cultural–religious field there was no need to strive to make such Arabs conscious of a common inheritance. They were already aware of it, and proud of it.

This cultural–religious inheritance had a social side in that it had created certain common forms of life which made it easy for an educated Arab to be equally at home in a dozen different Arab cities. Accepting the great division of power between the land-owning families and the bedouin sheikhs as a division within a single society which had always contained both, the nationalist could imagine the existence of an Arab unity which, in reality, was very far from the fact.

While these facts made possible the extraordinarily rapid spread of nationalism they were in themselves dangerous, for they made it appear that all that was needed was a single act of political emancipation for a new, united, and democratic state to come instantly into existence. A certain democratic equalitarianism had always existed in the Arab world, particularly among the bedouin, but exemplified also in the village council. But it was the democracy of Anglo-Saxon rather than of nineteenth-century England, the democracy of a simpler social life, untroubled by responsibility for major political decisions, and entirely unfamiliar with the ballot box, the political representative, or the machinery of party politics. After 1908 Arab representatives sat in the new Turkish parliament, but as a training in democratic election or action, such an experience was negligible, and in any case lasted only eight years and affected a few dozen effendis.

It is these facts which explain the unusual phenomenon of a national movement which had no foundations in the prepared soil of either popular religion or popular education, which had no economic or social programme, and scarcely a vestige of even local administrative experience, which was exclusively political in the narrowest sense, and showed little awareness of the day-to-day problems which would arise if its political objective were reached.

The earliest beginnings of the movement are traced by George Antonius in *The Arab Awakening* directly to the University of Beirut and to other foreign colleges. Apart from a revolutionary poem, circulated from mouth to mouth in 1857, the first serious steps were taken when a group of five Christian students at the college in 1875 formed a secret society with revolutionary aims. They established contact with friends in Damascus, Tripoli and Sidon, and took as a method of action the pasting up of proclamations on the walls of their respective towns. These posters could count on rousing some popular sympathy, for Abdul Hamid had in recent years disappointed his subjects by his immediate withdrawal of the constitution he had himself proclaimed in 1876. But on the other hand, he was rather successfully posing as a champion of Islamic unity and piety in terms which flattered his Arab subjects, and the posters produced no more than a passing excitement. During the next twenty years the spies of the government made it unsafe to stay in Syria, and the nationalist movement took root in Egypt – where its first leaders were Syrians, including al-Kawakebi – and there it developed an entirely independent programme.

It was not until the Young Turks' revolution in 1908 that activities recommenced among both Muslim and Christian Syrians. For a brief moment the revolution had caused a wave of enthusiastic fraternization among all the peoples of the empire; but this moment soon passed as it was realized that the Young Turks were set on carrying out a policy of turcification, and were capable of doing it more efficiently than Abdul Hamid. Four main societies came into existence at this period, and it is at this moment that the names of Arabs from The Land are first found among the nationalists. It is interesting that none of the movements originated on Syrian soil. Two were formed in Egypt, and showed how much more mature the nationalist movement had become in that country. They aimed at the decentralization of the empire, and at the development of either provincial autonomy or a dual monarchy. Among the members of these societies were several from The Land who were later executed during the First World War – Salim Abdul-Hadi of Jenin, Hafiz as-Said of Jaffa, and Ali Nashashibi from Jerusalem. A third society, of which Jamal Husseini of Jerusalem was a member, was formed in Constantinople. The fourth and most extreme, Al-Fatat, was formed in Paris and included among its members Auni Abdul-Hadi and Rafiq Tamimi of Nablus. In the few years which remained before the outbreak of war none of these societies managed to secure any satisfactory concessions from the Young Turks, who had become as adept at evasion as Abdul Hamid; and in 1914 an Egyptian officer, Aziz Ali al-Mazri, formed from their membership a secret group (Al-Ahd) composed almost entirely of army officers. Through them he hoped, at the appropriate moment, to secure adequate military support for an Arab rebellion. For if he secured the officers he believed that the Arab conscripts would follow them in fighting the Turks.

It will be seen that few from The Land had become directly involved in the nationalist movement at the outbreak of the war, but these few represented some of the most important families in the country, and their influence could be considerable. The movement had scarcely gone further, though later events proved that some understanding of what was at stake had begun to penetrate through the urban section of the population. It had not reached any numbers of the fellaheen, and it still lacked any social or economic policy of the kind which would be likely to attract them. In this the Syrian movement remained well behind the Egyptian which was still following an independent course.

One feature both shared : a profound and increasing distrust of the European powers. Though the Syrian movement would certainly not have come into existence at all without the work which had been done by educators from all the western countries, yet, with the sole exception of the Americans, all these powers were suspected of pursuing ulterior political aims in their willingness to spend large sums on educational and medical work in the Middle East. The ambitions of Russia were scarcely veiled. The *mission civilisatrice* of France, as exemplified in North Africa, alienated all except the Maronite and Melkite Churches of the Lebanon which looked to French support against the eastern Christians. The arrogance of Britain in Egypt and the Sudan, and her refusal to treat Egypt as an equal and independent power, damned her equally with France and Russia. And had Italy entered into consideration, her conquests in North Africa would have turned the Arabs against her.

CHAPTER FOURTEEN

The Jews and the Beginnings of Zionist Settlement

AT the beginning of the nineteenth century the Jews of The Land were possibly fewer than they had been at any time since the beginning of this history. The most populous centre was Safad, where they numbered some thousands. But Jerusalem, when it was visited by Sir Moses Montefiore in 1827, had less than a thousand. In 1839, however, we have the advantage of a report on the Jewish situation made by the first British consul in Jerusalem. This shows that the situation was then reversed, and Safad had sunk to the second place. It had passed through a series of disasters, of which an epidemic of plague in 1812 and an earthquake in 1837 were the most serious. In consequence Jews went increasingly to Jerusalem instead of to the northern holy city. The consular report gives the following figures for the Jews throughout the country. Jerusalem stood first with 5,000. Safad came next with 1,500. Of the two other holy cities, Hebron had 750 and Tiberias 600. A certain number of Jews, presumably engaged in trade and commerce, lived in the three sea-coast towns of Acre (200), Haifa (150) and Jaffa (60). Apart from the holy cities, the only inland town in which Jews were discovered was Nablus, where there were 150. In the villages there were estimated to be about 400. This gives a total population of round about 10,000.

At the beginning of the period the largest community was that of the Sephardim. Since its establishment after the expulsion from Spain it had absorbed earlier elements, and it continued to absorb most of the Jews from the east who came to the country. The Ashkenazim increased rapidly during the nineteenth century, and in 1857 secured the right to build a new synagogue in Jerusalem through the mediation of Sir Moses Montefiore. There were also smaller communities from countries within the Turkish Empire and other Arabic-speaking lands. Of these three communities the Ashkenazic was the most abnormal, in that it largely consisted either of elderly persons who desired to die in the Holy Land, or of young students, whose passage thither had been financed in order that they might concentrate exclusively on pious study. All communities alike lived in extreme poverty, for even those who desired to earn their own livings had few openings for doing so. They were very largely dependent on external support. Many of the Ashkenazim brought some funds with them. These they deposited with the community and received in exchange a pittance on which to live; but many depended entirely on the annual collections made in the synagogues of the Diaspora (the Halukkah). As these contributions were irregular, the community contracted what were, for them, enormous debts with local non-Jewish moneylenders, and the payment of interest (usually fifty per cent or more) formed the first charge on money sent from abroad.

In addition the method by which these monies were collected was extravagant and unsatisfactory. The rabbis of Jerusalem licensed collectors to visit different parts of the world and to receive the collections made. They had to deduct the costs of travel – often for a period of one or two years – out of the funds received, and, in addition, expected to receive up to a quarter of what they finally brought back as honorarium for their work. In 1880 these collections were found to amount to an annual sum of about £60,000. But, once the various costs were deducted, the amount received by the individual Jew was inadequate to keep body and soul together. Yet to the Turkish authorities and the Muslim and Christian inhabitants of Jerusalem the reception of sums from abroad gave the impression that the Jewish community was wealthy, and they increased their exactions accordingly. In the hierarchy of misery and exploitation, the place of the Jews was at the top. The Christian might be ill-treated with impunity by the Muslim. But the Jew had to suffer from both the Muslim and the Christian.

Like all other sections of the population they owed the first steps in the improvement of their condition to the work of foreign visitors. It was in 1827 and 1838 that Moses Montefiore (1784–1885) made his first pilgrimages to Jerusalem, and excited the amazement of the whole population, Muslim and Christian as well as Jewish, by the sight of a Jew who was not only a man of wealth and standing among the 'Franks', but was the personal friend of Mehmet Ali, and received with an official welcome by the governor of the city. Throughout his long life Montefiore laboured unceasingly for the good of the Jews of The Land. He made seven visits to the country, and in 1840, at the time of the ritual-murder accusation in Damascus, he procured a valuable firman denouncing the accusation. This was of great value when in 1847 a similar charge was launched from the Orthodox convent against Jerusalem Jews. In his earlier visits Montefiore made various plans which would, he hoped, lead to a resettlement of Jews in the country. But the impossibility of obtaining satisfactory conditions from the Turkish authorities turned his mind more and more to the immediate problems of rescuing those already living there from the demoralizing effects of Halukkah, and of finding some means to enable them to earn their own living. He was able somewhat to improve living conditions, partly by the erection of a group of cottages outside the Jaffa gate; and he made tentative, though not very successful, experiments in the agricultural field. But his main contribution lay in none of these precise plans, but in the impression made by his personality, as a distinguished English Jew, on the authorities and Jewish population of Jerusalem, and in the interest in the Jews actually living in The Land which his visits aroused in western Europe.

The greatest practical results in these early days came, not from western Jewish efforts, but from the establishment of a British vice-consulate, soon raised to a consulate, in Jerusalem in 1838. On 31 January 1839, Mr Young, the first to hold the post, received the following brief minute from the Foreign Office:

I am directed by Viscount Palmerston, to state to you that it will be a part of your duty as British Vice-Consul at Jerusalem to afford Protection to the Jews generally: and you will take an early opportunity of reporting to his Lordship upon the present state of the Jewish population in Palestine.

In November of the same year he received further instructions, explicitly permitting him to extend his protection to Jews who were subjects of other European powers, did the consuls of these powers at Alexandria (he was still the only European Consul in

Jerusalem) request him to do so. The actual setting out of which such instructions arose will come to be considered later in the chapter; but their value to the Jews already resident in the country, and to Jewish immigrants who arrived there, is obvious. It was the first time that any European power had definitely interested itself in their lot. France protected Latin Christians; Russia had pretensions to exercise the same authority over members of the Orthodox Church; but the Jews had had nowhere to turn for the representation of their interests, or their protection from local injustice. Though to a varying and diminishing degree, this protection of Jews was one of the most onerous and important tasks of the Consulate. It was also an extremely delicate task, and not infrequently involved the consuls in difficult negotiations with both the Turks and the other European consular offices. In the end the matter dropped, but from 1839 to 1893 it played a considerable part in local Jewish history.

The presence of such a consul in Jerusalem from 1839 onwards rendered that city for the first time a relatively safe residence for members of the Jewish and Christian minorities. Christian activity has already been described. What The Land meant to the Jewish people can be seen from the statistics of the population of Jerusalem. During the decade preceding the Consul's arrival the Jews probably numbered about 3,000 out of a total population of about 11,000. Ten years after his arrival a Christian deputation from Malta's Protestant College gives a total population of 15,000 with the Muslims at 6,000, Jews at 5,000, and Christians at 4,000. In 1872 the Jewish population just outnumbered the combined Christian and Muslim inhabitants (Jews 10,600, Christians 5,300, Muslims 5,000). In 1899 the comparable figures were: Jews 30,000, Christians 10,900, and Muslims 7,700. Figures for the Jewish population in the whole country in the nineteenth century are more difficult to obtain, but an estimate of 1888 put it at 45,000.

The most interesting of the consuls on whom the duty of protecting Jewish interests devolved was James Finn, who occupied the office from 1845 to 1862, and whose wife was the daughter of Dr Alexander McCaul, the most learned and prominent leader of the London Society for Promoting Christianity among the Jews. This meant that Finn and the missionary station in Jerusalem were in very close contact with each other, a situation which had obvious disadvantages, as well as assets. The disadvantage lay in the suspicion which was inevitably aroused among the rabbis and Orthodox Jews of Jerusalem that all the activities of the British Consul were tainted with designs for their conversion. The advantage lay in the voluntary support which Finn was able to enlist for various projects for the betterment of the Jews, and in the fact that both Finn and his wife were accomplished Hebrew scholars. Jews who came to the Consulate were sure of being assisted with a devotion which went far beyond official demands. He was, in fact, constantly being rebuked by his superiors for having exceeded his duties and powers in the services he rendered the Jews of Jerusalem. Like Montefiore, Finn was always seeking opportunities to enable them to earn their own living, and during the distress caused by the Crimean War he provided several hundred with agricultural work both at Urtas, south of Bethlehem, and at Talbiyeh outside Jerusalem, and these schemes were completely free from any proselytizing activity.

In the visit which he paid to Cairo and Constantinople in 1840 at the time of the ritual-murder accusations at Damascus, Montefiore was accompanied by Adolphe Crémieux, a leading member of French Jewry, and from that time onwards French Jews also became interested in the difficulties of their brethren in the Holy Land. Members of the French branch of the house of Rothschild undertook projects similar to those of Montefiore. The founding of the *Alliance Israélite Universelle* in 1860 made it possible to lay a foundation firmer than the benevolence of individuals, and the *Alliance* gradually came to represent the philanthropic interests of British and American, as well as French, Jews in all matters affecting the lot of their brethren in the east. In 1870 the *Alliance* bought a considerable tract of land outside Jaffa, and there founded an agricultural school, Mikveh Israel, which has endured till the present day. Ten years later they began to establish primary schools for boys, but by that time the situation had changed, and the emphasis was passing from work for the already existing Jewish community to projects of resettlement which led in turn to a new form of agricultural activity.

The transition was provided in 1875 by the pioneer purchase of land north of Jaffa for agricultural work by a group of Jews from Jerusalem. The site was named Petah Tikvah (gate of hope), but the site was swampy and malarial and, like all other early projects, it only survived with the aid of outside help. But that does not lessen its importance as a first effort, made by Jews of The Land by themselves, to build a new life on a foundation of agriculture. The experiment was quickly followed by similar efforts undertaken by Jews from Romania and Russia. In order to understand this development we need to go back to a much earlier period and follow the discussions, among Christians as well as Jews, as to the possibility of resettling substantial numbers of Jews on the soil of the land of Israel. In chapter eight the continuity of the Jewish relation to the Promised Land, and the various forms which that relation took, have already been discussed. In the nineteenth century the perennial hope expressed itself in new ways and with a new intensity.

The action of Lord Palmerston was in large measure due to the influence of Lord Shaftesbury, who had become convinced that a Jewish resettlement would be advantageous not only to the Jewish people, but also to the sultan, who could count on the loyalty of new subjects who would, at the same time, restore a desolate province to prosperity. At the time when the powers were decided to compel Mehmet Ali to abandon Syria, but were still uncertain of its future, the project was mooted of creating a Jewish commonwealth in the southern half of the country – i.e. in the area of Biblical Israel. That nothing came of these projects was in some measure due to the fact that western European Jewry was primarily engaged in the struggle for its emancipation and its consequent assimilation, and saw no point in the political re-establishment of a Jewish nation.

While, therefore, practical programmes of resettlement, largely initiated by benevolent Christians, languished for a period in the West, the struggle was taken up within Jewry. A number of rabbis in Germany and Poland, of whom the leader and most distinguished was Rabbi Zvi Hersch Kalischer (1793–1874), put before their depressed and persecuted brethren the idea of resettlement in the land of Israel. The main opposition which Rabbi Kalischer found himself compelled to meet arose from the belief that such an idea, effected by human agency, was in conflict with the messianic beliefs of orthodoxy. In 1860 Kalischer called a conference at Thorn, where he was rabbi for forty years; and in 1861, as an outcome of the conference, there was founded 'The Society for the Colonization of the Land of Israel'. It was partly due to the influence of Kalischer and his followers that Mikveh Israel was founded by the *Alliance* in 1870. Meanwhile a Jew of a different type, Moses Hess (1812–75), was expressing similar ideas. Hess had been a political journalist, and at one time a colleague of Marx and Engels. He took part in the revolution of 1848 and after its failure withdrew from politics and went to live in Paris. There in 1862 he produced *Rome and Jerusalem*, a book which laid the intellectual foundations of Jewish nationalism.

It was nearly twenty years before there were practical consequences from these and similar books and projects, whether of Christians or of Jews; and by that time the scene had shifted farther east, to Romania and Russia. The Jewries of these countries were largely ignorant of the earlier discussions in western Europe, and came to the idea primarily through their own troubles. In both countries their lot was exceedingly miserable. They possessed none of the rights of citizenship, but were expected to shoulder most of its burdens; while their own social and economic existence was curbed and limited in every direction by administrative and legislative action designed expressly to keep them in a state of poverty, ignorance and subjection. Two events brought matters to a crisis.

In 1878 the Congress of Berlin attempted to ensure that the Jews of Romania should be guaranteed equality of citizenship with the rest of the population. Though they sought to make this grant a condition of recognition, the Romanian government evaded its obligations successfully right down to the outbreak of the First World War. Instead of citizenship the Romanian Jews saw their position continually deteriorate, and the thought of emigration became urgent in many Jewish homes. Three years later an even more signal disaster overcame the Jews of Russia. In 1881 the Tsar Alexander II was murdered, and the bureaucracy, seeking a scapegoat, laid the blame on the Jews. Pogroms, inspired by the authorities, broke out in many towns, and on top of mob violence the Jews found themselves subjected to even more rigorous restrictions than those from which they had previously suffered. The result was a mass emigration, amounting in the end to millions. The greater part fled westwards to the industrialized centres of Europe where work could easily be found, or to the new world. The Jewish community in the United States grew annually by tens of thousands of members. But a few turned their thoughts away from a further life in the Diaspora to the idea of settlement in the land of Israel, and listened willingly to the summons which was being issued from many centres by various Jewish voices.

There had come into existence in Russia a movement known as *Chibbath Zion* (Love of Zion), supported by such men as the novelist and journalist Perez Smolenskin (1842–85), Moses Leib Lilienblum (1843–1910), the reformer, Eliezer Ben-Yehuda (1857–1922), who out of the ancient language and all scraps of modern usage, recreated Hebrew, and Leo Pinsker (1821–91), the author of the rousing pamphlet *Auto-Emancipation*. Societies of *Choveve Zion* (Lovers of Zion) sprang up in many cities, and began to spread rapidly to the West, and even to America; and in the same year, 1881, a group of Jewish students of Kharkov University toured the country with the slogan 'Oh house of Jacob let us go forth'. The initial letters of this slogan in Hebrew formed the letters *BILU*, and they were known as the Biluim. The organization spread so rapidly that in 1884 it summoned a conference in Kattowitz to discuss methods of supporting the settlements which were already being established, and as a result of this conference a central office, charged with raising funds, was set up in Odessa under the chairmanship of Pinsker. At about this time one of the most sensitive critics and, at the same time, profoundest writers of the early years of the movement made his appearance, Asher Ginsberg (1856–1927) who wrote under the name of Achad ha-Am. His first article was a call to fuller preparation, spiritual as well as material, before colonization could be pushed forward.

Meanwhile the first steps had been taken in The Land itself. From a Romanian committee in Galatz two groups had actually set sail and arrived early in 1882. One settled at Samarin (later re-named Zikron Yaakob) in the hills south of Carmel and the other at Rosh Pina (Cornerstone) on the road from Tiberias to Lake

Huleh. Only a short while afterwards the first two colonies of the Russian Biluim were established at Rishon le Zion (First in Zion) and in the temporarily abandoned Jerusalem colony of Petah Tikvah. A fifth settlement, founded by Jews from Poland, was established in the following year north of Rosh Pina. We have an account by Laurence Oliphant of the first days of the settlement at Samarin, and a report a year later from Mr E. F. Veneziani, a member of the central committee of the *Alliance* who was visiting the east in connexion with the *Alliance* schools. From these two accounts it is easy to see what difficulties the new settlers faced and with what naïve inexperience they faced them. Oliphant, who was a thoroughly sympathetic witness, speaks of the Romanian Jews as 'effeminate be-ringletted townsmen' forming an extraordinary contrast to the fellaheen on whom they relied for cooperation in the actual agricultural work. Mr Veneziani a year later found the colonists at the point of starvation and on the brink of abandoning the whole project. Nor was the situation any better in the other colonies. The colonists brought enthusiasm, but neither experience nor the physique which could resist the rigours of the climate, especially the malaria which resulted from the swamps and undrained rivers.

To increase their difficulties the Turkish government opposed itself firmly to the whole movement, and for the first time in history Jews were subjected to an ordinance that they might visit the country on pilgrimage, but that they were absolutely prohibited from acquiring the ownership of land or taking up permanent residence. For a short time it was uncertain whether the Russian government might not insist on the extension of the right of all Russian subjects to acquire land in Palestine – a right guaranteed by treaty – to cover Jewish immigration; for Russia was not averse to Jews leaving the country. But in the end nothing was done, and in most cases the settlers had to acquire their land by a number of more or less inconvenient subterfuges. At first the local population was often as hostile as the Government, and the settlers had to suffer from attacks both from the bedouin and from the neighbouring fellaheen. But at this moment, when the whole project seemed doomed, a French Jew, the Baron Edmond de Rothschild, came to the rescue.

The next fifteen years were years of difficulty, of internal hesitations and of conflicts. Some new settlements were built, and some new settlers arrived. But many left in disgust, for in their enthusiasm the propagandists had painted rosy pictures of the wealth and prosperity which could be immediately attained. In the settlements to which the Baron gave his assistance there were difficulties of another kind. Convinced that the settlers needed the guidance and control of experienced agricultural experts, the Baron confided the direction of his enterprise and the disbursement of the vast sums he provided to men with whom the settlers were frequently at variance, and who tried to carry matters with a heavy hand, relying on the paternal authority of the Baron. Their conception of agriculture was a western European one, relying largely on exports and not concerned to develop a subsistence industry largely consuming its own products; and they followed also the western capitalist idea of seeking the cheapest labour for their production. Such labour could evidently be more easily provided by Arabs than Jews, so that many of the settlements ended in the spectacle – utterly at variance with the original ideals of the Choveve Zion – of a Jewish 'planter class', protected by bribes paid to the most powerful sheikh in the neighbourhood, working under the strict direction of French or other experts, with Arab labour, for the production of goods which needed to be exported in order to be used. Vines were one of the main crops on the Baron's settlements, but he was sometimes obliged to buy the whole vintage himself, since it proved impossible to find a market for it.

The year 1897 marked the opening of a wholly new phase in Zionism. Up to that time it had been a mainly eastern European movement, resting on the twin foundations, one idealistic, that of seeking a rebirth under conditions of freedom of the Jewish tradition and culture, and the other practical, that of seeking some spot where it was possible to earn a decent living. But in that year a congress was summoned at Basle of members of the Jewish community throughout the world to deliberate about their future. The summoner of that congress was Dr Theodor Herzl, and he was almost wholly unaware of the events in Russia, Romania and The Land already described. That such a situation could arise was evidence of the anomalous position of the Jewish people in the nineteenth century. That which lay behind the action of Dr Herzl was the evidence of Jewish insecurity even in lands where political equality had been granted. From 1879 onwards a new anti-semitic movement had been making considerable headway in Germany and Austria–Hungary, and Herzl himself had experience of it in his home, Vienna.

It might, however, have seemed to so completely assimilated a Jew as was this Austrian journalist and playwright to be a mere political flash in a pan which could not long survive German stolid commonsense or Austrian culture. But in 1894 Herzl went to Paris as correspondent of the Viennese *Neue Freie Presse*, and found himself reporting the Dreyfus trial. The sight and hearing of the French crowds howling like wild animals for the blood of Dreyfus and the Jews provoked a profound revulsion; for France was the pioneer of emancipation and boasted itself the centre of civilization and culture. Herzl had no knowledge of Jewish culture or tradition; he suffered no economic hardship; but he became convinced that his political security and self-respect could not be assured so long as Jews lived in the anomalous position they occupied in their dispersion. He had no particular interest in the land of Israel but was convinced that Jews must have their own state somewhere to which they could turn if life was made intolerable in other lands.

Eastern European Jews, and Palestinian settlers were, at first, sceptical of the activities of Herzl. They were present at all the Zionist Congresses, but gradually drew round themselves a party called the 'practicals', opposing the schemes of supporters of Herzl who were dubbed the 'politicals'. They wished to see the settlements extended by every possible means, and regarded as temporary and unimportant the subterfuges and difficulties which the actual purchase and settlement of land involved. To Herzl and his followers these difficulties not only deprived the settlement of proper dignity, but involved dangers to the whole of his scheme for the achievement of security by the establishment of a Jewish state. For Turkey continued to reject all demands by which the Zionists sought legally to purchase land in The Land, and had gone so far as to prohibit it by law in 1882 and 1891. Though the law was never strictly enforced, it gave officials opportunities for unlimited demands for bribes to wink at its evasion. When the Young Turks succeeded Abdul Hamid they were no more favourable to settlement, and more efficient in putting obstacles in its way. Herzl desired to meet this situation by direct diplomatic intervention with the Porte, and by securing an open agreement by which an autonomous Jewish colonization on a large scale might take place. This objective stands first in the programme enunciated by the first Congress of 1897, and remained the official programme of the Zionist Organization up to 1914:

The aim of Zionism is to create for the Jewish people a home in Palestine secured by public law.

The Congress contemplates the following means to the attainment of this end:

1. The promotion, on suitable lines, of the colonization of Palestine by Jewish agricultural and industrial workers.

2. The organization and binding together of the whole of Jewry by means of appropriate institutions, local and international, in accordance with the laws of each country.

3. The strengthening and fostering of Jewish national sentiment and consciousness.

4. Preparatory steps towards obtaining government consent, where necessary, to the attainment of the aim of Zionism.

In his efforts to secure the recognition in 'public law' which he sought Herzl attempted to interest the Foreign Offices of Europe, and had several interviews with the sultan. When this was evidently not going to lead to practical results, the British Government in 1903 offered the Zionist Organization opportunities for settlement, first at al-Arish in the Sinai peninsular and then, when that proved impossible, on a stretch of land in the highlands of East Africa. This offer provoked a violent controversy between the practicals and the politicals. The latter were for considering it, and they included some disillusioned settlers; the former would consider no other country, and in this they were supported by the idealists to whom the rebuilding of Zion could take place in no other land than the land of Israel.

In the following year Herzl died at the early age of forty-four. There was no one of his stature to succeed him in his political activities, and power gradually shifted to the practicals, with the result that various developments took place in the building up of the new Jewish community.

In the meantime the 'non-Zionists' had also been active. The early settlements survived entirely by the generosity of the Baron Edmond de Rothschild; but their complete dependence on his philanthropy meant in effect merely a new kind of Halukkah, and was almost equally demoralizing. In 1899 he handed over all his interests to the Jewish Colonization Association (known as ICA). They reformed agricultural programmes as well as economic conditions in the settlements, with the result that they began steadily to improve. Meanwhile the *Alliance* continued its work of establishing schools. Between 1882 and 1898 schools of various kinds for boys and girls were opened in Jerusalem, Haifa, Jaffa, Acre, Safad and Tiberias. The *Alliance* was followed by other philanthropic bodies from western Europe and America.

In the early years of the twentieth century a crisis developed in both these fields of activity. The settlers complained that the overseers and experts appointed by the ICA deprived them of all independence, and that their administration was overbearing and bureaucratic; and at the same time the complaint was raised in the educational field that the French schools merely set out to create little Frenchmen, the German schools little Germans, and so on; and that none of them gave adequate or, in many cases, any place to instruction in Hebrew which was the language of the settlements. In consequence of these conflicts a new type of settlement emerged, and a new set of schools was developed.

The new settlements were the product of a new party within the Zionist Organization, the *Poale Zion*, a socialist party seeking to build settlements not on a 'planter' and individualist basis but as cooperatives in which no paid labour was employed, and all profits were equally shared among the members. The first of these settlements were Kinnereth and Dagania, on the southern shore of the Lake of Tiberias, founded in 1908-9. Only three others were founded before 1914, but it became a standard type of settlement after 1918. During the same period an attempt was made to solve the problem of cheap labour, by building Jewish workers' villages in the neighbourhood of the old individualist settlements, where by small holding, as well as by working on ICA estates, the worker might maintain a decent standard of living. The arrival of a number of Yemenite Jews helped in this direction. For they were hardy workers, spoke Arabic and were accustomed to the standards and the climate of the country.

The new schools started by, or in cooperation with, various sections of the Zionist Organization, all made Hebrew the foundation of their system. The language, however, was not introduced by them into the country. It is clear from many statements of Mr and Mrs James Finn that Hebrew was constantly employed by local Jews for their intercourse with each other, and that one of Finn's great assets as consul had been his ability to speak and write it fluently. He even reports that in the neighbourhoods of Safad and Tiberias the language was spoken by many of the fellaheen. The leadership in spreading schools wherever there were Zionist settlers was taken by the Odessa Committee. But a big step forward followed a conference of Hebrew teachers summoned in 1903 by Menahem Ussishkin, chairman of that committee and later one of the leaders of the community in The Land, at which an association of teachers was formed who took charge of the education service by forming themselves into a teachers' cooperative. It was the only such organization in the world. It was the teachers who in 1907 created in the Herzl Gymnasium in Tel Aviv the first Hebrew Secondary School.

The influence of the Zionist schools led to pioneering in new fields. In some of the old Orthodox Talmud Torahs modern subjects were introduced on to the curriculum. Arabic came to be taught in many Jewish schools. In 1909 the Bezalel School of Arts and Crafts was established in Jerusalem to develop native craftsmen and artists. In 1914 a Technical School was established in Haifa; but this was the cause of a considerable disturbance. For it was under German auspices and at the last moment the Board of Directors, who were appointed by the German organization, the *Hilfsverein der deutschen Juden*, decided that education should be in German. As the *Hilfsverein* had hitherto accepted Hebrew as the medium for instruction in the many schools in the country for which it was already responsible, this led to a strike of teachers and pupils. The outbreak of the war put an end to the controversy; but it also put an end to the use of European languages as the basis for instruction in purely Jewish schools. Though no beginnings had been made with the establishment of university teaching before 1914, land had been bought on Mount Scopus and funds were already collected. In this work one of the leaders was Dr Chaim Weizmann, who even earlier had pleaded at Zionist Congresses for a Hebrew University.

In the Zionist Organization the victory of the 'practicals' over the 'politicals' led to it taking an increasing responsibility for direct work in The Land. So long as the politicals were in power they had refused to involve the Organization in such questions until they could obtain a sure legal standing from the Porte. The practicals, realizing that this was not going to be achieved, set up a Palestine Office in 1907 at Jaffa, and at once advanced funds from the Jewish National Fund for the beginnings of Tel Aviv. They also established the Anglo-Palestine Banking Co. in the country, where it was the first modern bank and, as such, quickly made use of by merchants of all sections of the community. In a very short time it found it possible to establish branches all over the country with the protection and approval of the Turkish authorities. Another company which established offices at Jaffa was the Palestine Land Development Fund, which aided individuals to secure land, and undertook the first stages of its development. It was often its task to make land ready for settlement for owners who were still abroad.

By 1914 some 12,000 Jewish settlers were occupying and working about 100,000 acres of land. Much of the work had not been done by the Zionist Organization but by the Baron and by the ICA which administered the funds he provided and the land he had acquired. These holdings accounted for much more than half the total holdings in the country. A school system had been developed, under an almost bewildering variety of auspices, with the natural result that there was a bewildering variety of schools from the completely religious to the completely secular. Agricultural research and settlement experiment were sufficiently far advanced for it to be possible to say by 1914 that the Jews had both proved their ability to restore a prosperous agriculture to the waste places, and had forged the skeleton organization necessary to carry it further.

While Zionist settlers on the land amounted to about 12,000 in 1914, these were by no means the only new Jewish settlers in the country. Many Zionists themselves lived in the towns. But there had also been a considerable immigration based on the improved security and on the increasing possibility of earning a living by trade or craftsmanship. The whole Jewish population had grown to between 90,000 and 100,000 by 1914, and of these 50,000 to 60,000 lived in Jerusalem, where they formed the majority of the inhabitants, 12,500 in Safad, and 12,000 in Jaffa–Tel Aviv. In Jerusalem the Sephardic community numbered about 20,000, the Ashkenazic about 40,000. The former community included substantial settlements from many parts of the Islamic world. The wealthiest were the Bokharan Jews and the poorest those of Yemen and Morocco. The Jewish population had spread widely outside the walls of the old town, from the prosperous suburbs of the Bokharans to the cooperative townlets, such as Mea Shearim, in which different national groups lived with relatively complete self-government.

During the period between the Napoleonic and the First World Wars the Jewish community had developed from a poverty-stricken and persecuted minority of less than 10,000 in a population of possibly 300,000 to 400,000 to a very varied but energetic community of 100,000 in a population of about 700,000. And it had become a community making a contribution to the life of the country as a whole. The days of Halukkah were not over, but the majority of the Jews earned their livings in trade, in various crafts and, on the Zionist settlements, in agriculture. A third of the orange trade was theirs, and they had made substantial contributions to the development of new and better products in many fields. The community was served by a wide variety of schools for both boys and girls, and by a number of hospitals in which increasingly successful attacks were being made on the two major evils of trachoma and malaria. Much of the educational work, and all the medical, was at the service of the whole population, and was used by Muslims and Christians as well as by Jews. Though they were still exposed to the thievery and occasional violence which were regarded as natural by the bedouins and the fellaheen, on the whole good relations prevailed between Jews and the rest of the population. Certainly there was ample room for both in the country, and, apart from occasional hostile articles in the press, the nationalist movement had not sufficiently developed to present a serious problem.

PART FOUR

The Restoration of the Balance

CHAPTER FIFTEEN

The First World War and its Effects

THE story of the local population, and the impact on the country of diverse foreign interests, between the Napoleonic and the First World Wars have been reviewed in the four preceding chapters. Throughout the period the initiative came from abroad – from Turks as governors, Christians as educators, missionaries and archaeologists, and Jews as educators and settlers. While the balance in the whole country was changed by these activities, the extent to which different elements were affected varied. The whole population benefited from an increase in security, and the beginnings of hospital and medical services. To a lesser extent the whole population benefited from the educational work done; it led to a new life among the local Christians, and enabled them to challenge the supremacy of Greek nationalism in the Jerusalem patriarchate; it led to a renaissance in the local Jewish population, and the development of means by which they could free themselves from Halukkah; it led to the beginnings of an Arab renaissance, accentuated by reactions against the attempt of the Young Turks between 1908 and 1914 to impose a Turkish education on the Muslim population, and against the imperialism which the educating powers were showing in other portions of the Arab world. Unfortunately the elements of the population least affected by all these changes were the peasant cultivators and the nomad bedouins, and numerically these comprised the majority of the inhabitants.

Parallel with these new influences on the existing inhabitants came other developments, emphasizing the unique relations to the country of the Christian and Jewish civilizations. The protection of the European consuls and the reforms of Abdul Hamid led to the restoration of many of the Christian shrines and monasteries scattered throughout the countryside which had been destroyed in the previous centuries of Islamic rule or abandoned through the insecurity of the land and the hostility of the local Muslims.

It was not only in Jerusalem, Nazareth and Bethlehem that such shrines were rebuilt, but in all parts of Judea, Samaria and Galilee. A similar movement had taken place within Jewry. The population of all the Holy Cities had grown enormously, and at the same time the recurrent emphasis on resettlement had taken on a new meaning under the impetus of Zionism. It had created new Jewish settlements widely scattered through the land.

That which was lacking was any parallel interest on the part of Islam. The reform movements of the Wahhabi and Sanussi had not been followed by any comparable revival among the Muslim millions who were peasants or townsmen. A few wealthy Muslims sent their children to Christian or Jewish schools; Muslims of all sections of the population took advantage of hospitals and clinics. But Islam had developed no social or educational programme of its own. It had not even attempted experiments which had failed. The Muslims had become more law-abiding because it had become more dangerous to be lawless. Otherwise they had not changed; fatalism and resignation still ruled the lives of fellaheen and bedouins alike.

One of the best informed Englishmen in the country during the nineteenth century had been Colonel Conder, chief of the land survey of the Palestine Exploration Fund. Writing at the end of the seventies he had expressed the hope that regeneration would come from a kind of feudal state, led by the old landowning families which had produced such men as Fakhr ad-Din and Dahir. Scions of these families had been brought into touch with Arab nationalism at Beirut, Damascus, Constantinople, Cairo or Paris. But there was no sign within the country of the revival which he hoped to see. Order had led, as he foresaw, to an increase of population; but it had led to no general change of spirit. There were, as happily there are in all human societies, individuals in all walks of life who were generous in spirit and noble in character. They were to be found among the religious leaders, the bedouin and village sheikhs and the townsmen and fellaheen, men who would gladly and worthily have taken their places in a new and reformed society. But they remained isolated examples of what Islam could produce, and lacked that extra incentive which would have made them leaders of a national revival.

Such was the general situation when the Turkish declaration in November 1914 brought the country into the war zone. The actual course of military operations has been described in chapter eleven. But the country was as much affected by the general war situation as by actual military events. The European consulates were closed; most of the European educators had to leave; the great religious establishments of France, Italy and other countries were emptied, and many of them were commandeered by the Turks. The leaders of the indigenous Christians, the Greek and Armenian patriarchs, with their staffs, were deported to Damascus; and the Anglican bishop had to remain in Egypt. The majority of the Jewish immigrants of the previous thirty years had either Russian or Romanian nationality, and thousands retired to Egypt, though the bulk of the agricultural settlers stayed on their land. For this reason it is quite inaccurate to base the Jewish percentage of the population on the position when the Balfour Declaration was issued. In 1914 it was approximately thirteen per cent.

The Turks ruthlessly suppressed all manifestations of Arab nationalism; and a number of prominent Arabs paid with their lives for their patriotic ideals. As the war progressed, and particularly as the Turks retired before the advancing forces of Allenby, the peasants also were drawn into the maelstrom. Many tens of thousands were called up as conscripts, and most of these were sent to distant fronts. Food and livestock were commandeered, trees were cut down for fuel, and the work of months often proved more effective than the neglect of centuries in destroying the agricultural foundations of village life. Nearly all the improvements of the previous fifty years were swept away. When the British entered Judea and Jerusalem they found a land on the brink of starvation, and for their first year of administration the feeding of the population, countrymen as well as townsmen, proved their most urgent task.

A certain number of the inhabitants were drawn into active participation in the war against the Turks. As the revolt in the desert gathered momentum it drew in some of the bedouin tribes of Beersheba and Transjordan; as the Turkish forces retired northward some of the fellaheen soldiers deserted and melted back into the countryside, where they welcomed and assisted the advancing British. A few hundred took a more active part, including the future mufti, Haj Amin al-Husseini. Of the Jews, some of those who remained on their land did valuable work for the Allies behind the lines, and some paid with their lives for their courage. In Egypt a Jewish volunteer unit, known as the Zion Mule Corps, was formed and saw service in Gallipoli. Later four battalions of 'Judeans' were recruited, though largely from Jews of England, and saw service in Allenby's campaign.

Meanwhile the future of the Turkish Empire was being discussed throughout the Middle East and in the allied capitals in the West. In most proposals The Land was treated simply as a part of a larger whole – Syria, the Arab world, or the eastern Mediterranean area. All agreed that the whole should be emancipated from Turkish rule; all desired the advancement of the Arabic-speaking peoples; but the type of regime which was to succeed the Turkish was seen very differently in different quarters.

The Arab nationalists – including those of southern Syria – dreamed of a vast and united Arab empire, embracing all the Arabic-speaking peoples, Christian as well as Muslim, and entirely independent of any foreign influence or control. Intensely proud of the great period of the Arab caliphate, and almost wholly ignorant of the complex problems involved in sovereignty and independence in the twentieth century, they ignored the diversity of the area over which they demanded sovereign control, and the absence of any tradition of political unity between its different parts; and they were unrealistically and optimistically indifferent to their own lack of political experience, to the absence of that educated middle class on which a modern state rests, and to the existence within their borders of genuine interests which were different from their own, and of responsibilities which they were incapable of assuming.

In sharpest opposition to these Arab plans were those of the French. With the southern and eastern portions of the area in which the Arabs sought independence they had no concern. But in Syria, including The Land, they claimed a traditional interest and a *mission civilisatrice*, going back to the time of Charlemagne's relations with Harun al-Rashid. The French had never forgotten that it was Frenchmen who had been the leaders of the crusading movement. From France had come the successive dynasties of kings of Jerusalem. With the coming of the Turks it was to France that was granted the right of protecting European interests and the Latin Christians. French was the language of polite society in Egypt and the Syrian coast towns. In 1860 she had intervened with her forces to protect the Maronites of the Lebanon. In addition to this concept of a *mission civilisatrice* she had more frankly imperialist aims. She sought a balance in the eastern Mediterranean to the recent Italian conquests in North Africa, and a counterpoise to British influence in Egypt. For these diverse reasons she considered herself entitled to the control of a vast triangular area whose western side extended from the future Turkish frontier in Asia Minor down to Egypt, and whose eastern tip reached the Persian frontier beyond Mosul.

The claims of Great Britain were of a somewhat different order. She had no desire to extend her responsibilities unnecessarily, and her main concern with the Middle East rested on its geographical position athwart the routes to India and to the oil of the Persian Gulf. Strengthened by the experience of the Turkish advance to the Suez Canal in 1915 she desired to establish herself on its eastern side, and the obvious place for this was the bay of Haifa–Acre. Here she desired to create a naval harbour and base. Aden she already possessed at the south-western tip of Arabia, and she was in treaty relations with the local Arab amirs round the western shores of the Persian Gulf. She desired to have Basra as a military outpost in that area, and to be sure that no power in Baghdad could menace her oil or her route to India.

Finally there were local interests. Of these the Jewish was the more positive and extended to a desire for the establishment of a Jewish state on both banks of the Jordan, corresponding to the territory described in the second half of the Book of Joshua as the patrimony of the twelve tribes of Israel. There was also the Christian concern in the Holy Places, of which the guardians were France, the Vatican and Russia, and which was confined to the negative role of opposing any regime which might seem hostile to the proper maintenance of the Christian shrines, convents, schools and hospitals, or incapable of assuring security of access to them for Christians from other countries.

Needless to say the satisfaction of any of these interests depended on a victory of the Allies; for Germany and Turkey equally had ambitions in the region whose realization was incompatible with the desires alike of Arabs, Jews, French and British. Before any results could be enjoyed, victory, therefore, had to be won by hard fighting against a powerful and resourceful enemy.

All these factors need to be taken into account in considering the position in the Middle East. For the whole situation was fluid. Only in the simpler societies in the southern portions of the Arabian peninsula were the Allies being asked to recognize situations which had already come independently into existence and proved their reality. Everywhere else they were expected to assist new and hitherto unproved situations to emerge, and they could not necessarily foresee future incompatibilities and shortcomings. Those decisions which proved mistaken or unworkable were not due to conscious hypocrisy or double-dealing; supermen, working in a spacious tranquillity, would have made mistakes; actually the work of planning was undertaken in the middle of an exhausting war in which the Middle East occupied but a minor place; and even within single countries there were different interests and points of view which might lead to different local action or conflicting proposals.

It fell naturally to the British to take the first steps in regard to the claims and hopes of the Arabs. The forces engaged in the Middle Eastern theatre of war were almost wholly provided by Britain, India and the Dominions, and it was in the office of the British High Commissioner in Cairo that the first steps were taken. The Arab movement was not unknown to either the British or the Indian governments. In consequence there was a background of knowledge and of sympathy and understanding, and it was not only from reasons of military advantage that the British were prepared to lend their support.

The military need was, however, great. By the declaration that the war was a *jihad*, a holy war, which it was incumbent on all Muslims to support, Germany and Turkey hoped to be able to make use of Pan-Islam against the Allies. Had this been done, it might have caused grave embarrassment in India, Egypt and other parts of Africa and Asia where both Britain and France had many millions of Muslim subjects. While a *jihad* would be declared by the sultan as caliph, the support of the sharif of Mecca, as guardian of the holy cities and of the Prophet's flag, was essential for its implementation. Hussain, Sharif of Mecca, became thereby the strategic centre of political intrigues.

While stalling for time with the Turks, Hussain set himself to explore all other possibilities. He was able to learn in January 1915 that the Damascus Arabs looked to him to lead an Arab revolt. Simultaneously he let it be known in Cairo that he would be glad to know what were the feelings of the British. In March he sent his son Faisal on a pretended mission of loyalty to Constantinople, but with instructions, in passing through Damascus, to get into contact with leaders of the nationalist movement. He was able to return with a sufficiently encouraging report for Hussain to enter into discussions with the British in Cairo. There followed the well-known Hussain–McMahon correspondence, an exchange of letters between July 1915 and March 1916 in which the claims of the Arabs were put forward and the lines of British–Arab cooperation laid down.

The area which Hussain claimed for the Arab kingdom had as its frontiers the Mediterranean on the west, Persia on the east, and a line drawn through south-eastern Anatolia on the north. It extended to over one million square miles and contained something under ten million inhabitants. McMahon was unwilling to be drawn into a discussion of frontiers, since in any case it was not for Britain alone to decide such matters. Hussain however insisted and, after asking for instructions from the Foreign Office, on 24 October he sent a definition of the British point of view. He desired to exclude from the area in which the British would be committed to supporting an independent Arab kingdom certain places in the Persian Gulf area, and the Mediterranean coastal region with its many minorities, its complex civilization and its European contacts. He pointed out that these districts were not wholly Arab. He reinforced the conclusion by saying that Britain could not commit herself on regions which at the time of writing were claimed by France; and, as has already been said, France at that time claimed the whole Mediterranean coast as her sphere of interest.

It would probably have been better if McMahon had merely used some phrase like 'the Mediterranean coastal regions', but he gave a rough definition by describing the area as west of four important inland cities, Aleppo, Hama, Homs and Damascus. Damascus was then the most southerly city in Syria, for Amman was but an unimportant village. The misfortune is that it is not east but north of the whole area with which we are concerned. While, therefore, it is clear to a Jew or a Christian that there are just as important non-Arab and non-Muslim interests in the southern half of the coastal region as in the northern (Lebanese) half, a Muslim Arab reader of the letter in Nablus (and Hussain circulated the letter almost at once) could honestly believe that he lived in the area which was promised to the forthcoming Arab kingdom. Nor could the problem have been solved by McMahon definitely excluding 'Palestine', for there was no such place on the political map of Turkey in 1916.

Hussain did not, and in the circumstances, could not, admit the reservation of special French rights in the Lebanon and the rest of Syria. But, having said so firmly, he consented to waive further discussions until after the war. The next development took place between the British and the French. The result was the Sykes-Picot Agreement, in which Britain and France divided up the Arab world in just the way Arab nationalists were determined to resist. The whole area north of the peninsula was divided into two spheres of influence. In Syria France agreed to the establishment of an Arab kingdom with capital at Damascus under French tutelage but in the coastal region she insisted on her right to a direct French administration. However, she resigned her claims to the land south of Tyre; and it was agreed that the British should hold an area round Acre and Haifa for a naval base, and that the area to the south of this should be reserved for an international administration, set up after discussions with the Allies, as representing the Christian powers, and the sharif as representing Islam.

Its general terms leaked out in the summer of 1917 and created a difficult situation for those British officers who were seeking to persuade Arab prisoners of war to enlist with the British against the Turks. They declared they had been betrayed, and that they would not fight the Turks unless the whole of their demands for independence were acknowledged. Sir Mark Sykes, who happened to be in Egypt at the time, and whose sincere devotion to the Arab cause was well known, could only reply that any independence at all would be gained only by a victory in which the British were already shedding their blood; and that the Arabs had to choose whether it was better to fight for the next step in their march to freedom, or to refuse to fight unless they were guaranteed everything in advance. The desert Arabs under Faisal and Hussain were likewise proving to be no easy allies. Though they were fighting for their own freedom, they had to be led, fed, armed and supplied by the British at British cost; and even then only fought when it suited their own plans, and when they had been paid in advance in gold on a scale which would have made mercenaries blush.

Even their most enthusiastic friends, including Lawrence himself, are quite frank about the difficulties which the Arab campaign involved for the British. The Arabs in Cairo, who mostly came from the Damascus and Baghdad areas, equally demanded the privileged position that the British should, at the cost of their own lives and treasure, secure an Arab victory in which any diminution whatever of their maximum demands should be compensated for in cash. No nation has ever won its freedom on such terms. However, for the time, the crisis was averted by Sykes; there was sufficient confidence in British integrity to ensure that there should be no wholesale return to the Turkish side, and the British turned to other problems.

Discussions with the Zionist leaders had been carried on in London in a somewhat desultory fashion since the beginning of the war. The British were moved by both immediate political needs, and by a genuine sympathy with Zionist ambitions. It was an identical situation to that which had led to the discussion with Hussain; and the fact that in certain countries Jews might have possessed political influence of importance to the allied cause no more invalidates the promises ultimately made than the fact that Hussain might have declared a *jihad* against the Allies deprived the British promises to the Arabs of moral foundation. That

Zionist leaders should have chosen to seek the approval and assistance of the British was natural, not only because the British were primarily concerned with Middle Eastern operations, but because Britain had, in the past, been the country which had shown the most practical sympathy with the plight of the Jewish people.

The Zionists were anxious for the recognition of a Jewish state in the 'Promised Land' of the Bible; and from now until 1948 it is reasonable to use the word 'Palestine' with the proviso that the area covered by the word did not become a definite political unit until the formulation and subsequent definition of the Mandate (which excluded the area east of the Jordan). The Jewish demand seemed to the British too extreme, for the Zionists were as inexperienced politically as the Arabs themselves, and the arguments against surrendering the Mediterranean coast lands to an independent Arab state equally precluded the immediate creation of an independent Jewish state in a land in which there were vast interests which were not Jewish. On the other hand Britain recognized that the Jewish assertion of a historic interest in the country rested on genuine foundations, and that the extension of Jewish settlement in the country was a legitimate and possible objective. In November 1917 they therefore communicated, in a letter from Mr (later Lord) Balfour, the Foreign Secretary, to Lord Rothschild, as head of Anglo-Jewry, their support for 'the establishment in Palestine of a national home for the Jewish people' and promised 'to use their best endeavours to facilitate the achievement of this object'. At the same time they indicated that it should be 'clearly understood that nothing shall be done which may prejudice the civil and religious rights of the existing non-Jewish communities'.

The Balfour Declaration for the first time established a unit called Palestine on the political map. But there were two essential elements in political realism which it could not create. In the first place the Jews, who had through all the centuries clung to their right to settle in their Holy Land, had been so reduced in numbers and importance that they were not a recognized and accepted presence to the rest of the population as were the Christians in the Lebanon. In the second place, though the word 'Arab' was rapidly coming to be accepted as covering the indigenous inhabitants who spoke Arabic, independently of their religious or ethnic affiliation, there was no such thing historically as a 'Palestinian Arab', and there was no feeling of unity among 'the Arabs' of this newly defined area. Hence the unfortunate phrase used to describe the majority of the population in the Declaration – 'the non-Jewish communities'.

The Balfour Declaration did not 'give Palestine to the Jews'. It recognized that there existed already a historic Jewish right, not *to* but *in* the country; and it promised to assist the Jewish people in its development in such a way that the other rights in the country were not endangered. It equally did not 'give away what belonged not to it but to the Arab people'; for it had already refused to recognize, also on historical grounds, that the Arab claim to be exclusive owners of the country was justified. The Jewish association had always been connected with settlement; Jewish settlement had always been accepted by Muslim rulers until the end of the nineteenth century; and the Jewish population of the country had always been large as its political and economic conditions made possible. It was reasonable for Jews to say that the facts that their numbers had been reduced to a few thousands in the beginning of the nineteenth century, and had risen to a hundred thousand at the outbreak of the war in spite of great difficulties and hardships, were evidence that time had not weakened their associations or dimmed their memories.

Even apart from the Jewish issue, it was not in the least likely that either Britain or the Christian powers generally would have tolerated the continuation of the humiliating conditions which Christian institutions and the Christian population had so long endured under Islamic rule and Arab insults. The Christian Holy Places are not confined to Jerusalem, Nazareth and Bethlehem, but are scattered throughout the whole land. That so many churches and convents which had been built in past centuries still lay in ruins, or had been turned into mosques, dwelling houses and stables by the intolerance of Islam and the savagery of the local inhabitants, was no ground for continuing such a state of affairs. Orthodox, Roman Catholic and Protestant Churches alike had been striving to improve the spiritual and social conditions of the Christian population of the country for nearly a century, and would have energetically rejected the idea that their future activities were to be at the mercy of Arab nationalism.

While there was a definite intention to give recognition to Jewish and Christian associations with The Land, there was no deliberate desire to ignore the rights of the Muslim population or to minimize the fact that Islam also had entwined itself around the Jewish and Christian shrines and memories of the land, until it had come to possess an undoubted holiness for Muslims also. The objective named in an Anglo-French Declaration of November 1918: 'To secure impartial and equal justice for all, to facilitate the economic development of the country by inspiring and encouraging local initiative, to favour the diffusion of education and to put an end to dissensions that have too long been taken advantage of by Turkish policy' gave in outline the programme which all the friends of the Arabs hoped to see put into effect as soon as possible, under the aegis 'of governments and administrations freely chosen by the people themselves'.

There was, however, not only an over-optimistic belief that time would solve the problems incapable of immediate solution in Palestine itself; but there was a conception of a new world society within which the development of Palestine should take place which was tragically belied by the facts of the inter-war years. Palestine was never thought of as a refuge for Jews fleeing from increasing antisemitism in a world of nation states whose gates were closed to immigration. It was expected that it would draw the idealists, the religious and the pioneers in a new and more just social order. It was expected that there would be ample time to build creative relationships with an Arabic-speaking civilization likewise arising from a glorious past which had been overlaid for centuries by the oppression and indifference of Turkish rule. The Jews of Europe, protected by the new minority treaties, were thought to be secure. The whole project belonged to the world of the League of Nations, and the idealism of President Wilson, Dr Nansen and Lord Robert Cecil. That this world was stillborn was not the fault of the Jews.

CHAPTER SIXTEEN

The British Mandate

THE British association with Palestine began as a military administration, and then became a Mandate under the League of Nations. As such it was governed by Article 22 of the League Covenant which laid down that

Certain communities formerly belonging to the Turkish Empire have reached a stage of development where their existence as independent nations can be provisionally recognized, subject to the rendering of administrative advice and assistance by a Mandatory until such time as they are able to stand alone. The wishes of these communities must be a principal consideration in the selection of the Mandatory.

While this clause was adequate to form a basis for the administrations of Syria and Iraq, it did not wholly fit the Palestine situation, except on the purely Arab thesis. Doubtless the Jewish national home was considered to form part of the 'community' whose development was to be a 'sacred trust of civilization'; but, as in so many of the statements dealing with the Arab world and the Middle East, this is not clear. Actually neither the French interpretation of their rights and duties in Syria, nor the British interpretation in Iraq, met with the approval, or won the confidence, of the Arab leaders in those countries; and the following year was marked by more or less serious trouble in all three areas. In Palestine there were riots in Jerusalem; and though they were not serious in themselves, they marked the first moment from which it is possible to recognize the existence of a sense of common interest as 'Arabs' uniting the Christian and Muslim indigenous population of all classes.

It is frequently said, even by some who believe that the Balfour Declaration was fully justified, that it inflicted a very great injustice on the local, especially Muslim, population. It would be truer to say that it was 'a very great misfortune' for that population that so searching and unusual a challenge to their future came at a moment when they were so completely ill-equipped to meet it. Only tiny minorities had the education or experience which enabled them to emerge from the stagnation of some seven hundred years of Mamluk and Turkish rule. Even the word 'Arab' was only just beginning to have a uniting influence over the whole area, and it had singularly little effective content. It accentuated their misfortune that no Arab leader arose who was capable of doing for the Arabic-speaking peoples what Kemal Atatürk was beginning to do for their Turkish neighbours. The war had inevitably brought Hussain, Sharif of Mecca, into the forefront, because it would lie with him to declare or to refuse to declare a *jihad* against the enemies of Turkey, but he in no way really represented the population of what became Iraq, Syria, Lebanon and Palestine. The intolerant and puritanical Abdul Aziz Ibn Saud, who captured Mecca and dethroned Hussain in 1924, would have represented them even less.

It doubled the misfortune for the Arabs with whom we are concerned that there had been no Turkish administrative unit whose frontiers corresponded to those familiar to Jew and Christian as those of 'Palestine', so that there was no natural bond of unity and loyalty between the residents of one part of what became a single country and those of another. Not unnaturally the first meetings of 'Palestinian' Arabs declared that they wanted to be part of an independent Syria, and not a separate country on their own. But it would have been 'unjust' rather than 'unfortunate' if the post-war settlement had refused to recognize the rights and interests of Jews and Christians on the grounds that those who had been responsible for the erosion of those rights were not yet ready to restore them.

Nevertheless it can be readily admitted that the attempt to redress a balance whose deviation was the product of centuries, and to do it without injustice to those who had reaped the benefit of the deviation, was not an easy task; it created what was possibly the most difficult administration ever established. The whole conception of such an attempt to redress a balance, tilted by a long historic process, by a deliberate political act and a government administration was a novel experiment. It was unique because the situation of Palestine was unique; but, once the British administration was created, it raised the issue as to whether the officials involved in it were to be expected to endorse it before being accepted for service. To ask a candidate whether he understood and accepted a decision based on the interpretation in a political programme of the unique history of Palestine would have been an innovation which appeared impossible both to the military administration which followed the British armies and the civilian administration which followed the military; but the result was that, all through the period of the British connexion with the country, the task of the mandatory power was made much more complicated by the presence of individual officials in Jerusalem who made no secret of their disbelief in the Balfour Declaration, and in the concession of a favoured position to the Jewish people. They regarded Jews simply as a minority in a normal majority-minority situation; and they showed open sympathy with the majority in their rejection of the Mandate.

There was the additional problem that, from the very beginning, the machinery of administration was itself inevitably complicated. The two sections of the population differed considerably in the level of their civilization, and in their social and political needs; and they not only shared no common tradition but each possessed its own strong individuality. Moreover the acceptance of the Zionist ideal necessarily implied an indirect administration of the Jewish section of the population. The Jews of the world were to be given the chance to show whether they could rebuild their national life. It was not to be done for them; and from the moment when the Zionist Commission arrived in the spring of 1918 they were in some respects an autonomous body – an *imperium in imperio*.

The administration of the Arabs, however, was throughout direct; and it is natural for an administrator to have most interest in, and sympathy with, those for whom he is directly responsible. This, however, was merely another aspect of the problem that the type of public servant required for the one administration was not naturally the type best adapted for the other. Palestine, once it was handed over to the civilians, was under the control of the Colonial Office. That Office could provide experienced men accustomed to deal with the problems which faced the fellaheen and other Arabs; they were not always at home with the Jews who were mostly Europeans, often as well educated as themselves. But while this might be true from an intellectual point of view, in so far as political experience went Jews were as inexperienced as Arabs; and the sometimes utopian enthusiasm of the one was no easier to deal with than the sullen resentment of the other.

In 1921 the Palestine Arab Congress, a native Palestinian organization under the leadership of the Husseini family of Jerusalem, was created and sent a delegation of protest to London. In reply to their protest, Churchill, then Colonial Secretary, issued a White Paper which, in the opinion of the British, defined their commitment to Zionism in terms consistent with their general obligation under Article 22 of the League Covenant:

Unauthorized statements have been made to the effect that the purpose in view is to create a wholly Jewish Palestine. Phrases have been used such as that Palestine is to become 'as Jewish as England is English'. His Majesty's Government regard any such expectation as impracticable and have no such aim in view. Nor have they at any time contemplated, as appears to be feared by the Arab Delegation, the disappearance or the subordination of the Arabic population, language or culture in Palestine. They would draw attention to the fact that the terms of the Declaration referred to do not contemplate that Palestine as a whole should be converted into a Jewish National Home, but that such a Home should be founded *in Palestine*.

While the White Paper left a vague possibility that a Jewish state might emerge – and Churchill himself giving evidence before the Royal Commission in 1937 said that he did not intend to rule out such a possibility – it made it clear that the kind of society which the British expected to develop, and which they were ready to help to develop, was one in which Jewish and Arab cultures co-existed within a bi-national Palestine in which the Jews would possibly be a majority. The statement was officially accepted by the Zionist Organization as the framework within which they would work; but it did not satisfy the Arab demands, and when Churchill tried to get them to cooperate in setting up a legislative council as the first stage towards the establishment of representative bodies, they refused.

The text of the Mandate was drawn up and published in the same year – 1922 – though it did not come officially into force until the autumn of 1923. It showed a grave underestimate of the importance of Arab opposition, or indeed of the existence of the legitimate Arab grievance that their position was almost totally undefined in the various policy statements of the British government and the Palestine Administration. For the language which was used was such as is used of a minority – their civil and religious rights would be safeguarded; they would be recognized as equal citizens in the future state, and so on – and not only had they no intention of becoming a minority but, in actual fact, they were not one at the time these statements were being made. The Mandate, in its preamble, quoted in full the Balfour Declaration, and quite truthfully added that the opportunity was being given to the Jews to reconstitute their National Home; but it made no reference to any promises made to the Arabs, or to the obligations assumed towards them, not only in successive British statements but in Article 22 of the Covenant. In one clause of the Mandate after another priority was given to the opportunities to be allowed for Jewish development, and this could be justified on the grounds that a new political experiment required precise definition. But there was too complete a silence about the relations of this experiment to the normal development of the whole community. This was doubtless due to the fact that it *was* an experiment, and there is certainly no evidence that it expressed any intention or desire to reduce the Arab population to a position of permanent inferiority.

The Churchill White Paper preceded the issue of the Mandate, and it was the constant claim of the British that it was possible to fulfil their promises to both parties, and reconcile the reasonable ambitions of both Jews and Arabs in a harmonious whole. It was therefore a grievous error in judgement that no positive statement was made which could form the basis of cooperation with Arab moderate opinion, or, indeed, bring a moderate opinion into existence by giving it a worthwhile objective consonant with the Arab sense of national dignity. The Mandate contained terms for the setting up of a Jewish Agency, which was given very wide powers. No comparable Arab body was called into existence; and the Agency's powers were not related to, or made dependent on, the establishment of any wider body representing the whole country. This had the ill effect that Arab politicians had no executive responsibility for the welfare of the Arabs of the country. They could give their whole time to nationalist propaganda and agitation and to the struggles for power between the different families, while the work which was largely done by the Jewish Agency for the Jews was done for the Arabs by the British. Transjordan was excluded from the area in which the clauses dealing with the National Home should operate, as a natural consequence of the inclusion of it in the area in which Arab independence was promised to Hussain. But it caused a shock to Jewish opinion, and ultimately led to the formation of the Revisionist Party which demanded a revision of the Mandate to include Transjordan in the National Home. From the practical standpoint of Jewish–Arab cooperation it also had the disadvantage that it still further intensified the feeling of Arabs in western Palestine that they were destined to be swamped by the superior power, wealth and numbers of the Jews.

While the Mandate could and should have made more reasonable provision for the rights and future of the Arabs, the difficult position of the British was to some extent inherent in its nature. A mandate was temporary; the mandatory administration was not intended to become the centre of national loyalty; it had none of the attractions which a permanent government can build around itself. And in this case it had to recognize two conflicting communities without really possessing sufficient authority to bring them together. Education was an affair of each community; religious courts had wide and independent powers. Moreover the Administration was not a government, but had to obey orders from Westminster, which in turn had to submit reports to the Mandates Commission of the League of Nations at Geneva. As to the natural loyalties of its 'subjects', the Jews looked to the World Zionist Organization, and that organization appointed the executive which formed the Jewish Agency named in the Mandate. Later on other Jewish bodies were brought in; but it still remained true that the members of the Agency were most of them not even subjects of the Mandatory, and that the Mandatory had no say whatever in their appointment. The Christians had a wide variety of loyalties, few of them inherently Palestinian. For the 'Arabs' the centre of loyalty was the more intangible, but still real, conception of Arab unity, supplemented in the case of the majority by the unity of Islam.

Before dealing with the causes of the ultimate failure of the Mandate it is only fair to record two fields in which it succeeded, and which sufficiently disprove the arguments of either side that the British were indifferent, were partisans of one side or the other, that they entered into commitments without sufficient care, that they made contradictory promises without scruple for their own advantage, and so on.

In the first place events amply justified their belief that there was room for both peoples in the Palestine of 1917. The whole period of the Mandate not only showed an increase of the Jewish population to three quarters of a million, but it witnessed also the steady increase in both numbers and prosperity of the Arab population. There was even a substantial illegal Arab immigration during the period. The Arab refugees of 1948–9 were not the result of overcrowding.

In the second place the whole population benefited materially from the British Administration. At the end of the First World War Palestine was in a most desolate condition. On top of the ruin caused by centuries of neglect, the exigencies of four years of war had brought it near to starvation. Agriculture was almost at a standstill and three quarters of the populace had to live off the land. By contrast, in spite of continuous disorder in the later years of the Mandate and the inevitable devotion of much of its manpower and finance to public order, the fellaheen at the end of the Second World War were, for the first time in centuries, free from debt; medical, social and educational services were more widespread than ever before, and great advances had been made in communications, in water supplies, and in the modernization of the towns and cities.

It is only fair to pay full tribute to the British administrators and their Jewish and Arab colleagues for this state of affairs, since it has to be admitted that they failed completely to help the different elements of the population to cooperate for the common good. To lay the blame exclusively on their shoulders would be grossly unfair. The basic fault lay with the British government in London. With the hindsight of half a century one can say that the *injustice* to the Arabs lay in the fact that the government which had issued the Balfour Declaration never offered them a reasoned explanation of why they had done so. It was a unique action, and it should have been explained. No doubt Arab propagandists would have rejected the explanation, but its existence would have provided a solid basis on which discussion could have taken place between all the parties involved.

At a secondary level blame for this omission must be shared with the recipients of the Declaration: the Zionist Jews. They were not in any sense anti-Arab, and the Diaries of Colonel Kisch, the first chairman of the Palestine Zionist Executive, reveal on almost every page the efforts made to secure cooperation with the Arabs at all levels. It was, perhaps, inevitable that Zionists should look back to the heroic period of the Maccabees and Bar-Cochba, but their real title deeds were written by the less dramatic but equally heroic endurance of those who had maintained a Jewish presence in The Land all through the centuries, and in spite of every discouragement. This page of Jewish history found no place in the constant flood of Zionist propaganda, much of it as violent as it was one-sided. The omission allowed the anti-Zionist, whether Jewish, Arab, or European, to paint an entirely false picture of the wickedness of Jewry trying to re-establish a two-thousand-year-old claim to the country, indifferent to everything that had happened in the intervening period. It allowed a picture of The Land as a territory which had once been 'Jewish', but which for many centuries had been 'Arab'. In point of fact any picture of a total change of population is false, as the previous chapters have shown.

A second error of Jewish propaganda, arising from the same deficiency, was to base their claim on *the legality* of the Balfour Declaration. The Declaration was unquestionably legal, and its embodiment in the text of the Mandate justified. But, set beside the omission of the promises to the Arabs, that legality was entirely valueless as an argument to convince Arabs of the moral rightness of their ever-increasing presence. The constant insistence on the prior acceptance of the Balfour Declaration in any practical discussions with Arab leaders was not dishonest, but it was extremely stupid when they had, in their continual presence and its reduction through oppression and local lawlessness in The Land, a far more cogent argument.

It is also a false perspective that regards the issue as a conflict between *two* rights. The Palestine Mandate covered *three*, not two, indigenous groups. The usual picture of the components of the problem being just 'Jews' and 'Arabs' should have found some public and official repudiation in an acknowledgement of the presence of an ancient and living Christian community which had held on to its presence in the Holy Land with the same courage and under the same miserable conditions as their Jewish neighbours under centuries of second-class citizenship. In actual fact it would have simplified, not complicated, the position of the British, had a very diverse but living Christian community, with its churches, schools, hospitals and congregations been recognized as partner in the future, instead of a collection of Holy Places governed by a Turkish *status quo* which rested on no morality but on the balance of ecclesiastical bribery at a particular date. For the native Churches of Palestine, as the Mandatory found them, had a century of foreign aid behind them which afforded further, and entirely non-Jewish, evidence that it was *not* a 'purely Arab country'. Actually, having no recognized status of their own, indigenous Arabic-speaking Christians were obliged in many cases to purchase their security during the violent troubles of the thirties by being more passionately pro-Arab than the Muslims. This is not suggested in the belief that some kind of 'Christian Agency' could have been easily created. It would have been extremely difficult to get the churches to acknowledge each other's existence, let alone cooperate. But the creation would have been worth the effort.

In 1921 an appointment was made which turned out to be the most disastrous in the history of the Mandate. Public office in Jerusalem had long been divided between the families of Nashashibi and Husseini. As there was a Nashashibi mayor, Haj Amin al-Husseini was appointed Mufti of Jerusalem and President of the Supreme Muslim Council. But both families were rivals for a wider influence. Early in the twenties the Nashashibis formed a National Party in which they grouped their followers for a struggle with the Husseinis. In the municipal elections of 1925 they won a number of seats. Yet another blow at the domination of the party of the Mufti was the formation of a number of local 'National Muslim Societies' representing the interests of the peasants against the landowners. These societies were, partly at least, inspired by Chaim Kalvarisky, an old pre-1914 settler who knew and was known to the Arabs as a realistic worker for Arab–Jewish cooperation. But none of these efforts really succeeded in countering the power of the Husseinis embodied in the Mufti, who, as head of the Supreme Muslim Council, disposed both of funds and influence with which no other Arab leader could compete.

The Mufti openly fanned religious fanaticism to further his ambitions, making use of false accusations, such as that which provoked riots in 1929, that the Jews had designs on the Aksa Mosque, and that the Haram ash-Sharif was in danger. This was all the easier in that the whole temper of the Arab world was rising, and violence was affecting all classes in Syria and Iraq, as well as in neighbouring Egypt, though this last country was not yet prepared to consider herself part of the Arab world. An inquiry followed the riots of 1929, and found inevitably that the basic cause was Arab resentment against the National Home, but it had no mandate to look into the fundamental problems of the conflict. It recommended restrictions on Jewish expansion, and the wisdom of this appeared to be confirmed by a report prepared by Sir John Hope-Simpson, who had been Vice-President of the Greek refugees settlement commission of the League of Nations. Hope-Simpson's findings were that there was no spare land for further Jewish settlement until there had been a reform of Arab holdings and a development of Arab methods of farming, after which he thought there should be room for another 20,000 families. He also connected Arab unemployment with excessive Jewish immigration. The report was violently attacked by the Zionists, who claimed that he had seriously underestimated the amount of cultivable land in the country; and subsequent events have justified their scepticism. Even more dubious was the linking of Arab unemployment with Jewish immigration; for it ignored the extent to which Arab employment, in private agriculture, industry, and government contracts, was almost wholly due to activities consequent on the existence of the Jewish National Home and the substantial contribution which Jews made to the revenue.

The government accepted the Hope-Simpson report in a White Paper which in its language was markedly unsympathetic to the Zionists. But it also, though perhaps unconsciously, marked a profound revolution in British thinking about the terms of the Mandate. For it treated the Jews throughout as though they were a normal immigrant minority who could only be granted such rights as would not interfere with the maximum demands and needs, present and future, of the majority. It is easy to understand the shock which this caused to Jewish opinion; for it was a denial of their basic position that they entered the country 'as of right and not on sufferance'.

There followed the most serious crisis which had thus far befallen the National Home, and it came at a time when their fortunes were at a low ebb. There were less than two hundred thousand Jews in the country; the economic crisis which had just smitten the world had reduced the Agency's income, especially from America; and this betrayal, as they regarded it, was the climax.

Dr Weizmann resigned from the Presidency of the World Zionist Organization, a position which he had held from the beginning of the Mandate, and other prominent members of the Jewish Agency followed suit. The depth of Jewish emotion seems to have surprised the British government; and, in a letter from the Prime Minister, Ramsay MacDonald, to Dr Weizmann an effort was made to undo the effects of the White Paper by a somewhat lame explanation that it did not mean any abandonment of the policy enshrined in the Balfour Declaration and the Mandate. While this consoled the Jews, it merely enraged the Arabs still further, and lent colour to their belief that Jewish influence was so powerful that any measure in favour of the Arabs was instantly cancelled. On this uneasy note Palestine entered the second period of the Mandate, from 1929 to 1939.

The period which stretches from the disturbances of 1929 to the publication of the White Paper of 1939 is one of paradox. It witnessed simultaneously the breakdown and abandonment of the Mandate, as it had hitherto been interpreted, and the signal justification of the relevance and value of that interpretation to the Jewish people to meet whose needs it had been designed. Moreover, while Arab anger and violence increased catastrophically during the same period, the Arab population and its prosperity both showed an unparalleled expansion which, but for strikes and violence, would have been even greater. The increase in the Jewish population had at no point been balanced by a decrease of that of the Arabs, and increased Jewish prosperity was, in fact, reflected in increased Arab prosperity.

In this decade a new factor entered which increased the tension and widened the gulf between the three groups. Each was submitted to violent outside pressure irrelevant to the others but which made accommodation and understanding even more difficult.

For *the Jews* the pressure came from Europe. In Poland a hostile dictatorship and severe economic stress immensely increased the number of Jews who desired to leave the country. In Germany a similar economic crisis had, in 1933, helped to bring Hitler to power and after 1933 the position of German Jews was desperate. Moreover the gates of immigration remained closed in almost all the countries of the world – except Palestine where it was their anchor of hope that they were entitled to enter 'as of right and not on sufferance'. *The British*, themselves experiencing the economic crisis of the thirties, were witnessing the rapid increase of an aggressive policy first by Mussolini, then by Hitler, which they lacked the power effectively to oppose, and were increasingly swept into the policy of appeasement which led to the surrender over the Abyssinian war and to Munich. *The Arabs* were subject to continual broadcasts from Italy and flattering approaches from Nazi Germany, which invited them to align themselves with those dictatorships against the decadent imperialism of the British and the Jews.

In such a situation it is the better men who lose heart; the second-rate are prepared to drift with the tide, to become themselves partisan, and so to accentuate the problem they have given up hope of solving. And such a situation encourages the bully and the corrupt. How grave was the malady is shown by the paradoxical fact that this deterioration was taking place under the eyes of the noblest and most devoted of the High Commissioners, Sir Arthur Wauchope (1931-8) who spent himself and much of his private fortune in efforts to bring together the two communities and to assist the development of each. But in the end it was Sir Arthur's unwillingness to believe that it was impossible to bring the Mufti and the Arab leaders of the rebellion of 1936 to reason, which led to his refusal to declare martial law and take the strong military measures which the situation required.

It was, of course, only gradually that the inner deterioration became revealed. The first years of Wauchope's period of office were years of prosperity for both communities. Jewish immigration which had risen to nearly ten thousand in 1932 soared suddenly, through the Polish collapse and the Nazi regime in Germany, to over thirty thousand in 1933, and even that figure was surpassed by more than ten thousand in 1934 and more than doubled in 1935. In addition there was an illegal immigration of some thousands in these years, and the Jewish community reached a total of between three and four hundred thousand. Many of the immigrants, especially from Germany, were able to bring some capital with them. This rapid rise resulted in speculation in Jewish circles and in the Jewish press that the National Home might soon represent a majority of the population. This, it was said, would entitle Jews to press for the termination of the Mandate, and the establishment of a 'democratic' constitution.

So foolish a speculation naturally aroused Arab fears that they would be swamped by the Jews, but it still remained true that these fears belonged exclusively to the future. The Arab population continued to grow at a phenomenal rate; there was a substantial illegal immigration of Arabs especially from the Hauran. Arab prosperity increased through the increased activity of the Jewish community and the many new openings for employment which it offered. It is a cherished belief of the townsman of the twentieth century that the peasant never likes to leave his land. In actual fact peasants, in Palestine as in every other country of the world, cheerfully leave their land when opportunities of earning a better wage are offered in the towns. What is, of course, true is that during slumps or urban unemployment many country-men return to their villages; and after an economic panic in 1935 many Arabs returned to the villages, and being unemployed readily took part in the disturbances of the following years.

Nationalism was still mainly an urban and middle-class pre-occupation, though the 1929 riots had shown how easy it was to rouse the fellaheen by appealing to their religious fanaticism. But the sudden recovery of the Jewish community from the slump at the end of the twenties, and its immense immigration in 1933 and subsequent years naturally roused widespread political fears; and if the peasants were not conscious of having already lost their land, they could easily see that a continuation of such an annual increase might imperil their future position. All through 1933 the Arab press indulged in inflammatory articles against the British for having become the tools of the Jews; in the spring there was a boycott which still further reduced Arab participation in the activities of the Administration. In October there were riots in Jerusalem, Jaffa, Haifa and Nablus, and these riots were directed almost wholly against the British.

In November 1935 the five Arab parties combined to present the Administration with three demands: a democratic parliament, the prohibition of land sales, and the cessation of immigration. To the second and third the High Commissioner replied with a refusal; but he announced that he had secured the consent of the British Government to the establishment of a Legislative Council in which the official element would be much reduced, and twelve out of the twenty-eight members elected. The Jews absolutely refused to cooperate, and the proposed Council was violently attacked as a betrayal of the Mandate in the British parliament. The Arabs were disposed to consider it – if only because they felt that anything which aroused Jewish opposition would be favour-able to their cause; and the rejection of a proposal of the British High Commissioner by the British parliament, because the Jews opposed it, raised their bitterness to a new level. In April 1936, as soon as the citrus harvest had been shipped, they declared a general strike, to continue until Britain changed her policy.

While the strike was the joint work of the five Arab parties represented in the Arab Higher Committee, the Mufti had also his personal ambitions; and during the summer he began to organize, behind the façade of the strike, a more serious and violent rebellion, designed to bring him personally into power. With so much of the country idle, there were many elements which could be drawn into his schemes, and bands, half brigands, half adventurers, began to assemble in the hills and to attack Jewish settlements. In August Fauzi al-Kaukji, who had had much experience of military and guerilla operations in other parts of the Arab world, was brought in to complete the organization and training of what had become a guerilla army of some five thousand men. The nucleus was paid by funds received from Italy – some of which were handled by Italian religious institutions in Palestine – and by the misappropriation of the considerable Waqf endowments which the Mufti controlled as president of the Supreme Muslim Council.

The British had announced that a Royal Commission would examine the whole problem of Palestine, and that it would not sail until order was restored, but they were not able to keep their word. The Mufti's rebellion in the hills had not been quelled and sporadic violence continued; but the strike terminated and measures against the rebel bands were stopped. No attempt was made to disarm them. The termination of the strike and the continuation of a smouldering rebellion in the hills brought about a rift in the unity of the Arab Higher Committee. The landowners and businessmen realized that they had lost much and gained little by the activities of 1936; and they were increasingly opposed to the dictatorial actions of the Mufti. By the end of June of the following year the Committee had broken up and the Mufti had turned on his Arab opponents with the same violence which he had used against the British and the Jews; and for two years he terrorized them much more effectively than either of his two other opponents. The months of respite granted him by the Administration were used in reorganizing his forces, training them and bringing them under unified control. The two main bands operated from the Galilean and Samarian hills, while a smaller band was centred in Hebron. In addition he had a private gang of assassins, and scarcely a week passed without the murder of a landowner, a businessman or a village mukhtar who had refused to pay the blackmail demanded, or had opposed him in some other way.

Up to the middle of June 1938 the Jewish community had exercised remarkable self-control, and had confined its action to strictly defensive needs. But in the end there was inevitably some break in this attitude and some elements in Jabotinsky's Revisionist Party sought to counter terrorism with terrorism. How many actions were to be attributed to the Irgun Zvai Leumi and the Stern Band, both of which were formed during the Arab rebellion, it is impossible to say; for the Mufti's assassins were also using terrorist methods against the Arab population, and some of the bombs which exploded in Jaffa, Haifa or Jerusalem may have been their work.

It was not until the autumn of 1938 that the military completed the task of making roads which would enable them to take the offensive against the headquarters of the bands in the hills, and in October martial law was at last declared in a modified form which yet gave the army effective control of the situation. Once the bands began to be defeated in open battle their powers of blackmail and terror over the towns and villages began to diminish, and in the spring of 1939 their power was at last broken, though isolated terrorist actions continued right up to the outbreak of war. But for more than a year they had held practically the whole country in their control, and had caused immense loss of life and property to all sections of the community.

When the Royal Commission reported in 1937, it offered a number of criticisms of the Administration but it coupled these with the statement that it did not believe that, if all it criticized were put right, it would make any fundamental difference. Without a radical change of policy the British could only meet the Arab demands with continuous and wholly sterile repression, which could, by its very nature, lead to no improvement. The expectations of Jews and Arabs had become irreconcilable, and the Mandate had become unworkable. Facing the situation on the basis of both Jews and Arabs possessing rights in the country, they proposed a geographical partition as the only method by which each would receive something of their fundamental demands for self-government and control of their own political destiny. The actual division which they suggested allotted Galilee and the plains of Esdraelon and Jezreel, together with the maritime plain to south of Jaffa (but not including that town), to the Jewish state, and the central hill country and the whole of the south to the Arab. Jerusalem and Bethlehem, together with a wide corridor covering road and rail communications with Jaffa they proposed to leave as a permanent international Mandate.

The report was immediately rejected by the Arab leaders. The Zionist Congress which met in the summer of 1937, while not prepared to approve it, authorized Dr Weizmann to explore the matter with the British, but not to commit the Zionist Organization without further consultation. The idea of partitioning the Holy Land caused a considerable shock to opinion, and in the succeeding months many discussions were entered into, in which private Jewish and Arab personalities were involved, to see if a *modus vivendi* could not be reached. But, though the Jews showed some willingness to compromise, the Arabs did not, and a minority position in an Arab sovereign state was a solution wholly unacceptable to all shades of Jewish opinion.

The British government, in publishing the Commission's report, had published a White Paper announcing their acceptance of it. But when it came to practical proposals no reasonable division of the country was put forward. A stalemate ensued, the Administration became more desperate, and, after a futile attempt at an agreed solution in 1939, the British put forward a scheme for a unitary government of Palestine. This was to be achieved within ten years by a gradual devolution of power, with safeguards for the Holy Places and the Jews as a permanent minority, though a certain amount of immigration would still be allowed during the transitional period. This was proposed at a double conference in St James's Palace in February 1939. The government invited Egypt and the Yemen, as well as Iraq, Saudi Arabia and Transjordan to join the Arabs of Palestine at the Conference, as the Jewish Agency represented the whole Jewish people, not merely the Jews of Palestine. The scheme was rejected by both sides, and various informal conversations led to no result. The British therefore announced that they would put forward their own scheme and enforce it.

In a White Paper the government announced that it could not agree that the commitments which it had entered into under the Balfour Declaration committed it to continual unlimited immigration in the face of Arab hostility. It therefore proposed a maximum of 75,000 to be admitted at an annual rate of 10,000 over five years, with an additional 25,000 refugees from Nazi Germany to be admitted as and when the High Commissioner considered that the situation warranted it. After the 75,000 were admitted, there would be no further immigration without Arab consent. Whether there was ever any chance that this consent might have been secured under the conditions of this time is exceedingly doubtful.

The emotion which this proposal caused throughout the Jewish world can only be understood on the background of the pressure of events in Europe. In Germany, Austria and Czechoslovakia a million Jews were already crushed under the heel of Nazism; their civic rights had perished, and they were subjected to ever-increasing violence and robbery. But that was not all. The terrible menace of war hung over all the other Jewish communities of Europe, in particular over the three million Jews of Poland. And the doors of the rest of the world remained closed. Already Palestine had been able to absorb into new and creative life more refugees than either the United States or the British Empire. That the White Paper was a death blow to their political aspirations was bad enough. But what struck home to the least politically minded or the most ardent advocate of concessions to Arab opinion was that such a regulation meant in all probability the condemnation of millions of Jews to physical extermination at the hands of the Nazis.

In the White Paper it was foreseen that regulations would be subsequently published to deal with sales of land. These were delayed until war had actually broken out, and were only published in 1940. The blow they struck at Jewish development was equally serious. Throughout the hill country land sales by Palestinian Arabs to Jews, or any but other Palestinian Arabs, were wholly forbidden. In the plains of Esdraelon and Jezreel and in upper Galilee they could only be permitted under stringent restrictions. Only in the urban areas and the maritime plain from a little south of Jaffa to Carmel were Jews to be allowed freely to buy land. A Zionist Congress, meeting just before the outbreak of war, denied its legal and moral validity, and refused any cooperation of the Agency in its enforcement. At the same time they denied that they desired a conflict with Great Britain, or that their opposition to the White Paper was a sign of hostility to the Arabs. Apart from anything else, they still recognized in Great Britain the best friend they had among the great powers, and realized that she would be the main defence of democracy in the war which was coming to the world.

It would be rational to expect that the events of the decade from 1929 would have led to the spiritual and physical withering of the National Home. On the one side was an administration which, unable to maintain the fiction that it was possible to carry out satisfactorily the dual obligation of the Mandate, was increasingly sympathetic to the demands of the Arabs; and on the other was the continuous insecurity of life and property which was the consequence of the British inability – or unwillingness – to come to grips with the Mufti and treat the 'disturbances' as open rebellion. But this is to forget the pressure under which Jewry lived during this decade. An inexhaustible optimism, born of desperation, continued to convince the masses of European Jewry that safety and self-respect lay only in Palestine; and, in fact, during these years the National Home reached new heights of creative development and, in so far as its internal life was concerned, justified all the hopes which were placed in it.

Of the immigrants who came from Germany a number were able to bring with them the relics of their capital and this, together with increasing contributions resulting from the appeals of the national funds and from private contributions from America and elsewhere, assured a sufficient flow of capital to allow for the rapid absorption of the immense flow of new inhabitants. It was to be expected that an economy developed so rapidly and under such a strain should show many ragged edges, and that many mistakes should have been made. On the other hand the immense investment of capital needed to develop the different kinds of agricultural settlement, while unjustifiable from a short-term economic standpoint, was socially justified, and, on a long term, not unreasonable even from an economic standpoint, when it is realized that the land had to be brought from desolation to productivity within a single generation, and that operations were performed in a few years which an ordinary farming community would spread over the accumulated work and expenditure of generations.

The number of agricultural settlements of all kinds doubled during this decade; and in many communal villages experiments were made in combining farming with industry, since this allowed them to absorb newcomers at an increased rate, while still maintaining the social life which gave these settlements a significance out of all proportion to the number who were able to live in them. A national-service scheme brought youngsters from the towns to work for a year in the pioneering on the land, and gave the whole community a common interest in the rebirth, out of the soil itself, of the National Home.

When the Arab rebellion brought all the villages into the danger zone, the work did not slacken. A new technique was devised by which a prefabricated village was erected between dawn and dusk by a cooperative effort of all its neighbours, so that when the first night came its stockade was completed, and its water tower, armed with a searchlight, stood ready as a watch tower for the pioneers. Many of the villages were founded in the blood of their first settlers and this increased the pride which the whole of the Yishub, and Jewry throughout the world, felt in the courage and steadfastness with which they pressed on unremittingly with the task of building new homes for the refugees from the world's oppression or indifference. When a small Jewish terrorist organization came into existence during the Arab rebellion, it was not from the villages that its members came but from the towns. The villages throughout remained faithful to the principle of self-restraint, fighting courageously, but only when attacked.

It was during this period that the Jewish Defence Force, the Haganah, came to be efficiently organized. Jewish defence has a history going back to the first days of Jewish settlement in the nineteenth century; and a volunteer force was built up in the early days of the Mandate, after the 1921 riots. It had to be done secretly, as, according to official policy, the villages were adequately defended by the police, and were allowed only a small sealed case of shotguns in case of need. Even these were withdrawn in 1928, and in the 1929 riots the Jewish casualties would have been much more numerous had the settlers not been able to make use of their 'illegal' training and arms to defend themselves. The shotguns were restored, but organized training remained illegal. It was 'provocative' to Arab opinion that Jews should be able to defend themselves. Even the restoration of the guns was made the subject of a violent press campaign by the Arabs that Jews were being armed to murder them, though there had been no case of the Haganah exceeding the bounds of pure defence.

After 1933 the Administration continued the policy of refusing to recognize the Haganah or the possession of more than the shotguns; but as the military gradually took over, they cooperated, if not openly, with the Haganah; and even the Administration had to accept some 16,000 of them as 'settlement police' when it was evident that the general police and military could not arrive at an attacked settlement in time to save it. In 1937 Captain Orde Wingate (later Major-General, and killed in the Burma campaign) organized, with the Haganah and the military, special squads which performed essential services in the rooting out of the Mufti's forces in their hill strongholds. But even then Haganah officially remained illegal.

The bulk of the immigrants of the thirties were urban; for agricultural development is both slower and more expensive. The towns of Tel Aviv, Jerusalem and Haifa all increased considerably in size, and a number of previously rural settlements, such as Petah Tikvah, Rehovoth or Hadera, assumed urban characteristics and took part in the industrial development of the country. The new industries were as much pioneering as the new agriculture; for while the emigrants from Germany, Austria and Czechoslovakia brought with them a good deal of technical skill as well as capital, the whole development of industry in a country lacking most raw materials involved a continuous process of trial and error. Actually the largest single industry during these years was inevitably building; and it was perhaps fortunate that this was the industry which involved the closest cooperation between Jews and Arabs. For if the clients and builders were usually Jews, the quarrymen and stonecutters were largely Arab.

It was difficult for political life to keep pace with the new responsibilities created by the immense and rapid growth of the Yishub. Though the period urgently demanded a fundamental rethinking from all parties, this fact was not reflected in the majority policies of any. Among the Arabs such moderates as remained were afraid to speak out in view of the Mufti's assassins; among the British they were rendered hopeless by the apparent impossibility of reconciling Jewish and Arab demands. Among the Jews they could not withstand the pressure of the European tragedy which laid on Zionist leaders one duty above all others – that of providing a refuge for as many Jews as by hook or crook could be brought into the shelter of the National Home. It was their tragedy that such a policy, in the conditions of the time, only alienated British and Arab opinion.

The Christian community during this period played but little part in the life of the country. Among the Arab Christians most had supported the Arab Higher Committee, and the same was true among the many Christian Arabs who were employed in the Administration. The Orthodox Church entered into a long period of crisis on the death of Patriarch Damianus in 1931. The conflict between the Greeks of the Brotherhood of the Holy Sepulchre and the Arab congregations was not resolved; and the election of a new patriarch aroused every existing feud within the community and was protracted year after year almost until the war. In the western Christian circles religion was often involved in politics, Italians supporting Mussolini, Germans supporting Hitler, and both secretly or openly assisting the Arabs in their resistance to the British. The younger members of the Templar colonies were largely won over to Nazi views. Among the Anglicans and British missionaries, linked as they were to native Arab Christian Churches and schools, pro-Arab views were also widely held. Dr Graham Brown, who became bishop in 1932, tried to mediate between the two communities and preserve an impartial standpoint, but his voice was little heard amidst the excited passions of Jews and Arabs, and had little influence on the increasingly disillusioned British officials.

The Royal Commission in 1937 had truly declared that the Mandate had become unworkable, but they had declared it to a world too preoccupied with other affairs to be able to think out seriously what should be done. The menace of war hung over the whole scene; and under that menace British officials had to carry on day by day an administration in which they could take no pride, and which could lead to no solution of their urgent problems. The psychological effects of this miserable situation were increasingly apparent in the years of heightened strain after the outbreak of war.

CHAPTER SEVENTEEN

The Mandate breaks down and is abandoned

FROM many standpoints the Middle East was an area of extreme significance in the strategy of both sides during the Second World War. It lay across the supply lines of Britain and America with the east; and it contained essential oil resources; but it also lay along the southern frontiers of the Soviet Union and within reach of her oil supplies in the Caucasus, and its acquisition might have enabled Germany to make contact with her eastern ally, Japan. The thrusts of Germany and Italy through the Balkans and along the coast of North Africa were parts of a vast pincer movement which would have enclosed Palestine within the Nazi sphere, had the pincers been able to close. The defence of the Suez Canal, of the oil of Arabia and of the Mediterranean, were the necessary British and American reply to this movement; and brought Palestine into the centre of the Middle Eastern picture.

Yet Palestine was only a part of that picture, and its administrators became a small section in an immense web of British officials, military and civilian, spread over the whole of the Arab world; and the conduct of those administrators had to be fitted into a general pattern suitable to the whole area. A dominant element in that pattern was, inevitably, the conciliation of the local population and the avoidance thereby of any increase in the commitments of the military power, first of France and Britain, then of Britain alone, finally of Britain and America, which was already stretched to the uttermost by the needs of the main theatres of war elsewhere. Without their needing to make any sacrifices or to commit themselves to the uncertain hazards of supporting one side or the other, the Arab power of pressure was immensely enhanced; whereas, in spite of their terrible needs in Europe and their inevitable loyalty to the anti-Nazi cause, the power of the Jewish community was correspondingly lessened.

How great was the Jewish need can be understood only by turning from the general considerations of world strategy necessitated by the war to the position of the Jewish people itself. After the peak year of 1935, immigration fell to 30,000, that is less than half, in 1936; and in the three following years averaged only 13,000. The White Paper of 1939 threatened still further to reduce this figure to 10,000 a year, and to 75,000 in all; for no Zionist leader believed that the Arabs would consent to further immigration, or that the British would take any steps to aid them to secure such consent. And yet all the time Jewish need was growing by leaps and bounds. Within a few weeks of the outbreak of war Poland was prostrate and the 3,000,000 Jews of that country were either under the Nazi heel or fugitives within the Russian zone. In the spring of 1940 western Europe was overrun, and flight westwards to the new world was cut off, even had shipping been obtainable. There remained only one possible way out of Europe, through the Balkans into Turkey and thence into Syria. Turkey, herself a poor country, could not undertake to house refugees indefinitely. She could only allow those to enter whom she knew she would be able to pass further on.

The British controlled her south-eastern gateway and kept it bolted.

It is this action, more than any other, that Jewry finds most difficult to forgive. How many tens of thousands might have been saved it will never be possible to know. But it is natural that every Jew of Palestine, and indeed of all other countries also, must think that those with whom he personally was concerned, his parents, husband, wife, brothers and sisters, sons and daughters, might have been among those who could have escaped had that door been allowed to open while it was still possible to reach it.

Since it was impossible to take the short and safe route across the Bosphorus, Jews tried to reach Palestine direct by ship. Actually even before the outbreak of war such ships had tried to reach the Palestinian coast and had been ruthlessly turned back. After the outbreak of war those whom the British caught were interned and released when there were certificates available; but in the autumn of 1940 the Administration announced that any refugees who did arrive would not be allowed to stay in the country. In November a number were collected on board the *Patria* in Haifa harbour for deportation, and the ship was deliberately sunk by Jewish extremists with the loss of over 250 lives. The survivors were allowed to stay in the country, but the succeeding arrivals were sent to Mauritius. In December of the same year a ship laden with refugees, the *Salvador*, sank with great loss of life in the Sea of Marmora; but the greatest shock was caused by the loss of the *Struma* in February 1942. The *Struma* was an unseaworthy Danube steamer on which nearly 800 Jews sought to reach Turkey. There was never any question of it being able to make the sea journey to the coast of Palestine. The Turks would not allow the passengers to land without the certainty that the British would allow them to leave Turkey for Syria, and this the British refused to do. Finally the ship put to sea again, and sank with the loss of 763 lives. There was one survivor.

The loss of the *Struma* was the direct cause of the decision of the Extraordinary Zionist Conference, held at the Hotel Biltmore in New York in May, to demand the recognition of a Jewish state in Palestine as an immediate war aim. News of the massacres in eastern Europe had already begun to penetrate to the West, though the Foreign Office dismissed them as hysterical rumours. The Jews took them more seriously and the conviction grew that nothing less than complete control of their own territory would allow them to rescue the survivors of the death-camps of Europe. It was a signal example of the difficulties caused by the different pressures to which the different elements in Palestine were subject. For the Biltmore resolution coincided with the German advance across the frontiers of Egypt, and the quiescence of the Arabs, who had sullenly watched the defeat of Rashid Ali al-Gailani in Iraq the previous year, was again in doubt.

At the end of 1942 the British finally opened the Turkish frontier, when the Germans had obtained complete control of the Balkans and flight had become almost impossible. Nevertheless some 6,000 managed to reach Palestine through Turkey between then and the end of the war, as part of the legal quota of immigrants.

In spite of their indignation and grief over the rejection of their pleas for mercy for the victims in Europe, the Jews of Palestine showed, from the very beginning, the utmost eagerness to take an active share in the war. At its outbreak Dr Weizmann had assured the British Prime Minister, Neville Chamberlain, that the Jews were anxious to play their part, and would do nothing to embarrass the British authorities. In Palestine the formula was evolved that 'they would fight the war as if there was no White Paper, and the White Paper as if there was no war'. Such a formula was natural in the circumstances, but it gave the excuse to the local officials to base their conduct more frequently on its second than on its first clause.

There were genuine difficulties about accepting the Zionist offer in the beginning, when the British had far fewer arms than they needed even for their home forces; but these difficulties were supplemented by the Palestine Administration in innumerable ways which could only have the intention of damping down the Jewish desire to serve lest it throw Arab indifference into too strong relief. Jews were first accepted into the army only as labourers and at a low scale of pay which made it necessary for the Agency to raise special funds to pay separation allowances. Parity had to be maintained with Arab enlistments, and as these were few the number who could serve was small. Nevertheless Palestinian units were in France before its fall. At the end of 1940, still on the basis of parity, they were allowed to volunteer for the infantry; but the slowness of Arab enlistment finally led to the abandonment of the principle in 1941. Mixed units were, however, maintained for some time longer, and one, the 51st Middle East Commandos, distinguished itself in the Abyssinian campaign. During the same year both the army and the navy began training wholly Jewish units for special services, and Jews were engaged in commando work in Syria, Iraq and East Africa. Later both men and women were trained to be parachuted into Europe. Of these special Jewish groups more than half gave their lives for the cause. 1800 Palestinian pioneers, most of them Jews, were left in Crete when that island had to be evacuated, and were taken prisoner by the Nazis.

In 1942 mixed units were replaced by wholly Jewish or Arab units. The role of the latter will be mentioned later, but the Jewish units saw much service in the African campaigns, and formed part of the armies which invaded Italy. In 1944 a Jewish brigade group was finally formed and took part in the occupation of Germany. In all almost 30,000 Jews served during the war. But the Palestine press was allowed to hear little of their exploits, and even when they were allowed to show the shield of David on their vehicles and shoulder badges on the field of battle, these had to be removed before they could enter the National Home, lest the sight of them should offend Arab feeling.

While many of the Jews who enlisted in the fighting services were drafted to units where their special qualifications could be best used, the industrial potentiality of the National Home was similarly geared into the war effort. Lack of minerals and other raw materials limited the scope of possible development, but Jewish factories turned out many of the immense range of articles needed for a modern army, and so saved invaluable shipping space.

But the disastrous political background inevitably created another and more sombre side to Jewish activity during the war. There had been little action on the part of the extremists during the years which culminated in the German pincer-movement reaching Stalingrad on the north and Alamein on the west. But the victory of Alamein on 2 November 1942, the landing of American and British forces six days later in North Africa, and the Russian counter-offensive on 19 November, all combined to alleviate the danger in Palestine; though at the same time the news from Europe made it ever clearer that the millions of Jews in the hands of Hitler were being systematically exterminated. The result of this double situation was an increase of political intolerance and terrorist activity, of attempts to secure means by which immigrants could reach the shores of Palestine, and of acquiring arms for a subsequent trial of strength with the Arabs and, if need be, the British. In addition Jewish extremists – particularly among the youth – began to treat disagreement within their own ranks as treachery to be countered with violence and brutality.

The attitude of the Agency towards these unwelcome developments was hesitant. While Jewish opinion generally strongly disapproved of terrorism, it was also deeply moved by the European news and the unwillingness of the Administration to make any concession to Jewish needs. It was not until the tragic murder of Lord Moyne in Cairo on 6 November 1944 crowned a whole series of political assassinations that the Agency effectively cooperated with the police for the suppression of the terrorists, and even then the cooperation was short-lived. For by that time it was too late to affect the conviction of the Administration that anything which might disturb Arab equanimity merited instant and ruthless action. Infamous as such a policy was in terms of human need, it appeared to them to be dictated by the circumstances; but even if history endorses their decision, it remains true that human beings involved in such a policy inflict on themselves psychological scars which impair their judgement and plunge them ever deeper into a tangle of rationalization, misrepresentation and self-justification.

Meanwhile the lot of the Arabs was very different from that of the Jews. The immense expenditure of the British and American forces in the Middle East brought to all Arab lands a period of great prosperity. In particular the peasants of Palestine, for the first time in centuries, were able to clear themselves of debts, because of the high prices they obtained for agricultural produce. From the political and military standpoints the Arabs were equally fortunate. Even desert warfare had changed completely since the days of Lawrence, and there was no particular desire on the part of the British for large-scale Arab recruitment, apart from the fact that Arab troops had proved unreliable in the dark days of 1941 and during the rising of Rashid Ali al-Gailani in Iraq. They could therefore follow, without arousing criticism, the policy which seemed most logical to them of waiting to see which side would win, and joining in at the last possible moment. It was in February 1945 that the Arab countries, including Egypt, officially declared war on the Axis. There were doubtless a number of individual Arab leaders who were sincerely pro-British, and in the early days of the war there was a genuine change of feeling among the majority of the Palestinian Arabs who up to that moment had regarded Britain as an enemy; but in the Middle East in general there was an equal number who were convinced that a German victory would be desirable; and the same was true of the younger generation.

The number of Arabs who actually joined the fighting forces was about 12,000, but by no means all of these came from Palestine, and, after the first period, few saw any active service.

Desertions were frequent, and there were those who joined merely in order to obtain a rifle with which they decamped. Some, who were taken prisoner by the Germans during the earlier part of the war, were later taken prisoner again by the Americans, having in the meantime joined the German army under the inspiration of the recruiting campaigns of the Mufti. The Mufti was the centre of Axis intrigue in the Middle East, though his concern remained for the Arab future, as he saw it, and not for the advancement of German world hegemony. When it became unsafe for him to remain in Syria, he moved to Iraq; and it is typical of the instability of the 'pro-British' element among the Arab leaders that Nuri es-Said, the Premier of Iraq and a sincere friend of Britain, gave him a state reception and extensive financial support during his stay in that country. When the rising of Rashid al-Gailani failed, he retired first to Iran, and thence made his way to Italy, until he ended in Hitler's headquarters. There he remained until the end of the war, organizing Muslim and Arab battalions for the Nazis.

In the fortunate position in which they stood, these activities did not harm the Arab cause in the eyes of the British; and they were able to continue their political demands without abatement. The only reply which could be expected to the Biltmore programme was the demand for an independent Arab Palestine; and this demand was made with the more vigour in that the British were concerned not merely to maintain the Arab position but to strengthen it. It was largely through British initiative that in September 1943 representatives of the Arab states met in Alexandria under Nahas Pasha of Egypt, and in the 'Alexandria Protocol' laid the foundations of the Arab League. But politically the Arab world is not easily united – except in its opposition to the claims of Israel. In 1945 the Arab League declared that *de jure* Palestine was already an independent Arab country by virtue of the Treaty of Lausanne which had been signed with Turkey in 1923 and had ratified the settlement reached after the First World War.

The war ended in Europe in May 1945, but this brought no relief to Palestine. For the next two and a half years – until the acceptance of partition by the United Nations on 29 November

1947 – the centre of the stage was occupied by the vicious circle created by Jewish terrorism on the one hand and, on the other, the inability, or refusal, of the British to make any gesture which would increase the power of moderate Jewish opinion or enable the Jewish Agency to take effective steps to assist in its suppression.

The Yishub in Palestine placed no limits on the sacrifices they were prepared to make in order to receive the shattered remnants of their people. They asked only the opportunity to receive them; and it was because of the consistent refusal of the British to make any gesture which would meet the situation that terrorism not only grew, but enjoyed a toleration from large sections of the community which no political objectives would have accorded it. The consciousness of duty well done during the war, contrasted with the supineness or actual disloyalty of the Arab population, and the knowledge that it was to conciliate Arab feeling that any gesture was refused, served to accentuate a situation already felt to be intolerable.

From 1939 onwards the view had become increasingly widespread, especially among the Revisionist elements, that the British rule had ceased to have legal validity. It rested on force alone, and as such, could be challenged by force. The terrorists claimed that they were fighting by the only means available to a weak power to wage war on a strong one. Many of them had fought in the resistance movements in Europe; many were themselves illegal immigrants who had avoided death at the hands of the Nazis by their own courage and resource. They held that they were at war with the British and, if captured, entitled to be treated as prisoners of war. But political fanaticism, and their belief in their right to turn all Palestine into a Jewish state, was an equally important factor in their outlook, and for this they had no legal foundation either in the Balfour Declaration or the Mandate. Hence the basic cause, that of rescuing their brethren in Europe, became overlaid with chauvinist politics; but the issue was so tangled, and tempers so strained, that few possessed a clear enough picture to form a reasoned judgement of the harm terrorism was doing to the Jewish cause.

In England the Labour Party, which alone could enunciate a

new policy for the Administration to follow, came into power in July 1945; but, in spite of their many pro-Zionist pronouncements in previous years and, indeed, at the party conference in the spring of 1945 itself, they maintained silence for almost six months on the issue. This long delay enabled the situation to worsen considerably. During the summer Arab political activity in Palestine increased; para-military formations came into existence and movements for the formation of a new Higher Committee were initiated. The increase of Arab political activity, as intransigent in character as it had been before the war, stirred Zionist resentment in all quarters. In America strongly anti-British pronouncements were made; and in August President Truman, in a letter to the Prime Minister, Clement Attlee, made his first request that the British take the first step towards the solution of the problem of European Jewish refugees by admitting 100,000 to Palestine. In view of Labour's frequent denunciations of the 1939 White Paper the request was not surprising, especially as, by the summer, the issue of the homeless Jews of Europe had become the main issue in Zionist policy, whether among the terrorists or the most moderate advocates of Jewish–Arab rapprochement.

The certificates still available under the White Paper were coming to an end in September, and the first batches of post-war 'illegal' immigrants were already arriving at the shores of Palestine. But the British showed no signs of acting; and the inevitable consequences followed. The extremists announced that they would take every possible step to aid refugees to enter the country; and the Haganah, with the backing of some at least of the members of the Agency, promised their support for this particular objective, adding that they would make every effort not to destroy life in the process. Attacks were mainly directed at coastguard stations and at communications, and this stage culminated at the end of October in a general attack on the railways in which many bridges were blown up.

Palestine had previously been regarded as the concern of the Colonial Office, but the Labour Government transferred it to the Foreign Office, which brought it under the control of Mr Ernest Bevin. Whatever his private sympathies, Mr Bevin had an unfortunate knack in every speech which he made on the Jewish question of interjecting some remark which showed either an astonishing ignorance – as when he announced that Jews and Arabs had been in conflict for two thousand years – or a complete lack of insight into the Jewish plight – as when he told them not to try to get to the head of the queue for his attention. Moreover in January 1946 he suddenly announced that Transjordan would become an independent state, and in March a treaty was signed giving the British extensive military facilities, and entirely ignoring the fact that the new state did not even pretend to be independent financially.

The policy which Mr Bevin announced on 13 November 1945 was not action, but the association of the United States with Britain in a fresh inquiry into the future of Palestine, as it affected the position of the Jewish refugees in Europe and the National Home. It is at least interesting that it was after the inquiry had been commenced, but before it had completed its work, that he suddenly announced and carried through the independence of Transjordan. The inquiry was to be made by a committee composed of six British and six Americans, with the right to make interim proposals, and with the general task of suggesting a final solution which could then be implemented under a trusteeship of the United Nations.

During the same period the intensity of the Jewish determination to let nothing stand in the way of their efforts to rescue their brethren in Europe – of which terrorism was only a single unbalanced expression – was made still clearer. In December Sir Alan Cunningham, the High Commissioner, had formally asked the Agency for its cooperation against the terrorists, and Mr Ben Gurion and Mr Shertok had replied that they could not cooperate with the authorities, for it was not the Jewish people but British policy which had created the movement. Shortly after this exchange the most considerable outrage yet attempted resulted in the blowing-up of the police headquarters in Jerusalem. Opinion again hardened on both sides.

Meanwhile the scene shifted to Europe and America. American Zionists launched a bitter campaign of abuse against the British, and the extreme wing of the movement openly encouraged the terrorists in their resistance. At the same time information began to accumulate of a wide-flung organization throughout Europe, largely backed by members of the American forces and endowed with very extensive funds, whose aim was the rescue of homeless Jews and their transfer by secret routes across Europe to Palestine.

While the shutting of the doors of Palestine constituted the main grievance of the Jews, the unwillingness of the United States to do anything other than ask for their opening, and the failure of that country and the rest of the world to make any alternative provision, was a natural cause of anger to the Arabs. There were, especially among certain members of the Arab League, moderates who sought some solution which would accept the presence in Palestine of the existing Jewish community, and grant it what, in their eyes, would be adequate local autonomy. But none were prepared to recognize that immigration into Palestine should be complacently regarded by the rest of the world as absolving them from all responsibility for, or participation in, a problem which was a world problem, and not, in any interpretation, a problem created by the Palestinian Arabs or the Arab states.

It was one of the saddest elements in the whole disastrous complex that there was a gulf which could not be bridged between the willingness of moderate elements among the Arabs to accept the fact of a Jewish community in Palestine and grant it the best they could offer of minority status, and the desire of moderate elements among the Jewish community to reach an accommodation with their Arab neighbours. The minority status envisaged by the Arabs fell far short of anything which would have enabled the Jews of Palestine to take any effective action to succour their European brethren; but there was also the fact that a minority status under a Muslim government entirely lacking in political experience, and containing many elements which were not 'moderate', offered the Jews no real guarantee whatever for their future.

In this unhappy atmosphere the Anglo-American Committee started its work. In four months its members visited the main refugee centres in Europe, as well as Palestine and the Arab capitals of the Middle East. Their report, presented at the end of

April 1946, showed remarkable insight into the whole problem, in spite of the brief period in which it was prepared. Although behind the scenes and in the press during these months there was much discussion of partition as the only permanent solution, the Committee did not propose the dismemberment of the country, but the continuation of a trusteeship until it was possible for a single government to take over. In striking language the Committee stated:

Recommendation No. 3

In order to dispose, once and for all, of the exclusive claims of Jews and Arabs to Palestine, we regard it as essential that a clear statement of the following principles should be made: I. That Jew shall not dominate Arab and Arab shall not dominate Jew in Palestine. II. That Palestine shall be neither a Jewish state nor an Arab state. III. That the form of government ultimately to be established shall, under International Guarantees, fully protect and preserve the interests in the Holy Land of Christendom and of the Moslem and Jewish faiths.

Thus Palestine must ultimately become a state which guards the rights and interests of Moslems, Jews and Christians alike: and accords to the inhabitants, as a whole, the fullest measure of self-government, consistent with the three paramount principles set forth above.

They rejected immediate independence because:

We have reached the conclusion that the hostility between Jews and Arabs and, in particular, the determination of each to achieve domination, if necessary by violence, make it almost certain that, now and for some time to come, any attempt to establish either an independent Palestinian state or independent Palestinian states would result in civil strife such as might threaten the peace of the world.

In proposing a continuation of a mandate or trusteeship they emphasized the need for serious efforts to step up the level of the Arab economy and education so as to rid the Arabs of their fear of the Jews, but at the same time they considered that continued immigration should be allowed and that the land regulations should be abolished, replaced only by adequate protection for the interests of smallholders and tenant cultivators. While these were their long term proposals, they proposed also the immediate admission of the 100,000 for whom Mr Truman had several times asked.

The report had an uneasy press with the Jews and was rejected by the Arabs. Mr Truman announced his support for the immediate immigration programme, but said nothing of the other proposals. But it was killed within forty-eight hours of its publication by Mr Attlee's pronouncement in parliament that the report would have to be considered as a whole and that no consideration could possibly be given to the admission of the 100,000 until *both sides* had completely disarmed. It is difficult to believe that the government seriously thought that the Arabs, in their present mood, would disarm in order that 100,000 Jews should be admitted to the country.

Announcing that they had evidence of their complicity in illegal and even murderous attacks on the government, the Administration on 29 June suddenly arrested all the Agency leaders and two thousand other Jews, and interned them in detention camps; at the same time arms searches in the settlements were stepped up in severity. The arrest of their leaders did nothing to make the Jews more compliant; and as the Administration found itself in the humiliating position that it could only still further embitter the situation by taking action against them, it contented itself with publishing documents showing the relations of members of the Agency with the terrorists. In the end, after some months, it was compelled to release them untried, and thereby suffered a further loss of prestige. But these were not the only consequences. If the Agency leaders had had contacts with the terrorists, they had also sought to exercise a restraining influence upon them. Freed from all restraint, and while the Agency leaders were under detention, the terrorists blew up the wing of the King David's Hotel which housed much of the secretariat and the army headquarters. There were a hundred killed, including nearly half of the senior British officials.

Meanwhile the British government, having buried the findings of the Anglo-American Committee, was engaged in discussions between British and American experts whence, at the end of July, appeared new proposals known as the 'Morrison Plan' through being first presented to parliament by Mr Herbert Morrison, Lord

President of the Council. The plan proposed a federal government with Jewish and Arab provinces, each province to have its own control of immigration; and it suggested the possibility of a large American gift and loan to assist the Arab economy on to its feet. But in the meantime there had been a radical change in the situation behind the scenes. In a speech in parliament on 31 January 1947 Mr Churchill, leader of the Opposition, demanded that Britain should abandon the Mandate and added that he knew no reason why she should wish to stay in the country. There had been apparently a change of mind on the part of the general staff and a rearrangement of their Middle Eastern strategy, for on 18 February Mr Bevin announced that Britain proposed to hand the whole matter over to the United Nations, but would not herself make any proposals for the future. It was the abandonment in failure and despair of a task which had become impossible.

On 25 February the question was officially submitted to the United Nations. On 2 April Britain asked that a special assembly might meet to appoint a fact-finding committee, in order that the full facts might be laid before the regular meeting in the autumn. The special assembly opened on 28 April, and was preceded by a government announcement that the British would not undertake to assist in carrying out the decisions of the United Nations if they did not approve of them.

From then onwards the British attitude became more and more self-righteous and hysterical. The Administration in Jerusalem was living behind barbed wire, almost wholly isolated from those it was supposed to govern. The outrages of the terrorists increased in violence, and the Agency found, too late, that it had no power whatever to control or influence them. Denunciation, impotent but sincere, only increased the fanaticism of the extremists, and the misery of the Jewish community almost paralleled that of the British. Yet the Jews, at any rate, could not afford the luxury of despair. Ever since the fighting had stopped legal immigrants had been coming in and had been absorbed into the life of the community; throughout 1947 new agricultural settlements were still planned and carried through; new industries were developed. In the non-political fields sudden generous inter-community actions, affecting Jews and Arabs or Jews and British, would vividly illuminate the world of might-have-been behind the hideousness of the political realities. Nor was all the wealth accumulated by the fellaheen during the war wasted in the political struggle. Though at a pitifully slow rate, new schools in the villages were being built; agricultural improvements and the terracing of more hill-sides were being carried on, and in many parts of the country, among both Jews and Arabs, life could appear almost normal.

When the special assembly met at the end of April the Arab states sought to put on the agenda the immediate termination of the Mandate and the establishment of a 'democratic' state in Palestine, but this was refused. The Jews had no legal right to take part in the meeting, but as it was obviously both just and necessary that they should be heard, it was decided that they should be permitted to take part in the meetings of the political committee in which, in fact, all the states present were repre-sented. It was finally decided to set up a fact-finding committee of eleven states, none of the great powers being members. By the middle of June the committee was in Palestine. On 31 August it presented its report. It was not too soon, for the situation was still deteriorating.

During the period of the United Nations inquiry two events had shown the barrenness of both the British and the terrorists. During July, in revenge for the execution of three of their number, the terrorists had kidnapped two British sergeants and hanged them. When the British found their bodies booby-trap bombs had been attached to them which exploded causing further casual-ties. In the same month a large transport of illegal immigrants had, as usual, been intercepted off the Palestine coast. But instead of their being taken to Cyprus, the British government, on the plea that there was no further room on the island – a plea which was not true, for subsequent shiploads were taken there – re-turned them to Germany and placed them back in the camp life from which they had sought to escape.

The tragic events of Palestine during these years are incompre-hensible save when it is remembered that the gates of the world were still shut, and that, more than two years after the end of the war, Hitler's unhappy Jewish victims were still outcasts camped in the country of their martyrdom. The emotion caused in the Jewish world, and among humanitarians who were not Jews, by this callous action can easily be imagined. It availed nothing for the British government self-righteously to say that the fault lay with those who sought to escape from Europe and those who aided them to do so. A regime so bankrupt had lost the justification for its existence.

It is not surprising that the first, and unanimous, recommendations of the United Nations committee were that the British Mandate should be terminated at the earliest possible date and the country become independent. On the nature of that independence the committee were divided. The majority favoured political partition with economic union, and the minority a federal constitution embracing both Jews and Arabs in a single polity. In the former scheme Jerusalem would become a permanent trusteeship.

In the autumn the assembly of the United Nations met, and the future of Palestine was discussed. Partition was accepted, largely on the initiative of the United States but with the agreement of the Soviet Union. An *ad hoc* committee fixed the frontiers, and decided on procedure. To this committee on 13 November Sir Alexander Cadogan, on behalf of the British government, made it clear that the British would give the United Nations no assistance in carrying out their plan, as it had not the agreement of both the Jews and the Arabs. They proposed to withdraw their forces by 1 August 1948, but reserved the right to terminate their administration at any earlier date which suited them. Until they had so done they would remain responsible for law and order and could not permit outside interference; after that they would only maintain order in the areas which their troops were still occupying and even in those areas they would take no part in the civil administration. The United Nations had meanwhile appointed a committee of five to attend to the details of the transfer of power; but the British refused to allow them to enter the country before 1 May. Their whole attitude was as unhelpful as possible, since it was evident that in two weeks it would be impossible for the United Nations to take any effective measures for the future.

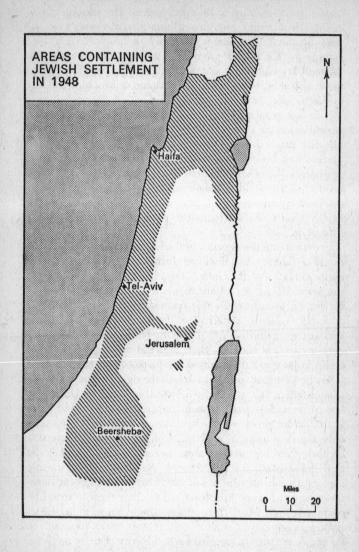

AREAS CONTAINING
JEWISH SETTLEMENT
IN 1948

N

Haifa

Tel-Aviv

Jerusalem

Beersheba

Miles
0   10   20

The partition scheme adopted by the United Nations was a curious one, and depended for its success entirely on the retention of economic unity between the two new states. The country was divided in chequer-board fashion into six 'squares'. In the north the Jews occupied the eastern square and the Arabs the western; in the centre the situation was reversed – Jews in the western, Arabs in the eastern; and in the south it was once again Jews in the eastern, Arabs in the western. At two points, one at Afula and the other south of Rehovoth, there were points of intersection. Jerusalem was left as an island, having no control of its road, railway or water supply, all of which passed through the Arab 'square'. Jaffa remained in the Arab state though situated in a Jewish square. The reasons for such a geographical curiosity lay in the distribution of the population, and the desire to give the Jews as large an area as possible, while yet containing as few Arabs as could be. Nevertheless, on the existing figures, in the Jewish state the Arab 'minority' almost equalled the Jewish 'majority'. It would contain 498,000 Jews and 407,000 settled Arabs of whom some tens of thousands were Christians. But, since it covered largely the plains of Palestine which are the areas through which the bedouin mostly wander, it would, at certain seasons, have 90,000 bedouins as well. If these are added there is a difference of only 1,000 between the two communities. It cannot be called other than a desperate solution for a situation which had thus far defied reason. On 29 November 1947 it was adopted by a vote of thirty-three states to thirteen, with ten abstentions; and the committee of five for its implementation was appointed.

The Jews accepted the scheme with thanksgiving, because at last they would be able to act themselves on behalf of the refugees of Europe, of whom over forty thousand were in Cyprus and some hundreds of thousands still scattered throughout that sombre continent. It was this fact that enabled them to accept nearly half a million Arabs in the proposed Jewish state. They knew that Jewish immigration would soon give them an obvious majority. The Arabs replied to the proposal of the United Nations by a general strike which immediately developed into open war against the Jewish community. The Haganah, at first, confined itself to the defensive; the extremists retaliated on the Arabs aggressively.

Two facts quickly emerged. The British claim that they would maintain 'law and order' until the conclusion of their administration was almost immediately shown to be vain; they were unable to maintain order even within Jerusalem or secure its access to the sea. Even more serious was the weighing of the scales between the combatants.

The Palestinian Arabs were from the beginning supported by the Arab League in their resistance; the headquarters of the rebellion was in Damascus, and operations were directed from there without any impediment. Armed forces of other Arab states entered the country from the north and east and nothing was done to stop them. By the beginning of the year some five thousand were in control of large areas. They were excellently armed, and amply supplied with ammunition. On the other side the Haganah still remained an 'illegal' body, and its soldiers were liable at any time to be stopped and their arms confiscated. Further, as the Jews could only obtain assistance by sea, it was an easy matter to prevent them from receiving either arms or recruits; and they were, in fact, effectively prevented from obtaining either.

By March 1948 the whole country was in disorder, and little 'law and order' was maintained anywhere. An advance party of the United Nations committee was permitted to come to Jerusalem, where they lived with little contact with anyone. But they soon became convinced that, unless the United Nations were prepared to supply adequate forces to implement their decision, it would be impossible to do so. The Jews were prepared to establish their own state; the Arabs refused to make any move to do so, or to accept the existence of a Jewish state. In these conditions, and in view of their unwillingness to supply troops themselves, the United States withdrew its support for partition, and suggested instead a temporary truce and a trusteeship pending a re-examination of the problem. The British replied that they would not oppose a trusteeship, but that they would close their administration on 15 May, even if it meant handing over the country to chaos.

No decision about a continued trusteeship was taken and, in spite of the hesitations of the United States, partition remained the only valid international proposal when on 15 May the British terminated their Administration. British action, and the armed conflict raging throughout the country, had made it impossible for the United Nations to take over responsibility.

CHAPTER EIGHTEEN

The State of Israel and the Palestine Arabs

THE withdrawal of the British Administration in May 1948 was carried out, on the orders of the British government in London, in a way which imposed an utterly undeserved humiliation on the British officials in Jerusalem, and the maximum difficulties on all sections of the population. They appear to have been told simply to abandon their posts, leaving offices and files behind them. It left both Jews and Arabs without any guidance or support. The recommendation of the Committee of the United Nations was not a legal mandate to create two new states. It was no more than a majority decision that this was the best thing to happen. For the Jewish community this was a matter of indifference, for they knew what they wanted to do and were adequately organized to do it. For the Arab population it underlines every weakness and deficiency of their leadership.

From the standpoint of international law the representative body of the Yishub, under the leadership of Ben Gurion, legally filled the vacuum which the British departure had created by proclaiming an effective state within the frontiers recommended by the United Nations. The Arabs of Palestine would have given themselves a legal corporate basis by declaring an Arab government in the territory allotted to them, and by creating an adequate organization to administer this territory. But they refused to recognize anything less than an Arab government of the whole of Palestine and declared immediately that they would meet any attempt at partition with force. In the confused situation which resulted, the vacuum was filled by King Abdullah, in regard to both the area allotted to the Arabs and the part of Jerusalem which came to be held by his forces (the Arab Legion, commanded by British officers). This is presumably of the same legal validity as the establishment of the state of Israel.

The action of Abdullah, however, was not just part of a peaceful and legal transaction. It arose out of the military situation created, not merely by Abdullah, but by the quite unorganized Arabs of Palestine, and by the governments of all the members of the Arab League. The 'armistice lines' which existed from 1949 until the Six Day War in 1967, incorporate more land into Israel than was recommended for her by the U.N. Committee, and are the result of the combined effort of the Arab world to enforce their will by military action. With the story of the war and the subsequent political history of Israel and Jordan we are not here concerned, but we are concerned with the traumatic effect of war and bitterness on all the inhabitants of The Land, Jewish, Christian and Muslim. On all they wrought fundamental changes, and on the Arabs these changes were an unparalleled and un-expected disaster.

The Christian issue is the simplest and can be taken first. The Committee had proposed that Jerusalem should remain as a separate entity under international administration, but entirely surrounded by Arab territory, and entirely dependent for food, water, and all other services, as well as communications, on Arab or Jewish goodwill. Neither Jew nor Arab was concerned to see this administration come into existence, and no outside power was sufficiently concerned to insist on it being created. In con-sequence the final armistice line ran through the centre of the city, leaving to Jordan the old walled town with almost all the Holy Places of the three religions, as well as the seats of the Greek, Latin and Armenian patriarchs, other heads of Churches, and the Anglican bishop (the see became an archbishopric in 1957). One corner of the city, containing various churches, Latin and Armenian especially, remained a battle-ground on Mount Zion, and some monastic establishments also became uninhabitable. But, on the whole, the Christians suffered less than either Jews or Muslims (Arabs), and when fighting stopped their property was respected by both states. Christians in Jordan, however, were made very conscious of being a minority in a Muslim Arab country and had no choice but to be *plus catholique que le pape* in their advocacy of the Arab point of view. The great ecclesiastics had little difficulty in passing from one country to the other to visit their flocks, and Arab Christians in Israel had, within limits, been able to make the Christmas pilgrimage to Bethlehem.

The most grievous suffering has been borne by Arab inhabitants of what became the State of Israel, together with those Arabs on the frontiers who were cut off from their lands by the armistice line. When the Arab world declared that it would meet by force any attempt to divide Palestine and establish a Jewish state, many military experts prophesied for them an easy victory. Quite apart from their Arab allies, the Palestine Arabs themselves outnumbered the Jews by two to one; they occupied all the hills, while the Jews were in the plains below them; they had copious supplies of arms available; they were surrounded east, south and north by their brethren who were actively supporting them. The Jews, on the other hand, were isolated except by sea – and they could receive help by sea only after the British had abandoned the country, for otherwise their supplies were stopped and confiscated by British patrolling ships. At the beginning they were very poorly armed, and had neither aeroplanes, artillery, nor armoured cars. It would be difficult to find a parallel to the pathetic flood of propaganda which has answered the question : *Why, in these circumstances, was there a flight of some half million Arabs?*

The old cry of 'injustice to the Arabs' has, of course, been raised, not only by the Arabs themselves but even more clamantly by the European 'pro-Arabs', whether workers in the refugee camps or not. But the answer is again misfortune rather than deliberate injustice. To a very large extent Palestinian Arab middle and professional classes 'emigrated' with most of their property as soon as it was proposed that a Jewish state should be established in the country. They found ample opportunities open to them in the rest of the Arab world. Consequently the rank and file in town and village fled because they had been deserted by those who should have been their leaders. Secondly they fled because they had had no training in defending their homes, fields and villages. The forces of the Mufti had been engaged in quite a different kind of operation, secret murder and sabotage, the ruthless blackmail and destruction of opponents, mob violence and ambush. Thirdly they fled because, though they had an ample supply of arms, there was neither training in their use, nor central plan in their distribution. But the most important reason is probably historical. The kind of warfare to which the villagers especially had been for centuries accustomed included *temporary* flight as an essential feature. When bedouins or rival fellaheen raided a village, then, as soon as the two forces became aware of each other's strength, the weaker immediately and sensibly took to flight. The raid was but temporary, stone-filled wells could be opened again, fields and houses restored. The only permanent casualties were trees, and fatalism accepted the increased poverty which resulted.

These facts are much more important than the nature or origin of the psychological pressure which was also undoubtedly used to persuade them to depart. It had been commonly believed for a number of years that an actual directive was broadcast from the Arab Higher Command, instructing them to retire temporarily from what might become the firing line so as to leave the way clear for the armies to sweep the Jews into the sea. But no evidence of any such command being *broadcast* has been discovered. The Jewish terrorist groups unquestionably copied Arab terrorism on one or two occasions, especially at Deir Yassin, as a form of ruthless psychological warfare; and the constant use by Arab broadcasts of Deir Yassin and exaggerated Jewish atrocities helped to create the atmosphere which encouraged flight. But one has to add '*in the Arab circumstances which have been described*'. Among the Jews, and among any people properly led and trained, such accounts would have doubled the determination to resist. Arabs are no more inherently cowardly than any other people. But the ordinary villagers and townsmen found themselves isolated in a crisis with which they could not cope.

This said as to the general situation, it has to be added that, especially in the later phases of the war, there were occasions when the Israeli army unjustly gave Arab civilians no choice but to leave at once with what they could take with them. This, for example, accounts for the flight from Ramleh and Lydda. On the other hand, the operations in Galilee during the last phase of the fighting left large pockets of Arabs especially round Nazareth, and Israel made no attempt to force these Arabs to leave. On the Arab side it seems that in the first stages of the war, 'the battle of the roads', villages in mixed areas were encouraged – or ordered – to leave by the guerilla forces operating at that time; and it is possible that it is from this limited fact that the later legend of a wholesale order to leave developed.

Whatever the balance of causes, however, it is unquestionable that some half million fled into the surrounding Arab territory, north, east or south of that held by Israel, and that they were immediately in need of support, for they took practically nothing with them. The Mediator at the time (Count Folke Bernadotte) demanded that *those who were prepared to live at peace with their Jewish neighbours* should be allowed by Israel to return. For the rest he demanded compensation for what they had left behind. Neither proposal was practicable at the time while active fighting was still continuing. When finally a truce was actually established and fighting ceased, the constant flow of wildly exaggerated hate-propaganda which followed, and with which the camps of the refugees and the whole Middle East have been flooded for twenty years, excluded the possibility of the Mediator's demands being met.

While Arab representatives at the United Nations constantly demanded their fulfilment, the Arab states themselves, by urging Arabs in Israel to act as a fifth column, made the fulfilment of the first demand impossible; and by expelling the ancient Jewish communities from their own lands they equally made a unilateral fulfilment of the alternative a demand which it would have been unreasonable for Israel, which had received these Jews, to accede to. The situation to which the word 'injustice' most rightly applies in the whole field of Arab–Jewish relations has been the exploitation of the Palestine refugees by the Arab governments. It is presumably intended to punish the western world for its support of Israel, but the Arab governments had many other ways of expressing indignation and causing trouble without victimizing their 'brother Arabs'. It remains a monstrous thing to be doing.

Moreover the figures presented to the United Nations organization, which feeds, houses, educates, and cares for the health of these victims, are unquestionably exaggerated. U.N. officials are not allowed to check the figures, which are given by employees who are themselves refugees, and have every interest in exaggerating the number of those under their care. Of the million and a half claimed perhaps one quarter are still genuine 'refugees', perhaps fewer. But this figure would include men and women who are now too old to find new occupations, and Israel has expressed a willingness to cooperate in giving these people some dignity and comfort in their old age.

When Israel occupied the West Bank in 1967 naturally many thousands again fled to still more miserable camps on the east bank of the river, fearing that the Israelis would do to them what for twenty years they had threatened to do to the Israelis. It is too soon to make definite statements about these new refugees, or those who fled from the Golan Heights, for their future depends on two unknown factors; when peace will be made between Israel and the Arab states, and where the frontiers will be between Israel and her neighbours.

What is new, and desirable, is that out of tragedy and confusion a Palestinian identity is beginning to emerge. We must not dismiss it because it has emerged as a terrorist movement. Algeria and Eire, to give only two examples, owe their freedom largely to such movements, and an Israeli government which includes the founder of the terrorist movement, the Irgun Zvai Leumi, could not reasonably refuse to negotiate with the Organization for the Liberation of Palestine (Al Fatah) led by Yasir Arafat.

This development makes it urgent that the Palestinians decide their attitude to Jordan. This is not an issue in which Israel has a claim to act, but inevitably she is concerned in the question of whether an economically viable state shares borders with her, or whether so narrow a definition of Palestine is adopted that another political unit is squeezed into the West Bank, a unit which could be neither economically viable, nor culturally a balance to Israel.

For those who fled twenty years ago, as well as for those who fled after the Six Day War, this involves new thinking. Of the former Jordan made those who were within her territory into citizens; but there is little evidence that those in the camps have accepted thereby integration within the Jordanian community. For them 'Palestine' still means that part of 'their' land which is occupied by Israel. While this may be natural, it is not necessarily realistic, even from their own point of view. All through the last half century the situation was bedevilled by the absence of an authentic Palestinian history and identity in which the Arabic-speaking population, whether Muslim or Christian, whether settled or refugee, could take pride and with which they could associate their own existence. The demand for repatriation has been sentimental rather than 'patriotic'. It has been an impossible demand to recreate the world of 1947, and the style of farming or urban life to which they were then accustomed, rather than a demand that they be allowed to share in the upbuilding of a genuine Muslim and Christian Arab 'Palestine'.

Al Fatah has already made statements in advance of any made on behalf of the refugees before the Six Day War. It has stated that it aims to create a single Palestine where Jew, Christian and Muslim share equal rights. In view of the different needs of the two peoples, it is surely better at present, at any rate, to have two political units, but the closer their links, the better for both. For the same reason, settlement in a prosperous Arab Palestine is a far wiser solution than repatriation to Israel into an identity which has become alien, with a level of life and taxation to which they would be totally strange. For it is the elderly and the less able who are still without a new home and new work.

If repatriation is no longer wise, the same is true about the claim for compensation. Not only is the vision of half a million separate claims to the re-creation of the situation more than twenty years ago apocalyptic in its impossibility of solution, but compensation to the Arabs cannot justly be considered apart from the compensation which would then be justly due to the Jewish population, equally ancient and equally authentic, which fled from all the lands of the Arab world. These are the 'oriental' or 'sephardic' Jews who now constitute more than a half of the Jewish population of Israel, and who, in almost every case, were expelled, or 'encouraged to depart' with no more than they could carry with them. Apart from a very brief period, when international funds were used to meet their needs, these Jews, whose numbers are approximately equal to those of the Arab refugees, have been supported entirely by their Jewish brethren, and are being slowly, and with many problems on both sides, incorporated into the State of Israel. They make nonsense, in 1970, of the pretence that Israel is a 'European imposition' into an otherwise homogeneous 'Arab' world.

The Jewish refugees do not desire, except perhaps in a few individual cases, to return to their position as unprotected minorities in the countries from which they have come; nor does the State of Israel intend to take any action to enforce their right to return. That a potential compensation to the Jewish refugees should, in a peace treaty, balance a potential compensation to the Arab refugees, remains a reasonable possibility. It is more important to assure the future than to wrangle over the past. But the basic injustice done by the Arab states to the Palestinian refugees passes almost from the tragic to the absurd when it is realized that Israel might accept back every refugee, give him Israeli citizenship and restore him to exactly the property from which he fled twenty years ago, *without in principle making the slightest change in the proclaimed attitude of the Arab states to the state of Israel*. Their misery and suffering has been an entirely wanton and inessential accretion to the Arab claim, made vociferously on every possible occasion, for the elimination of Israel itself.

No doubt the Arab moderate genuinely desires that such Jews as survive the elimination should be fairly treated as a minority within an Arab state. But Arab propaganda, by its constant appeal to violence and murder, has made the survival of any substantial number of Jews on the shores of the eastern Mediterranean an unlikely accompaniment to an Arab victory. King Hussain is regarded as the most moderate of the Arab rulers. His last broadcast in 1967 before the cease fire of the Six Day War included the words: 'Kill the Jews wherever you find them. Kill them with your hands, with your nails and teeth.' This is not said to create new hostilities, but to emphasize that no patched-up arrangement is likely to secure peace. It is only by a Jewish and an Arab recognition of the basic right of Jews, Christians and Muslims equally to dwell in what is now divided between Israel and Jordan that the fair decision as to *how* they are all to live in the territory is likely to be achieved.

It is important to recognize that this has to be a *Jewish* as well as an Arab conviction. For, while the average Israeli has no profound enmity towards the Arabs, either Muslim or Christian, there have been statements from the extremists and the Israeli religious leadership implying that the whole territory should be exclusively Jewish. It would be a help in the present position if there was an unequivocal declaration by the Israeli government that they recognized the right of the members of all three religions to equality within The Land, whatever divisions there were in its political government.

A future which is really a 'peaceful future' is a future which is creative and exciting for *all* the dwellers in The Land. It is not made by there being an Arab and Islamic rump tagging on behind an exciting and progressive Israel. What needs to happen is that, just as Israel is exciting to Jews all over the world, and as there is a *mystique* for Christians all over the world in the sites of the earthly life of the founder of Christianity, so also there needs to be a *mystique* for the Muslim that he is dwelling in creative fellowship with the older monotheisms which drew Muhammad and his earliest followers from the paganism of Arabia to the revelation of the Koran; and this *mystique* should give him a significance all through the world of Islam.

Such a vision is equally true if we speak in terms, not of religions, but of the Arab and Jewish peoples. Just as the establishment of Israel set new problems – not all yet solved – in the meaning of Jewishness, so we should look forward to an Arab presence as bringing with it a full measure of Arab vision and potentiality. And there, at once, there is for the Arab as there was for the Jew, the challenge of a choice which will be discussed in the final chapter: whether he sees his future in terms of a selfish nationalism or of a creative harmony such as was manifested in the great Arabic-speaking civilization which followed the Arab conquest.

CHAPTER NINETEEN

Arab Palestine, the Christian Community, and the State of Israel

I. THE PAST

THE Royal Commission of 1936, in its Introduction, stated that 'no other problem of our time is rooted so deeply in the past'. Every succeeding examination of the situation, whether by the Anglo-American Committee or by the United Nations Special Committee on Palestine, has reinforced this verdict of the Royal Commission. Only from a completely Marxist and materialist point of view is it possible to divorce the situation as it was in 1917 or 1948 and is in 1970 from the reasons which produced it.

There are few countries with so long a continuous history, there are few countries where the changing role of history is more obviously and inescapably reinforced by the unchanging role of geography. The Land is part of the bridge between three continents. It is narrow and small. On one side is the sea, on the other the desert. Such a land cannot be the permanent home of any single unchanging human group which desires to isolate itself from the world around it. It is no good seeking to decide what the result ought to be on an analogy with some other territory, for it is unique, and must be interpreted in terms of its own demands, and not by some false analogy with somewhere else.

In all the 3,500 years of its recorded history it has never been exclusively the house of a single people. Even when the Children of Israel regarded it as their promised land, they very quickly grew out of the idea that they would be the exclusive dwellers in it. They started indeed by proclaiming that their God called them to destroy Amalek and the other previous inhabitants. But they abandoned this idea more than 2,500 years ago when an Israelite author wrote the exquisite book of Ruth, showing that the grandmother of King David was a Moabitess, when an editor accepted into his text the statement that the wife of Moses was a Midianite

(Exodus ii, 21), and when a prophet could say to his brethren 'thy father was an Amorite and thy mother a Hittite' (Ezekiel xvi, 3).

Two thousand years ago a Maccabean king tried to make all the inhabitants into Jews; five hundred years later Justinian tried to make them all Christians; the mad caliph Al-Hakim wanted them all to be his brand of Muslims. None of these attempts succeeded. Today it is not a demand for religious uniformity which is made, but that it be considered 'an Arab country', primarily a Muslim Arab country, with Christians and Jews enjoying such minority rights as the Arab Muslim majority concedes them.

This demand is usually made on the basis that there has been a change in the population, that it can be agreed that it was once inhabited by Jews, but that for a period varying according to the author concerned, sometimes from the Arab conquest, sometimes from the fall of Jerusalem in 70 C.E., it has ceased to be a Jewish country, and has had a new population of Arabs. But the fact is that there never has been any sudden and basic change of population. There has been change of religion, but Jews, Christians and Muslims all have roots in The Land which go back to neolithic times, and all have had the widest variety of accretions through the centuries. It appeared to the casual observer at the time of the Balfour Declaration to be 'an Arab country', not because all Christians and Jews had left it, voluntarily or by compulsion, but because Turkish misrule, bedouin violence and fellaheen fanaticism and lawlessness had reduced the Christian and Jewish population to tiny minorities, just as these same qualities had reduced immense areas of a fertile land to little more than a marsh or a desert. It is a curious conception of 'justice' which then considers that Christians and Jews have thereby forfeited any rights to inhabit it, except as minorities with such privileges as the Muslim majority concedes them.

A great deal is constantly made of the imposition of the West in various forms upon an oriental country powerless to resist. Of course it is true that Europe was the dominant world power in the nineteenth century; but the main sign of that power in the area with which we are concerned was the establishment by American Protestants in Beirut of the first university at which young Arabs could receive higher education, a university in which actually the

Arab renaissance was nurtured, if not born; and this was very quickly followed by the establishment by European Roman Catholics of a second university in the same city, with a primary interest in the ancient 'Arab' Christian churches. It is equally true that, at the time of the First World War, the West was still the dominant political force in the world. But from this standpoint, Arabs as well as Jews depended on a European political decision; and Arabs, just as much as Jews, were favoured by the hostility of the victors of 1918 to the Turks, and by the already visible dependence of the victors on the oil which they could obtain primarily from the Arab world. Much is often said of the presence of Jews, and the absence of Arabs, in *some* British political constituencies. This is true. But the need for oil, and for careful treatment of those in whose country oil flowed, was an increasingly important factor in *all* constituencies.

A careful study of the successive decisions of either Westminster or Jerusalem, as to either the interpretation or the administration of the Mandate, reveals not so much a difference in goodwill towards Jews and Arabs on the British side as an extreme difference in the handling of their approach to the British by the Jewish and Arab leaders. When the time came to put wartime promises and expectations into practice, neither side received all they wanted to, or expected to. The Arabs, in addition, had a problem on their hands (which did not affect the Jews) in the ambitions of France, and the open or concealed dislike between the British and French administrations. But Jewish and Arab techniques for meeting these difficulties were in complete contrast. The Zionist leaders, especially Dr Weizmann, considered at each point what they could achieve with the possibilities which were actually opened to them by British action or consent. The Arab leaders continuously and unvaryingly demanded the immediate grant of their interpretation of the maximum; and this demand was inevitably refused. But the consequence was that, as each succeeding crisis emerged, the Jewish position was stronger than it had been before, and the Arab position was 'still at square one'.

Coupled with Arab intransigence in their political demands, two slogans gradually emerged which still more deflected any understanding of the real position by the Arab population. One was that Britain had 'given Palestine to the Jews, and in so doing had given away what was not hers to give'. The other became common after the immense increase of the Jewish population which followed the advent of Hitler. It was that 'an innocent Arab world, which had always treated Jews well, was being made to pay for the sins of Europe towards them'. Neither of these slogans is, in fact, true, though both were effective propaganda outside as well as inside the Middle East, because they *could have been* the explanation of observable phenomena.

As to the first, Britain neither gave land to the Jews, nor gave them any special privilege in buying it. Having recognized, in the Balfour Declaration, that a historic Jewish right existed in the country she administered, she naturally allowed Jews to buy land in it. But Arabs were free to sell or not to sell, and to demand what price they liked. In fact, Jews were indignant because Britain would not even 'give' them favourable rights in disposing of the substantial amounts of crown land she inherited from the Turkish regime. Previous chapters have shown how real that Jewish right was, and with what courage and suffering it was maintained all through the centuries. What Britain did recognize is that there was room for the Jewish purchase of land without inflicting injustice on the existing inhabitants. But the land was bought in the open market.

If what is meant is not the actual purchase of land, but the recognition of a public, corporate Jewish presence in The Land, represented by the phrase 'National Home' and the constitution in the Mandate of a 'Jewish Agency', then again it must be recognized that such a recognition did not get its justification from a British 'gift'. It is justified as a British recognition of facts which Jewish history had created. Nevertheless it is important to recognize that both British and Jews committed the injustice of not explaining the British reasoning to the existing population. This has already been stressed (p. 263 f.).

As to the second, the *observable phenomenon* was the great increase in the Jewish population after 1933 and again after 1948, in the first case as the result of European antisemitism, and in the second because no other doors were opened to receive the victims of a European crime. In both cases a good deal of Jewish comment, and in the latter case Israeli government policy also, were such as to justify Arab alarm that they would have no future in The Land if such Jewish activity continued unabated, and that Jewish 'imperialist' ambitions were boundless. So far as the facts are concerned, however, the increased Jewish immigration in the three years after 1933 was accompanied by an increased Arab immigration, because of the increased opportunities for employment. As to the situation after 1948, when Israel received something like a million refugees from Hitler's Europe, it might be thought that this was possible only by the expulsion of the Arabs from their lands. In fact it is said that the Arab refugees were the intended victims of this policy. But in the same years Israel was able to accept half a million Jews from the Arab world, and gradually filter them into the overall activity of the country, without any accession of territory or the displacement of the Arab citizens within it.

In both cases it was quite clearly the Jews who bore the burdens involved in the new arrivals. In the first case the Arab population benefited from increased money in the country, and increased opportunities for employment. In the second it resulted in no change of frontiers, or even a demand for change of frontiers. That a problem of population might arise in the future, out of Israeli policy, is dealt with below.

Finally the whole situation in the Middle East has been bedevilled by the underlying conception of 'a great Arab civilization while Europe was still barbarous'. In historic fact it was *a great Arabic-speaking* civilization, of which Arabs were the catalysts, but neither the creators nor the communicators. By an unexpected turn of history the Arab people became inheritors both of Greece and Byzantium on one side and of Mesopotamia and Persia on the other. The civilization which resulted flourished while Arab worked side by side with Greek, Syrian and Persian, while Jew, Christian and Muslim had scope to exercise their talents. It was killed by a narrow fanaticism which was part-Arab, part-Berber, and wholly Muslim. It will revive when the Arabs once more become open to the influences inherent in their situation between East and West.

II. THE FUTURE

There are three groups to be considered, though the Christians present much less of a problem than either Israel or the Muslim Arabs. If a solution can be found, and peace established, between Israel and the Arab world, the problem of the Christians should be easily capable of satisfactory solution.

It has already been said that it was a great misfortune for the indigenous population that there was no Turkish unit by which they could identify themselves when they became part of the British Mandate for Palestine. They became officially 'Palestine Arabs', but even so were almost immediately submitted to another new delimitation, for those across the Jordan became 'Transjordanians' under Amir, later King, Abdullah. These latter forthwith acquired a corporate identity and administration, but those on the west side of Jordan were, through their own refusal, administered by the British until 1948. When partition was recommended they again refused to accept or create any corporate identity for themselves. Those who remained in their homes became either Israeli citizens, or Transjordanians. But half a million fled for reasons already described and remained refugees, and it is primarily to them that the term 'Palestine Arabs' is applied. The largest number of these are in Jordan – as Abdullah's kingdom became when he annexed the area not in the possession of the new state of Israel. But there are also some tens of thousands in Syria, Lebanon and the Gaza strip, which was administered until 1967 by Egypt. From 1917 to 1970 decisions vitally affecting their future have been taken without their participation. In some way they must become the principals in any future and permanent settlement.

It is not easy to see at present how this is to be done, for their identifiable core – those who have lived in the refugee camps – has been separated from reality for twenty years. They have been fed on a propaganda of hate, and allowed to think only of one future – return to a no longer existing home in what is now Israel. Consequently it is with the settled Arab population on the west bank of the Jordan that the main responsibility lies for decisions about their future. There are at present two alternatives under discussion : the creation of some kind of autonomous Arab region under ultimate Israeli control, or permanent membership of the kingdom of Jordan, where as many as possible of the refugees should be incorporated with external help. It is difficult not to press for the latter of these two solutions, which would lead to a natural independent entity, as homogeneous as any Arab country is, and viable if it lived in harmonious relations with Israel. For this would mean access to a Mediterranean port, a link with a kind of 'East Pakistan' in Gaza – possibly an enlarged Gaza, capable, with suitable desalination projects, of sustaining a considerable population.

An argument for permanent membership of the kingdom of Jordan lies also in the consideration of the future of its substantial bedouin population. Relations have never been, and today are not, easy between the bedouin and the settled population. But the advent of the internal combustion engine has irremediably destroyed the mainstay of the traditional bedouin economy, the breeding and trade in camels. Increased population, increased demand for the full cultivation of the soil, still further endanger it. A great deal of 'sedenterization' has already taken place, in Jordan as in Syria and Iraq. But in many cases the registering of land as being that ranged over by a tribe was made in the name of the sheikh, and he had consequently, in fact, merely become a very wealthy individual, employing fellaheen to cultivate his estate, while, except for increasing poverty, his tribe continued unchanged its nomadic life. For a forward-looking Palestinian Arab, there is a much larger problem in the welding together of East and West Bank farmers with the bedouin tribes, who in a wide variety of economies and social structures, occupy immense areas of the 'desert' in the territory. Though it probably contains many sources of mineral and other wealth with modern possibilities of development, it is likely that the traditional occupations will for a long time continue to have their social and economic value.

Any solution is possible only with the agreement of the Arab states, for we have the paradox that it is not the Arabs of Palestine themselves who decide their future, but those who have made themselves their 'agents' – the Arab League powers. Whatever may be said *against* their violent propaganda, their false accusations, their encouragement of terrorism, and their aggression in 1948 and 1967, this must be said *for* them: that they have involved themselves in an immense expenditure of men and money in a quarrel in which no citizen of their own has suffered any injury whatever. Whatever the faults of individual Arab countries, they have acted in this case to right a wrong, as they see it, to 'a' brother Arab'. I confess that I find a world in which such altruism is possible – however mistaken this particular example may be – infinitely preferable to the cold selfishness of the famous utterance of de Gaulle, that France had neither friends nor enemies abroad, but only her own interests.

Nobody can tell how firm the present Arab attitude is, for Arab attitudes can change suddenly. But, though Israel at present can do little directly, there are two statements of her position which she can make, and which I believe it is incumbent on her to make. The first is a public recognition that she claims no exclusive rights in The Land, that she recognizes that she shares it with Christians and Muslims who now think of themselves together primarily as 'Arabs'. The second is more complex. It is a re-examination of her relations with Jews elsewhere.

In this re-examination the internal structure of Israel becomes a very important factor in the situation. As a historic fact it was eastern Europe that provided the central group of pioneers responsible for turning the dream of Zionist hopes into the fully organized National Home capable of assuming the responsibilities of an independent state in 1948. Not unnaturally quite a number of attitudes to life which were in fact eastern European were assumed by these pioneers to be essentially 'Jewish'. The most obvious example is the political structure with its multiplicity of parties, and a parliament built up from party lists, not from the separate representation of geographical constituencies on the western European model.

The same eastern European identity is also observable in matters which are purely Jewish. The whole development of Judaism which resulted from western European emancipation in the early nineteenth century was never a reality to the Jew of eastern Europe. If Israel is really to be the dynamic centre of the whole

Jewish people, then it must in itself embody the whole of Jewish experience. Moreover, if one can say of some Jewish features of Israel that they are eastern European rather than Jewish in origin and essence, it is today a much bigger problem that an increasingly evident strata of experience is 'middle eastern' rather than Jewish. The Jewish community in The Land has always contained a very varied group of Jews whose experience and culture have not been European. They have come from areas as far apart as Bokhara and the Yemen, Afghanistan and Morocco. But they were able to form small and dignified communities of their own until the hundreds of thousands of Jews arrived in a matter of a very few years from the Arab world.

On the surface these latter were as unacquainted with the modern technological age as were the Moroccans, or Egyptians or Iraqis among whom they lived. But it is no good just turning them into Europeans, or to some extent eastern Europeans. They not only possess ancient and magnificent Jewish traditions but could also be a bridge to the 'Arab' neighbours with whom Israel will ultimately live in creative peace. It is no easy problem, and at present there are a great number of complaints on both sides.

There is another real problem which needs to be faced. There are well over a dozen million Jews in the world. By law any Jew has a right to settle in Israel. At present those who wish to do so are not sufficiently numerous to make unreasonable demands on the territory at the disposal of the Jewish people in Israel before the Six Day War. But it is possible for an Arab to say: 'Supposing the Soviet Union expels its three million Jews; will Israel then offer to take them all, and demand more territory to do so?' There are those in Israel today who demand that Israel retain all the territory she has occupied with just that kind of fear – or hope – in mind. Because on two occasions the Israelis, by the development of their economy, were able to absorb an immense increase of population, it does not mean that the concept of indefinite expandability can be viewed without alarm by her neighbours. The Arab accusation of Israel's possession of 'imperialist ambitions' certainly uses a silly word in calling it 'imperialist'. But the fear is independent of the word, and is genuine.

If the slogan 'Palestine is an Arab country' is untrue, the slogan

'Palestine should be a Jewish country' is equally untrue. The original demand of Ben Gurion, constantly reiterated by his successors, for unlimited Jewish immigration into Israel, the conception that a full Jewish life can be lived only in Israel, the somewhat contemptuous attitude sometimes adopted by Israeli youngsters to Jews who lived in the Dispersion – all this feeds the flame of Arab hostility, and it is time that Jewry should examine whether these demands of Israel are justified. It is perfectly reasonable that during the last fifty years the main interest of the Jews in dispersion has been the building up of an independent Jewish centre, but it is now time that the centre began to consider how and in what manner it has an inescapable responsibility towards the Dispersion, and thereby for feeding Jewish experience into the non-Jewish world. Either Jewry consists of a Homeland and a Dispersion, both equally alive, or its religion sinks into a Levantine tribalism, while abroad there is no future for Jews except complete assimilation and absorption. This again is not an easy problem. If one considered the Jewish situation by itself, one might well argue that it is a question which can be left to time, or, at least, postponed till easier days. But the whole creation of Israel imposes certain obligations on Jewry as a whole, and this question of the growth of Israel and its relations to its Arab neighbours is obviously of importance to the whole Arab world.

If justice is to be done, then the Christians, both native and as a world community, deserve also to be considered. Territorially they present no difficult problem. The freedom of genuine equality, not the freedom of a separate government, expresses their basic need. It has not been pleasant, either under Muslim Arabs or under the Israeli government, to be a 'native' Christian. Under the former there was their inferior status laid down in fundamental Arab tradition; under the latter there was the unhappy record of the Christian missionary societies and of Jewish converts in the past, which naturally resulted in the feeling that in some way a Jew, by becoming a Christian, was 'letting down' his brethren and his history. A changed atmosphere in the area as a whole would solve both these problems.

Secondly there is the interest of the world-wide Christian community in the land where the founder of Christianity lived and died. The various partitions proposed since 1937 provided for an internationalization of Jerusalem, but Jerusalem has nothing significant to nations as such. Its significance is to religions. What would fulfil its role is an 'interreligiousization'. For it is a fact of history that it is the only place in the world where the three ethical monotheisms meet, each being there in its own right, and not as the guest, however honoured and welcome, of one of the others. If we are to be factual, however, we must still make a distinction. Each is there by its own right, but each is not there because Jerusalem is the heart and nerve centre of its world-wide community. That applies only to Jewry and Judaism.

That Jerusalem should remain united and within the political sovereignty of Israel is right and proper; for, though both Christendom and Islam venerate it as a holy city, neither religion could claim that it has ever had the place in their thought that it has had for nearly three millennia of Jewry. But it would be a gracious act if Israel established, probably within the old walled city, some kind of triumvirate in which its triple religious life could be developed. What kind of regime this would involve depends on whether Jerusalem be regarded primarily as a collection of existing holy places whose traditional rights must be safeguarded, or primarily as a unique centre where three twentieth-century religions, each with world-wide relations, meet for their mutual advantage, and for the spiritual advantage of the world as a whole. If it is to safeguard holy places, then the triumvirate would necessarily be chosen from among the clergy of Jerusalem. But if it is to develop the world significance of the city, then it would be wise that the triumvirate – who might well be called Regents, for that is a title of dignity without political overtones – should consist of laymen, and that none of them should be chosen from the Middle East.

For each of the three actors in the drama of The Land the future cannot be easy. For the Palestine Arab the task is to find his own identity, and to develop the whole organic expression of that identity in ways more creative than terrorism. For the Arab states it is not easy to stand back and allow the Palestinian Arab to choose for himself, while it is so much easier to provide him with weapons and vicious propaganda to spur him on to redeem vicariously the honour of the Arab people after their humiliating defeat. For Israel it is a long task of adjustment in which she is bound to be involved, once she is able to convince her neighbours that she is not insatiably seeking more land, but recognizes that she is one part of an ancient common history within a small territory.

That that territory lies at the centre of one of the world's cross-roads is obviously true, and obviously complicates life for all the actors involved. But its political implications are not the subject of this book, though they are inevitably a central preoccupation of all the actors whose place in The Land over the centuries it has set out to describe. It may take a long time before justice is really done, but when it is, it will be rooted firmly in the history this book has described.

Bibliography

General

Smith, Sir G. A., *The Historical Geography of the Holy Land*, 25th ed. (revised), Hodder and Stoughton, 1931

Political History

Avi-Yonah, Ed., *A History of the Holy Land*, Weidenfeld and Nicolson, 1969

Hitti, P. K., *History of the Arabs*, 8th ed., Macmillan, 1964

Runciman, Sir S., *A History of the Crusades*, Peregrine Books, 1965

Muir, Sir W., *The Mamelukes or Slave Dynasty of Egypt*, 1260–1517, Smith Elder, 1896

Eversley, Lord, *The Turkish Empire from 1288 to 1914*, extended by Sir Valentine Chirol from 1914 to 1924, 3rd ed., T. F. Unwin, 1924

Sykes, Christopher, *Cross Roads to Israel*, Collins, 1965

Palestine Royal Commission Report, 1937, H.M.S.O., Cmnd. 5479, 1937

Jerusalem

Cust, Sir L. H., *Jerusalem, an Historical Sketch*, A. and C. Black, 1924

Hollis, C., and Brownrigg, R., *Holy Places*, Weidenfeld and Nicolson, 1969

Margoliouth, D. S., *Cairo, Jerusalem, Damascus, Three Chief Cities of the Egyptian Sultans*, Chatto and Windus, 1907

Kollek, Teddy and Pearlman, Moshe, *Jerusalem: Sacred City of Mankind*, Weidenfeld and Nicolson, 1968

Thubron, Colin, *Jerusalem*, Heinemann, 1969

Israel

Ben Gurion, David, Ed., *The Jews in Their Land*, Aldus Books, 1966

Parkes, James, *Five Roots of Israel*, Vallentine, Mitchell, 1964

Prittie, Terence, *Israel: Miracle in the Desert*, Pall Mall Press, 1967

Eisenstadt, S. N., *Israeli Society*, Weidenfeld and Nicolson, 1967.

Bibliography

Jordan and the Palestinians

(It is very difficult to keep to books in which the facts themselves are not so distorted that the general reader cannot form his own judgement. In the following books there are different points of view, but they help, rather than obfuscate, the reader.)

Furlonge, Geoffrey, *Palestine is My Country: The Story of Musa Alami*, Murray, 1969

Meinertzhagen, Richard, *Middle East Diary 1917–1956*, Cresset Press, 1959

Storrs, Ronald, *Orientations*, Nicholson and Watson, 1945

＊

Glubb, Sir John B., *The Story of the Arab Legion*, Hodder and Stoughton, 1948

Kirkbride, Alec, *A Crackle of Thorns*, Murray, 1956

Morris, James, *The Hashemite Kings*, Faber and Faber, 1959

The Six Day War

Churchill, R. S. and W. S., *The Six Day War*, Heinemann, 1967

Lall, Arthur, *The UN and the Middle East Crisis, 1967*, Columbia Press, New York and London, 1968

Laqueur, W., *The Road to War, 1967*, Pelican Books, 1969

Warburg, James P., *Cross Currents in the Middle East*, Atheneum, New York, 1968

Index

Another Pelican book by James Parkes is described
on the following page.

Also by James Parkes

A HISTORY OF THE
JEWISH PEOPLE

This is the fascinating story of a unique people and their religion through 4,000 years. Dr Parkes, who is perhaps the foremost Christian authority on Jewish affairs, tells this story as 'the successive or simultaneous encounter of Jewish people with different non-Jewish societies'. Beginning with the Kingdoms of Israel and Judea and the dispersion, he then treats the way of life of the Jews as they come into contact with Rome, Islam, medieval Christendom, secularism, and nationalism. The last chapter brings the account up to date with the heroic survival of a people in the face of persecution, and their rebirth in the new state of Israel.

'James Parkes has written a work of importance and also of distinction. He has triumphed magnificently over the difficulties of covering almost four millennia of world events'—*Daily Telegraph*